F

Dr. Joseph R. Mancuso is the founder and director of The Center for Entrepreneurial Management, Inc. (CEM), the world's largest nonprofit membership association of small-company presidents. He is also the founder of The Chief Executive Officers Clubs (CEO), an organization of CEOs who run businesses with sales between $1 million and $50 million annually.

As a "compulsive entrepreneur," he has launched seven businesses, and he serves as a board member and advisor for a score of entrepreneurial ventures. Dr. Mancuso holds a bachelor of science degree in electrical engineering from Worcester Polytechnic Institute and an MBA from the Harvard Business School, and he earned a doctorate in education from Boston University. He is the author of fifteen books, including *Fun and Guts; The Entrepreneur's Philosophy;* his classic best seller, *How to Start, Finance, and Manage Your Own Small Business,* now in its second edition; and his current best seller, *How to Prepare and Present a Business Plan.* Articles by Dr. Mancuso have been published in such diverse magazines as *Playboy, The Harvard Business Review,* and *The Journal of Small Business.*

Dr. Mancuso is a popular luncheon speaker and has appeared on numerous TV and radio programs. As a lecturer, he has delivered major seminars in thirteen foreign countries as well as in more than one hundred U.S. cities.

JOSEPH R. MANCUSO

How to Write a Winning Business Plan

A FIRESIDE BOOK
Published by Simon & Schuster
New York London Toronto Sydney Tokyo Singapore

To the naive entrepreneur, who is surprised to discover when submitting the business plan to the bank that the people who write the advertisements for the bank don't work for the bank.

FIRESIDE
Simon & Schuster Building
Rockefeller Center
1230 Avenue of the Americas
New York, New York 10020

Manufactured in the United States of America

10   9

Library of Congress Cataloging-in-Publication Data

Mancuso, Joseph
How to write a winning business plan

Includes index.
1. Small business   Finance.   2. Venture capital.
3. Corporate planning.   I. Title.   II. Title: Business plan.
HG4027.7.M36   1985   058.1'522   84-18286

ISBN 0-671-76358-X

Contents

Introduction

Reader of Plan / Type of Plan

Venture Source — Equity
Loan Committee (Banks) — Debt
Executive Committee (In-House) — Corporate Financing
Peer Review — Planning
You — Personal Planning

For whom are business plans written and what purpose do they serve?

As you can see from the above chart, only the smallest percentage of business plans are written to raise venture capital. However, these plans are the most comprehensive and the most demanding. The reason for this is clear: Venture capitalists always seek to minimize the risks inherent in any investment. And, taken on its own, that isn't bad advice. *If you can write a winning business plan for a venture capitalist, you know how to write a plan for anyone.* The venture capital plan begins with the most risk, banks are second, and corporate plans are third in initial risk. Corporate plans include a history of the people carrying the corporate ball, whereas venture plans usually put together people who don't have experience working as a team. A bank's plan is usually less risky, as well, because a debt plan measures:

1) Ability to pay bank
2) Collateral

The second category is used only if you fail to pay back the debt. In most venture capital deals there is no collateral—so they must be even more accurate in assessing the first category. Hence, venture capital business plans are usually, but not always, the most comprehensive and difficult to write.

Portions of this book have appeared in *How to Prepare and Present a Business Plan* by Joseph R. Mancuso, © 1983 by Prentice-Hall, Inc., published by Prentice-Hall, Inc., Englewood Cliffs, NJ 07632.

The original business plan of Storage Technology Inc. is reprinted with permission of Jesse I. Aweida of Storage Technology Inc.

The original business plan of Shopsmith, Inc. is reprinted with permission of John R. Folkerth of Shopsmith, Inc.

The original business plan of *Venture* magazine is reprinted with permission of Joseph Giarraputo.

Pages 7–9 and 184–86 ("Projection of Financial Statements") are reprinted with the permission of Robert Morris Associates.

Appendix E is reprinted from Osgood and Bangs, *The Business Planning Guide* by permission of Andy Bangs, Upstart Publishing Company, Portsmouth, NH 03801. The forms were originally supplied by General Business Service, Inc. of Rockville, MD.

chapter 1

The Perfect Business Plan

PREPARING YOUR PLAN

People are always telling me that they'd like to see the perfect business plan. "Would you mind handing me that business plan over there? Right—the perfect one. You see, I'm in a hurry and I don't want to spend a whole lot of time writing one, so I'll just take advantage of someone else's hard work. Just show me the perfect plan and I'll copy it."

Can you imagine the results? What you'd end up with would be a program for a word processor that types out "John went to _____ _____ high school in _____, and then he went to _____ _____ college," and so on. All you do is feed in a few magic words and change the business from computers to a restaurant, or a restaurant to construction, or construction to software, and you're ready to go. The program has all the boiler plate stuff in it already, so abracadabra, you've got the perfect business plan. In fact, there's a company in Los Angeles that does just that. I'll bet it does pretty good business with accountants, lawyers, and other business plan preparers. As far I'm concerned, a plan like that is just a waste of time. It's like saying, "Let me see a work of art that's perfect. I want to have the Mona Lisa in my house, so give me a paint-by-the-numbers kit."

It's foolish to think that you could paint the Mona Lisa by numbers. And when it comes right down to it, a business plan is a work of art in its own right. It's the document that personifies and expresses your company. So when people ask me whether it should be five pages or fifty, I answer them by saying, "Who knows?" Some people might type up three-page plans and raise a million-and-a-half dollars. I could show you one that's only seven pages long that raised more than a million. But most business plans are "wheelbarrow" plans. You have to put it in a wheelbarrow to carry it, and that doesn't even include the appendix that you left back at the office.

I like to use the example of someone who was my hero when I was a kid growing up. His name was Joe DiMaggio, and he played baseball for the Yankees. The guy looked great and acted great, and when he hit the ball, his swing was level perfect. Even in the outfield, he was a beautiful and graceful person, and his lifetime batting average was .325. At the same time, there was a guy over in St. Louis who stood at the plate with his fanny sticking out, his arms tilted, and his knees bent. It looked like he'd either fall over from the wind off the ball or get hit by the first ball thrown his way. His name was Stan Musial, and even though his stance was completely different, he had a lifetime batting average of .331. The message is the same when it comes to business plans.

I can't give you a magic formula: Copy this and you'll have the perfect plan. In fact, the perfect plan is probably one that was turned down. The ones that get financed are seldom perfect, but they are always sweet. That's why my advice is called the "Frosting on the Cake Principle." I start out with the assumption that most entrepreneurs can write a business plan that's about an 8, on a scale of 1 to 10. And that's not bad because most business plans aren't even 8's. Most plans are about 6's, but it doesn't really matter whether a plan is an 8, a 4, a 6, or a 2 because the ones that get financed are 10's.

Let's say business plans that are "found in nature" are 8's. As I said, a plan that's an 8 is a good plan, but 8's don't get financed. So if you start with an 8, how do you put the frosting on the cake? Read another book? Go back to fundamentals? That's fine for bringing a 1 up to an 8, but how do you go from an 8 to an 11? It's like golf. It's a lot easier to bring your score to 80 from 100 than it is to bring it down to 70 from 80. It looks like a linear scale, but it's not. An 8 is an entrepreneur's plan as it's "found in nature." If you add an accountant and a lawyer, another two months and another three grand, you come up with a 9. But a 9 is no better than a 6 because neither one of them gets financed. So if a 10 is a plan that gets financed, what's an 11? The answer is, an 11 is a plan that's so good you have to turn back money.

If you actually take in too many checks and have to explain to an investor why he or she is being cut out of the deal, that's an 11. And this book is designed to tell you how to take a 9 and turn it into an 11 with *magic*. If you ever did magic tricks as a kid, you'll know what I'm talking about. The first question a magician hears after having done a trick is, "How did you do it?" And if the magician finally gives up and shows how to do it, what does the audience say? "Oh, is that all? I knew that all the time!"

So what I'm going to tell you about business plans isn't very different from common sense, but the problem with common sense is that it isn't always that common until someone else explains it.

NINE QUESTIONS THAT MUST BE ANSWERED

Before I go any further, it's time for you to do some of the work. Please answer the following questions:

1. What is the single most important aspect of the business plan, according to the venture capitalist?

   _____

2. List, in chronological order, the six steps in presenting a business plan.

   1. _____   4. _____
   2. _____   5. _____
   3. _____   6. _____

3. Name two elements of a business plan that can bring it from the 7 to 9 range, up to a 10.

   1. _____
   2. _____

4. List the five questions that a venture source needs an answer to.

   1. _____
   2. _____
   3. _____
   4. _____
   5. _____

5. In what order are the parts of a business plan read?

   1. _____
   2. _____
   3. _____
   4. _____
   5. _____
   6. _____

6. Rank, in order of importance, these ten sources of linkage people for introducing your deal to venture capital sources.

   1. Entrepreneur in the venture portfolio   _____
   2. Another venture capitalist   _____
   3. Accountant familiar with a venture source   _____
   4. Lawyer familiar with a venture source   _____
   5. Banker familiar with a venture source   _____
   6. Friend of a venture source   _____
   7. Blind letter to a venture source   _____
   8. Customer of a company familiar with a venture source   _____

9. Investor in a venture capitalist's portfolio _____

10. Telephone a venture source _____

7. Identify the nine members of an entrepreneurial team and circle the most important player.

1. _____
2. _____
3. _____
4. _____
5. _____
6. _____
7. _____
8. _____
9. _____

8. What should be found on the summary page of the business plan?

1. _____
2. _____
3. _____
4. _____
5. _____

9. What are the six most common debt/equity instruments available to a lender or investor?

1. _____
2. _____
3. _____
4. _____
5. _____
6. _____

Dr. Edward B. Roberts, the David Sarnoff Professor of Management and Technology at MIT, did a study of 20 business plans submitted by high-tech, start-up companies to venture capitalists in the Boston area. Here are some of the results of that study:

1. While all 20 plans stated an overall objective, only 14 had a specific strategy that appeared rational and achievable.

2. The central thrust of the plans broke down as follows:

Product	47%
Market	29%
People	24%

3. Profitability and growth were not discussed in detail in 45% of the plans.

4. Three-quarters of the plans failed to identify details about their competitors.

5. The marketing plan was consistently the weakest element of the 20 plans, while the R&D aspect was consistently the strongest.

6. Marketing research and selling were given very low priority in three-quarters of the plans, and little background in these areas was evidenced. (It is interesting to note that earlier research by Professor Roberts showed an inverse relationship between product success and a firm's ability to do market research. It concludes by stating that if time exists for market research, you're already too late for the market.)

7. The financial projections offered in these plans broke down as follows:

None	10%
Data not available	5%
1–3-year income statement only	10%
4–5-year income statement only	40%
1–3-year income statement and balance sheet	15%
4–5-year income statement and balance sheet	10%

Roberts concluded the report on his research with the following statement: "One critical aspect of the business plan is that if you don't do it right, there is a high likelihood that you will never do anything beyond it. Business planning needs to be undertaken seriously, if for no other reason that it is a major tangible representation of who you are, what you are, and what you want to be to the financial community. It may also even relate to later business success."

TIPS ON FINANCIALS

I'm going to give you two tips on business plan preparation. These are great tips. They won't turn an 8 into an 8.1, and they won't help you to get financed, but you need them just the same.

For some reason, convention dictates that all the words and romance in a business plan go up front, while the financials are always in the back. I've always thought that the front page should be the balance sheet, and the back pages should tell where you went to school, what you plan to do, and so on. Instead, the balance sheets always go in the back so that you have to shuffle the plan around to get to them. All the same, it's those back pages that get *read*, so the way they are presented is a key issue.

Of course, many entrepreneurs present financial information the same way they present plans—home-cooked. They dream up their financial format in such a way that the balance sheet becomes the hardest part of the plan to read. But bankers and financial people are going to be the people who read your plan, so it pays to prepare it in terms they will understand. When

Thomas Edison invented the light bulb, he described it in terms of candle power. By using the already accepted terms to describe his new invention, he made it easier for his invention to gain acceptance. It made the conversion from gas to electricity smoother.

My point is: Prepare your financials in such a way that bankers and financial people will be able to understand them easily. How do you do it? Let me give you a roundabout explanation. When little commercial bankers want to grow up to be big bankers, they get their training from Robert Morris Associates (sometimes from the American Banking Association), an association of commercial loan officers.* And what do venture capitalists most often share (besides their need to make a profit)? A common background. While entrepreneurs come in all shapes and sizes, venture capitalists all look as if they came out of the same mold.**

I always say (and I joke when I say it) that venture capitalists are born with a step-by-step chart to follow. First, they go to prep school, then they go to Princeton, and from there they go on to Harvard Business School. After that, they spend two years at a bank, two or three years with a major consulting firm, then they go to work for an SBIC. After all those steps, by the time they turn 35, they are ready to be stamped "venture capitalist" and to go to work with one of the private (nonSBIC) venture funds. While the pattern may not be exactly the same for every venture capitalist, the one thing that they most often have in common is the "two years at the bank." What does that mean? They all have been trained by Robert Morris Associates at one time or another. Robert Morris is *the* training arm of the banking industry. So when little bankers are trained to become commercial lenders, they are trained on Robert Morris (or Bank Administration Institute) forms.

Therefore, it's helpful to financial people if entrepreneurs prepare their financials on Robert Morris (or equivalent) forms.*** These forms contain all three of the fundamental financial tools. The income statement is at the top, the balance sheet is at the bottom, and the glue that holds them together is right in the middle—that's the cash flow statement. On one page you have all three financial forms, so you can get all of the financial information at a glance. It's a one-sweep system, and it reminds me of a three-sweep oscilloscope. If you've ever seen a three-sweep oscilloscope, you know if one sweep goes up, one goes down, and one goes sideways; when you sweep them together, you see the interaction. The same goes for financials. Reading them one at a time doesn't give nearly as clear a picture as is gained by watching their interaction.

*Robert Morris Associates, 1616 Philadelphia National Bank Building, Philadelphia, PA. 19107.
**By the way, I use the pronoun "he" throughout the book, not out of any chauvinistic choice, but to avoid the awkwardness of "he/she."
***You may order forms and samples from BANKERS SYSTEMS INC., Box 1457, St. Cloud, MN 56302.

PROJECTION OF FINANCIAL STATEMENTS

SUBMITTED BY _____

			ACTUAL	PROJECTIONS →											
SPREAD IN HUNDREDS ☐	DATE														
SPREAD IN THOUSANDS ☐	PERIOD														

© 1984 Robert Morris Associates · Form C.117 Rev. 8/84
ORDER FROM Bankers Systems, Inc., St. Cloud, MN 56302
Successor to Cadwallader & Johnson
These forms are intended for use in commercial lending transactions.
Where any other use is contemplated, it is suggested that a careful review
be made to ensure compliance with applicable laws and regulations.

LMa

PROFIT and LOSS

1	NET SALES	1
2		2
3		3
4	Less: Materials Used	4
5	COST OF GOODS SOLD	5
6	GROSS PROFIT	6
7	Less: Sales Expense	7
8	General & Administrative Expense	8
9	Depreciation	9
10		10
11	OPERATING PROFIT	11
12	Less: Other Expense	12
13	Add: Other Income	13
14	PRE-TAX PROFIT	14
15	Income Tax Provision	15
16	NET PROFIT	16

CASH PROJECTION

17	CASH BALANCE (Opening)	17
18	Add: Receipts: Cash Sales & Other Income	18
19	Cash Sales Plus Receivable Collections	19
20		20
21		21
22	Bank Loan Proceeds	22
23	Other Loan Proceeds	23
24	TOTAL CASH AND RECEIPTS	24
25	Less: Disbursements: Trade Payables	25
26	Direct Labor	26
27	OPERATING & OTHER EXPENSES	27
28		28
29	Capital Expenditures	29
30	Income Taxes	30
31	Dividends or Withdrawals	31
32	Bank Loan Repayment	32
33	Other Loan Repayment	33
34	TOTAL CASH DISBURSEMENTS	34
35	CASH BALANCE (Closing)	35

BALANCE SHEET

36	ASSETS: Cash and Equivalents	36
37	Receivables	37
38	Inventory (Net)	38
39		39
40	CURRENT ASSETS	40
41	Fixed Assets (Net)	41
42		42
43		43
44		44
45	TOTAL ASSETS	45
46	LIABILITIES: Notes Payable-Banks	46
47	Notes Payable-Others	47
48	Trade Payables	48
49	Income Tax Payable	49
50	Current Portion L.T.D.	50
51		51
52	CURRENT LIABILITIES	52
53	Long-Term Liabilities:	53
54		54
55		55
56	TOTAL LIABILITIES	56
57	NET WORTH: Capital Stock	57
58	Retained Earnings	58
59		59
60	TOTAL LIABILITIES AND NET WORTH	60

7

HOW TO USE THIS FORM

RMA's Projection of Financial Statements, Form C-117, may be completed by the banker, the customer, or both working together. It is designed to be flexible and may be used as a:

1) Projection tool to provide a picture of the customer's present and future financial condition. Actual and estimated financial data form the basis of the calculations.
2) Tool for analysis of the customer's borrowing needs and debt repayment ability.
3) Budget to aid in planning for the customer's financial requirements and repaying the banker's credit accommodation.

INSTRUCTIONS: In the first column, enter the actual PROFIT AND LOSS STATEMENT and BALANCE SHEET of the date immediately prior to projection period. Then, in each subsequent column, covering a projection period (e.g., month, quarter, annual):

- Enter on the "date" line, the ending date of each projection period (e.g., 1/31, 3/31, 19____)
- Enter on the "period" line the length of each projection period (e.g., 1 mo., 3 mos., 12 mos.)
- Then, follow the line-by-line instructions below:

Line No.	Title	Instructions
	PROFIT AND LOSS STATEMENT	
1	NET SALES	Enter actual or beginning net sales figure in the first vertical column. We suggest you project future net sales based upon a % sales increase or decrease. Estimate acceptable % figure and record here ____%. (This % is generally calculated based on historical changes in net sales. However, consideration must also be given to factors, such as general business conditions, new products and services, and competition.)
2 through 5	COST OF GOODS SOLD	Enter all relevant components of customer's cost of goods sold calculation. Project future cost of goods sold based upon % increase or decrease. Estimate acceptable percentage figure and insert here ____%. (This figure is generally estimated as a percentage of sales based on prior years.)
6	GROSS PROFIT	Line 1 minus line 5.
7 through 10	Sales Expense; General and Administrative Expenses; Other	Enter all items. Project future expenses based on an increase or decrease. Estimate acceptable percentage figure and insert here ____%. (This figure is generally estimated as a percentage of sales based on prior years. Anticipated increases in major expenses, such as lease, officers' salaries, etc., should also be considered.)
11	OPERATING PROFIT	Line 6 minus the sum of lines 7 through 10.
12 through 13	Various adjustments to Operating Profit	Enter all items and estimate future adjustments.
14	PRE-TAX PROFIT	Line 11 minus the sum of lines 12 through 13.
15	Income Tax Provision	Common methods used for calculating Income Tax Provision include the most current year's tax as a % of the Pre-Tax Profit.
16	NET PROFIT	Line 11 minus the sum of lines 12 through 15.
	CASH PROJECTION CALCULATION	
17	CASH BALANCE	Enter opening cash balance. For subsequent periods, enter the closing cash balance (Line 35) from previous period. Or enter an adjusted amount to reflect a desired cash balance.
18 through 21	Receipts	Enter total cash sales & other income plus receivables collected. Receivable collections must be calculated separately. This requires an analysis of the customer's sales and collection patterns:

    (1) Estimate the portion of each month's sales collected in that month and subsequent months.

    (2) From the sale's figure last month and the previous month(s), calculate how much of the existing receivable figure will be collected in the current month.

    (3) Deduct the collected receivables balance calculated in (2) above from the month-end balance of accounts receivables.

    (4) Add this month's sales figure to the remainder of receivables calculated in (3) above. This figure is the new accounts receivable figure for the end of the current month.

EXAMPLE Assumptions:

Projection calculation - monthly

Monthly Net Sales:	9/30 - $250M
	10/31 - $300M
	11/30 - $150M

| Accounts Receivable balance: | 9/30 - $250M |
| | 10/31 - $367M |

The average collection period is 45 days. This means that 66.7% (30 days ÷ 45 days) of each month's sales will be collected the following month and the remaining 33.3% in the second month.

To determine receivable collections for November --

			Accounts Receivable balance, 10/31		$367M
	Deduct:	66% of 10/31 sales	200M		
		33% of 9/30 sales	83M	283M	
					84M
	Add:	11/30 sales			150M
			Accounts Receivable Balance, 11/30		$234M

Line No.	Title	Instructions
22 through 23	Bank Loan Proceeds/ Other	Enter actual or projected bank loan proceeds on line 22. Enter any other receipts on line 23.
24	TOTAL CASH AND RECEIPTS	Enter sum of lines 17 through 23.
25 through 33	Disbursements	Enter actual or estimated cash disbursements on these lines.
34	TOTAL DISBURSEMENTS	Enter sum of lines 25 through 33.
35	CASH BALANCE (Closing)	Line 24 minus line 34. Note: The closing cash balance on line 35 may be entered on line 17 in the next column. However, if the closing cash balance is negative, or below the desired opening cash balance, then bank loans (line 22) may be needed to raise the closing cash balance to zero, or to the desired opening cash balance. The bank loan necessitates planning for repayment (line 31 and 32) in subsequent columns.

8

BALANCE SHEET

(36 through 44)		**ASSETS**	
	36	Cash and Equivalents	Enter cash and readily marketable securities--current year only. For subsequent years use the closing cash balance (line 35).
	37	Receivables	Enter actual receivables in the first column. To project, use previous receivables figure plus projected net sales (line 1), minus projected cash sales and receivables collections (line 19).
	38	Inventory	Enter actual inventory in the first column. To project, add purchases to beginning inventory. Then, subtract materials used to calculate the ending inventory amount (lines 2 through 4). If the inventory purchase figure is not available, balances can be calculated based on historic turnover ratios.
	40	Current Assets	Enter sum of lines 36 through 39.
	41	Fixed Assets (Net)	Enter fixed assets. To project, add previous year's fixed assets and any fixed asset additions. Then, deduct estimated accumulated depreciation.
42 through 44			Enter other non-current assets (stockholder's receivables, intangibles, etc.).
	45	TOTAL ASSETS	Add lines 40 through 44.
(46 through 56)		**LIABILITIES**	
	46	Notes Payable-Banks	Prior period balance plus loan proceeds (line 22), less repayments (line 32).
	47	Notes Payable-Others	Prior period balance plus note proceeds (line 23), less repayments (line 32).
	48	Trade Payables	Prior period balance plus purchases less payments (line 25). If the inventory purchase figure is not available, balances can be projected based on historic payables turnover.
	49	Income Tax Payable	Add prior period balance to income tax provision (line 14) and deduct income taxes paid (line 30).
	50	Current Portion Long-Term Debt	Estimate current maturities by entering the sum of prior period debt's maturities and additional bank loan proceeds scheduled repayments.
	51		Enter the sum of any other current liabilities.
	52	CURRENT LIABILITIES	Enter the sum of lines 46 through 51.
53 through 55		Long-Term Liabilities	Enter long-term liabilities here. Calculate long-term debt by adding previous period long-term debt (line 53) to loan proceeds (line 22 & 23), and subtracting current maturities (line 50).
	56	TOTAL LIABILITIES	Enter sum of lines 52 through 55.
(57 through 59)		**NET WORTH**	
	57	Capital Stock	Enter current capital stock figure. An increase will occur if capital stock is sold; a decrease will occur if existing stock is repurchased or retired.
	58	Retained Earnings	Add prior period retained earnings to projected net profit (line 16), and deduct dividends or withdrawals (line 31).
	59		Enter other equity items.
	60	TOTAL LIABILITIES AND NET WORTH	Enter sum of lines 56 through 59.

If you want to have some fun with your banker, put a Robert Morris form in front of him, then count the seconds it takes for his eyes to come to rest on lines 35 and 36. You won't get past 2 because these lines are called *cash*. That's my message about using a standardized accounting format. The second advantage is best appreciated when the entrepreneur makes a financial presentation to the venture capitalist. This is the same for any of these standardized accounting forms, not just Robert Morris. Your job is to discover the preference of the reader before you prepare your financials.

Now that I've told you all about the Robert Morris forms, let me add one caution. With the arrival of the desktop computer have come the VisiCalc fanatics. And the VisiCalc fanatics are even worse than their Robert Morris counterparts. While the group is still small, you might try to find out which presentation is preferred. Seven out of ten will want the Robert Morris forms, but those three exceptions won't be comfortable until they see the VisiCalc (or equivalent) printout. Also, other programs are now becoming popular, and the VisiCalc people may soon outnumber the Robert Morris old-timers.

Tip two is just as valuable as tip one, but it alone won't get your plan financed either. It's called "How You Price the Deal." Remember, if you have the wrong price for the wrong thing, you're in real trouble.

How much stock you give up to obtain how much money is the unanswerable question in a venture capital deal. You don't want to give up too much (after all, it's *your* money), or too little (after all, it's *their* money). The final ratio will undoubtedly be determined after some long-term and dead serious negotiating, so it's important that you know some rules of thumb.

1. With most entrepreneurial companies, you simply cannot use the price/earnings ratio (P/E) of similar companies because they will seldom offer an accurate equivalent to your situation.

2. A venture source wants to earn about 45% compounded annual return on all funds invested. Offer them much below 40% and they're usually not interested. If your projections are much over 60%, they'll become very skeptical. So in order to get financed, business plans should offer a 45% compounded return on investment (ROI). Here's a sample of how that works on a $1 million investment (all figures are in millions):

YEAR	VALUE OF AMOUNT INVESTED
1	1.45 M
2	2.10 M
3	3.05 M
4	4.42 M
5	6.40 M (5th year gain)

3. A 44% compounded ROI is approximately equivalent to six times your money in five years. That's the goal.

4. The total value of your company is determined by multiplying your after-tax earnings in the fifth year by an acceptable (usually low) P/E ratio. The most commonly used P/E ratio is 10. (More on this later.)

How to Price a Venture Capital Deal.
Here is a visual representation of the same data. As we explained, venture sources usually want a 45% Return On Investment (ROI)—6 times the investment over a five-year period.

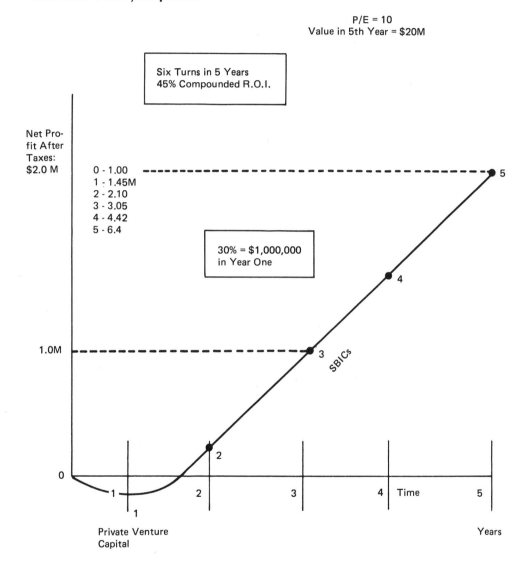

P/E = 10
Value in 5th Year = $20M

Six Turns in 5 Years
45% Compounded R.O.I.

Net Profit After Taxes: $2.0 M

0 - 1.00
1 - 1.45M
2 - 2.10
3 - 3.05
4 - 4.42
5 - 6.4

30% = $1,000,000 in Year One

1.0M

SBICs

Time

Years

Private Venture Capital

Hence, if your business projects after-tax earnings of $2 million in the fifth year, and you need $1 million now to launch your venture, how much of the company do you have to surrender to the venture capitalists? The answer is roughly 30%. Now, let's go over the way we arrive at that figure. First, multiply the standard P/E (10) times the after-tax earnings ($2 million). Then figure that if the venture capitalist gives you $1 million in *year one,* he'll require roughly $6 million in value by the end of *year five.* So if the value of the company, given a P/E of 10, is $20 million, and assuming the venture capitalist wants an ROI of about 44%, you will have to give up 30% ($6 million in value) of the company for $1 million in start-up money. That's the basic arithmetic.

What exactly is a P/E ratio? First it's the price per share divided by the earnings per share. But when an investor looks at a company's P/E, what does he or she see? Sex appeal. The P/E is a company's sex appeal. To an investor, the Ford Motor Company is a little unsexy these days because its P/E is down around 4. IBM, on the other hand, is very sexy because its P/E is up around 18 or 20. Are you beginning to get the picture?

Let's talk about one of the sexiest companies of all times: H. Ross Perot's Electronic Data Systems (EDS). When EDS went public, its P/E was 120. That means that for every dollar EDS earned, the value of the company increased by $120! To put that in perspective, let me give you this example. Let's say the Ford Motor Company earned $1 billion last year. If you multiply that by their P/E, you come up with a value of $4 billion. On the other hand, if EDS earned just 10% of that, $100 million, their value would be calculated at $12 billion, or three times that of the Ford Motor Company! Now that's what I call a financially sexy company!

chapter 2

Romancing the Money Men

ROMANCE AND THE BUSINESS PLAN

It is well established that you can't raise money without a business plan. If you ever try to raise money without one, the financial source will listen to your song and dance, then say, "Come back and see us again when your plan is ready." Over the last 10,000 years, God has been working overtime to create people, and in that time he's created all kinds of people. Someone said he created 20 billion people of all sorts and he created four people a second in 1983. But what has always fascinated me is that in all that time and with all that hard work, God has *never* created an overfinanced company!

Therefore, every company that has ever existed has had to start with some kind of plan. Maybe it's called a feasibility study or maybe it's called *the deal*, but it is a business plan by any name. One of the best ways to prepare yourself to prepare a business plan is to remove yourself from your own business. Step back as far as you can and take as objective a look as possible. One good way to help yourself gain this kind of objectivity is to examine other people's business plans before you go to work on your own. Moreover, you should look critically, examine exactly what is there, and try to figure out what is missing. Later, you should examine your own plan in the same way.

*How to Start, Finance, and Manage Your Own Small Business** has been a perennial best-seller primarily because it contains five different business plans. That's why I've put three new plans into this book.

I know better than to fool with success. But before you study those plans,

---

*Joseph Mancuso, *How to Start, Finance, and Manage Your Own Small Business*, rev., (Englewood Cliffs, N.J.: Prentice-Hall, Inc., 1984).

let me tell you how money men read a business plan. The thing they're really looking for is the romance. And it's an entrepreneur's job to bring the romance into the plan because most bankers and venture capitalists become bored with looking at the same thing again and again. The financial side will get their attention, but the romance is what is going to do the selling.

Moreover, don't copy someone else's plan, even those you judge to be perfect, like the three big winners at the back of this book.* Each plan, like every snowflake, must be different. Each is a separate piece of art. Each must be reflective of the individuality of the entrepreneur. Just as you wouldn't copy someone else's romancing techniques, so should you seek to distinguish your plan for its differences.

However, before I tell you what the romance is, it will help if I tell you one thing that it isn't. It isn't a plan's physical appearance. Entrepreneurs sometimes think they can disguise the flaws in a plan by putting it in a fancy package. I've seen plans that were bound in leather with gold printing on the front and plans with a lot of fancy typesetting, but believe me, if a plan isn't any good, none of that is going to help sell it. In fact, whenever I see a fancy package, it automatically sends up a red flag. I want to know what's wrong with the plan. The plans that are bound as a book are also a red flag.

The romance isn't in what the plan looks like. Rather, it's in what it says. The romance is the hook, and anyone who knows anything about romance knows what it's like to get hooked. It's the sizzle in the steak. So let's look at what is going to make a venture capitalist fall in love with your plan.

A History of Success.   More than anything else, the venture capitalist wants assurance of success. And nothing succeeds like success. If you (or team members) have done it once, they'll believe you can do it again.

A Well-Recognized Market.   Cures for cancer or herpes come with an automatic market. A restaurant doesn't. Sure, you say, but everybody has to eat. Of course, but unless you can show why people will want to eat *your* food (and I'm talking about an in-depth analysis, not just a few dozen great recipes), you're going to come up short in the romance department.

Somebody Big Is in It.   There's no better way to make a venture capitalist fall in love with your plan than to show him that someone else already has. That's not just romance; that's sex appeal. It's the attraction for what others possess.

Potential for Going Public.   In this respect, raising capital is a lot like the fashion business. In the fashion business, buyers try to decide what the public is going to want to wear in two years. The venture capitalist wants to speculate

*Venture Magazine, Inc., Storage Technology, Inc., and Shopsmith, Inc.

that your stock will appeal to public investors in three to seven years. You see, investors need to be liquid and to be highly profitable, too.

I Don't Want Your Money as Much as I Want Your Advice.   This one's tricky, but it's won many an investor. It sounds like flattery, and in a sense it is. The point is that you have to let them know that you want them on your board—that their experience and expertise is at least as necessary to your success as their money is. Don't worry—money always follows advice.

If Your Company Dies Tomorrow, Is the World Going to Suffer?   Before there was a personal computer, no one knew they needed one. Now it's a billion dollar market. If you have a plan for a product that will create a permanent market, you've got the romance.

THE MEN WHO MANAGE MONEY

The funny thing about money is that the only thing you can't buy with it is money. But you can buy money with stock. The only question is how to come up with the conversion rate to turn your stock into money. H. Ross Perot gives you one share of stock, and you give him $120 (when EDS's P/E ratio was 120), and what you're buying with that $120 is one dollar's worth of earnings. Remember, a good story is worth more than a marginal track record.

More venture capital is available today than there was last year. And there was more available last year than the year before that. Venture capital is a growth industry. And as more and more people get involved in venture capital, it begins to look more and more like the trend of the 1980s. It's becoming a glamour industry as well as a growth industry. And as the amount of venture capital goes up, so does the quality of the business plans being financed. That means that this year's 11 is just that much prettier than last year's. More money attracts more competition, and more competition raises the level of the game.

It's like mile runners. These days milers are coming in with times well under four minutes, but when Roger Bannister first broke the four-minute mile, it was really an awesome thing. Milers are getting faster and business plan preparers are getting better. The business plans in this book are all at least seven years old. So if you look at your plan in relation to these plans and find that your plan is lacking, you are in trouble!

		YEARS OF PLAN
1.	*Venture* Magazine	1977 October
2.	Storage Technology	1969 June
3.	Shopsmith	1971

The most valuable skill to learn when raising capital is the art of reducing risk. When I go to Las Vegas, I like to take all my chips to the roulette wheel, bet half of them on red and half of them on black, and pray that zero doesn't come up. What a venture capitalist wants to see is even better odds against losing, combined with a much bigger promise of return. At the same time, it's important to remember that venture capitalists make emotional decisions. (I'm sure some of you will say that venture capitalists have no emotions, but the truth is that no decisions about money are unemotional.) Very often, the seemingly coolest decision will be made emotionally, then justified with logic. Aristotle discovered this truth years ago, and if you are skeptic, please follow this little story for emphasis. It is important.

The weekend is coming up, and you're expecting company for dinner on Saturday. Now it's not Ronald and Nancy Reagan, but you still have a special reason for looking nice. It's an old friend that you haven't seen in years, and you're afraid that you just don't have the right clothes.

So you hop in your car and head for Bloomingdale's. You know they're having a sale, and you're hoping you can find something nice for under $1000. Suddenly, you notice a manikin wearing a very attractive dress that has been marked down from $2 million to $400, which is one hell of a markdown. The salesperson comes over to you while you're trying it on and says, "By God, Jennifer, you look great in that dress. In fact, you look fantastic."

You look in the mirror and conclude that she's right. Instead of just plain old Jennifer, you look fantastic. So you turn to the salesperson and say, "I have to take this home and let my husband see it. If he doesn't like it, I'll have to bring it back." She replies, "At Bloomingdale's, you can always bring it back." You buy the dress and bring it home.

Later, when your husband comes home from work, you fix him a nice dinner. After dinner (his belly is full) you say, "I bought a new dress for Saturday night." Before you have a chance to model it for him, he says, "How much did it cost?" Without answering him, you try it on (let the dress sell itself), and he says, "You look great Jennifer, but how much did it cost?"

"It was marked down from something like $2 million. I saved a fortune." He continues, "Never mind that, how much did it cost?" So you say, "It was only $400. I saved you $1,999,600!" And he says, "Oh come on, it's just your college roommate and her husband. I was planning on wearing jeans."

This goes on for quite awhile, and you say things like, "I can wear it for four seasons, and it doesn't even have to be dry cleaned so it will practically pay for itself." Then he says, "Honey, the kids are going to need braces soon, and we just can't afford it." Finally, you come up with the clincher. "Dear, this is the same size that your mother wears, and she's already told me that she wants to borrow it."

The decision to buy the dress was made as soon as she tried the dress on. After that, it was just a matter of justifying the decision. Almost everyone has had an experience like this, and believe it or not, venture capitalists have this experience more often than the rest of us. That's why the romance of the business plan is so important. The plan has to be so sexy and so exciting that the venture capitalist falls in love with it. For if a venture capitalist falls in love with a deal, he'll do the rest of the selling for you. Just the opposite also holds true. If the venture capitalist doesn't fall in love with your plan, no amount of selling is going to help it.

NINE QUESTIONS ANSWERED

1. What is the single most important aspect of the business plan, according to the venture capitalist?

   Management

2. List, in chronological order, the six steps in presenting a business plan.

   1. *Prospecting*
   2. *Approach*
   3. *Qualifying the source*
   4. *Presenting the plan*
   5. *Handling objections*
   6. *Gaining Commitment*

3. Name two elements of a business plan which can bring it from the 7 to 9 range, up to a 10.

   1. *Answer the negatives*
   2. *Answer sheet: 2(a) It's just like... 2(b) If it goes bad... 2(c) The other guys have deep pockets.*

4. List the five questions that a venture source needs an answer to.

   1. *What business are you in?*
   2. *How much money?*
   3. *For what percentage of the business?*
   4. *Who is in the deal?*
   5. *What is unique about the deal?*

5. In what order are the parts of a business plan read?

   1. *To determine the characteristics of the company & industry*
   2. *Terms of the deal*
   3. *Balance sheet*
   4. *Caliber of people*
   5. *To find the USP (Unique Selling Proposition)*
   6. *Once over lightly*

6. Rank, in order of importance, these ten sources of linkage people for introducing your deal to venture capital sources.

   1. Entrepreneur in the venture portfolio — *1*
   2. Another venture capitalist — *2*
   3. Accountant familiar with a venture source — *6*
   4. Lawyer familiar with a venture source — *7*
   5. Banker familiar with a venture source — *5*

6. Friend of a venture source _3_
7. Blind letter to a venture source _10_
8. Customer of a company familiar with a venture source _8_
9. Investor in a venture capitalist's portfolio _4_
10. Telephone a venture source _9_

7. Identify the nine members of an entrepreneurial team and circle the most important player.

1. *Partners*
2. *Lawyers*
3. *Accountants*
4. *Advertising Agencies*
5. *Consultants*
6. *Bankers*
7. *Board of directors*
7. *Manufacturer's agents*
9. *(Controller / VP Finance)*

8. What should be found on the summary page of the business plan?

1. *Percentage of the company being sold*
2. *Price per share VS last price pd share*
3. *Minimum investment (number of investors)*
4. *Total valuation (after placement)*
5. *Terms of placement*

9. What are the six most common debt/equity instruments available to a lender or investor?

1. *Common stock*
2. *Preferred stock*
3. *Debt with warrants*
4. *Convertible debentures*
5. *Subordinated convertible debt*
6. *Straight debt*

Now it's time to start talking about how to turn a business plan that's an 8 into a business plan that's an 11. One way of doing it is what I call "The Footwork Necessary."

THE FOOTWORK NECESSARY

How's your broken field running? Raising venture capital often parallels trying to make a touchdown through the best defense in the league. It takes fancy footwork to work your way over that goal line.

Let's say you want to raise $250,000 for 25% of your company in a private placement. First, you must get a venture capitalist lukewarm about your situation. No one will be really enthusiastic after only one visit. I've heard that Digital Equipment Corporation (DEC), of Maynard, Massachusetts, shopped around for quite a while before American Research and Development Corporation (AR&D) finally committed itself to the tune of $70,000, an investment which, rumor has it, is worth $200 million today.

Venture capitalists see dozens of deals a day, so it will not be easy to turn them on to your proposition. Besides, they are like sheep. They'd rather follow than lead. You have to be the sheep dog to keep the pack moving.

So, once you've got the first party lukewarm, plan your strategy carefully.

One strategy that usually works begins on the second visit when you say, "I know you're not in a position to go first in this package, but I have a proposition that should interest you. I already have other investors subscribed for the first $200,000. You can have the last $50,000. You don't have to sign anything—just give me a verbal commitment contingent on my getting the other $200,000 first."

If he agrees, repeat your story to anyone else who seems to be lukewarm and proceed to sell the last $50,000 five times. You have to deal from strength.

This example may be a little farfetched because someone has to go first. He's the one who counts, and he's the hardest one to find—not a sheep but a true venture capitalist.

This is the man who'll set the pace for the rest of the deal. Ask him for some sort of tentative percentages and terms and, after you've negotiated the terms, get a letter of intent for $50,000 spelling out the terms of the placement. You may have to make a few extra concessions to him, but once you have his pledge on paper or even verbally, your placement is in the bag and you should have the rest within two months. Touchdown!

Always talk to potential investors as if your deal is all but closed, and you may have to eliminate two or three investors from the package. Never act as if you need their help or you'll be tackled before you reach midfield; rather, suggest that this one time you'll accept their money. I can't overemphasize the need to *deal from strength*!

ANSWERING THE NEGATIVE

By now, you should be able to bring your plan up from an 8 to a 9. Answering the negatives will bring it up to a 10, and 10's get financed! As I've emphasized, raising capital is not the art of selling dreams, it's the art of reducing risk. Venture capital flows in an inverse relation to the level of risk involved.

So, whenever I put a business plan together, I begin by listing all the negatives. Then I answer them; first with a tape recorder, then on paper. The result should be consistent and concise descriptions of the negatives. As you plan to turn them around into opportunities, you see a problem is just an opportunity turned inside out.

Don't avoid it, don't sidestep it, and don't ignore it. Answer it. Head on! A great entrepreneur I worked with in Boston went bankrupt with an early company. Later, he developed a new company and went after venture capital. On the front page of his new business plan, he states that a past company of his went bankrupt. Now, rather than hemming and hawing when a venture capitalist says, "I hear you went belly up last time around," he's prepared to deal directly with the negative. And believe me, he doesn't answer by excusing his way out of responsibility: "First this conservative pension fund money fell through, then my partner was involved in a messy divorce, and that's just the beginning." Even if it's true, it sounds like sour grapes, and nobody ever raised money with sour grapes.

Instead, he practiced his answers to all the negatives, and when the question of the bankruptcy comes up, he says, "You know, I did go belly up last time, but I've started five businesses and I probably learned more from that one than from all the rest put together." One only need look to entrepreneurs like Henry Ford, Walt Disney, and Milton Hershey for prime examples of men who failed at least once before launching billion dollar businesses. John DeLorean's biggest problem was that DeLorean Motor Cars was his first failure, and he's already experienced too much success in the corporate world to learn how to be comfortable with failure. Sometimes, failure can be the biggest force behind a positive thinking entrepreneur.

You have to take the negative and make it a positive. If you try to explain it any other way, you'll get creamed. So I say, "Take your negatives and turn them around." For instance, if you're trying to raise money for a service business, the venture capitalist might say, "Why should I invest in a service business? Service businesses don't make money." Then you can say, "Well, you've heard of Frederick Smith and Federal Express, haven't you? What's that if not a service business? He's delivering packages overnight; I'm delivering flowers." He then might say, "You'll never pull this deal off because of a, b, c, and d." If you're well prepared, you can turn all those negatives around, and he'll finance your deal. That's the way you turn a 9 into a 10—by answering the negatives.

THE ANSWER SHEET

Now to turn those 10's into 11's takes another magical element. It's nicknamed "The Answer Sheet." The idea is that every business plan should contain an answer sheet that summarizes the key aspect of the plan. If you don't read any other part of the plans in this book, read the answer sheets! These three examples will show you how the answer sheet works for you in your business plan.

1. It's just like . . .
2. The other guys have deep pockets.
3. If it goes bad . . . .

It's Just Like . . .

Example 1.   Let's take a venture capitalist I know up in Boston who heads up the New England Venture Capital Company. We'll call him Peter. Peter is the dean of venture capital in the New England area. He's been at it for 30 years, and he runs about $150 million in several funds. Over the past 20 years, his average rate of return has been 46%. He's invested in Wang Laboratories, Unitrode, and Damon Engineering, just to name a few. But the two deals he missed (both in Massachusetts) are Digital Equipment (DEC) and Data General (DG), and those are two of the biggest venture capital deals in history. So when Peter goes home at night, his wife says, "How are you sweetheart? Nice to see you. Did any deals come along today that look like Digital or Data General?" So if the front end of your plan looks like DEC or DG, Peter is immediately interested.

On the other hand, there's a fellow in San Francisco who brought out Apple Computers. He runs a huge fund of venture money and is America's premier venture capitalist with an endowed chair at the Harvard Business School. Apple was only one of his big successes, and he now is listed in *Forbes* magazine as one of the richest people in the U.S. Let's call him Arthur.

Arthur dosen't need money, but thousands of people made millions of dollars investing along with Arthur. So when he goes out socially, his friends always pester him and ask, "Arthur, have you seen any more young Apple Computers . . . "

The Other Guys Have Deep Pockets.

Example 2.   This is the story of In-Line Technology, a company located in New Bedford, Massachusetts, and run by Gene St. Onge and Hank Bok.* Gene and Hank went to see a famous New York venture capitalist's Fifth Avenue apartment. During the breakfast, which lasted about two hours, the venture capitalist spent an hour and a half discussing a new painting that his wife had just purchased, then he spent a half hour discussing the business. But at the end of breakfast, the venture source agreed to put up half of the $200,000 that they were trying to raise. However, he made two conditions. The first

*See p. 350 of *How to Start, Finance, and Manage Your Own Small Business,* (rev.), by Joseph Mancuso (Englewood Cliffs, N.J.: Prentice-Hall, 1984).

condition was that he would not visit the company and analyze it because that alone would cost him another $25,000. The second condition was that they shouldn't call him if they ran out of money. "I'm going to make a little investment with you guys and see how it works," he said, "but I can't afford to spend a lot of time with your people."

Here's where the second principle of the answer sheet emerges: "The other guys have deep pockets." Having a secured a promise of $100,000 from a well-known venture capitalist, Gene and Hank had no problem raising the second $100,000. In fact, their deal was oversubscribed and they had to turn back some of the money. You see, everyone assumed that the other guy had deep pockets so the deal was safe. When the Rockefellers, General Electric, or whoever back your deal, you get credibility. That helps lower-level investors (friends and relatives) sponsor your deal. Fred Smith claimed the early commitment from General Dynamics was crucial to launching Federal Express—because everyone knows they have deep pockets.

If It Goes Bad . . .

Example 3.   Continuing with the story of In-Line Technologies, after about six months they did run out of money (not an uncommon experience for an entrepreneurial venture). And though they remembered the venture capitalist's instructions not to call him for help, they also knew that your best investors are your current investors. *By the way, you might want to go back and underline that sentence.* It's easily the most important in this book! So they picked up the phone and said, "Hello, Mr. Venture Capitalist, this is Gene and Hank. Right. The ones who had breakfast with you and looked at your wife's new painting. Well, the news is that we're out of money and we need another $200,000 to keep us going."

As you might expect, the venture capitalist wasn't quite as cavalier as he appeared when he first made the investment because before he put up the money, he sent the business plan to a portfolio company on the West Coast where he was a director. This company needed the technology that In-Line had developed, and the venture manager and the executive vice-president had both said, "Gee, this business plan looks interesting." You see, the venture capitalist had his backside well covered because one of his portfolio companies was willing, able, and even anxious to pick up the company *if it ever went bad!*

To make the long story short, the West Coast company flew East and bought In-Line Technologies in a 30-day period, and all of the In-Line investors wound up with a healthy profit on what turned out to be a short-term investment. So the third message on the answer sheet should always be a contingency plan. In other words, *if it goes bad . . .*

Three ways of many to create an answer sheet were just presented. But it's up to you to consider ways. Don't limit yourself to only these three choices.

Just remember, an answer sheet is so valuable to a business plan that you only need read it to be excited enough to invest. The plan is necessary, but the answer sheet provides the compelling motivation to be a part of this deal.

NARROWING YOUR FOCUS

When searching out a venture source, it's important that you quickly focus on locating the sources most likely to arrange capital for you. Making a thorough presentation to a venture source can be an exhausting process, so there's little point in wearing yourself out trying to sell a restaurant to someone who specializes in high-tech, or vice versa. You are selling to the wrong person. You need to locate the right person to have any hope of selling the business plan.

There are five categories of potential investors for every venture capital deal.

1. People who are *familiar* with you, your product, and your industry.
2. People who are *familiar* and have *made money* with you, your product, and your industry.
3. People who are *familiar* and have *made money* with you, your product, and your industry and *have money* to invest.
4. *Gap Analysis*—A financial source who is overinvested in the industries. He is most familiar with and seeking initial investments in new industries.
5. *New Boy on the Block*—Dozens of new venture funds are being formed every year. Each fund has to have a *first* investment, and it's easier to be the first investment in a fund than to be the last.

These five categories are windows of opportunity for those seeking venture capital. And while no hard statistics exist, my estimate is that the appeal of each of the five is as follows:

1	10%
2	25%
3	50%
4	10%
5	5%
Total	100%

In other words, 25% of all completed venture deals would fall most closely into category 2, while only 5% would most readily fall into category 5. But each of these five categories of reasons to invest are equally viable to the entrepreneur beginning a search for capital.

COMMON SENSE

When I train venture capitalists in reading business plans, what type of tricks do you think I show them to trip up unprepared entrepreneurs? Believe it or not, the best and most telling way to find out if an entrepreneur knows his stuff is to ask these three common sense questions. Good venture sources ask them intuitively. Please answer them below.

1. On a scale of 1 to 10, what's your plan? _____

   _____

2. What business are you in? _____

   _____

3. Have you shown this plan to anyone else? _____

   _____

The answers to question aren't as easy as you think, so stop and think a minute before you answer. Please list your answers before you read my comments. It will make what you are about to read more useful.

1. An honest answer might be, "Hell, we've been working on this plan for three months now and we were afraid that if we just didn't get it done, we'd never get any money." Stop right there. Never tell a venture source you haven't brought him the best plan you know how to write. You should always tell him it's a 10, or if you're really confident, an 11. (If you're not overconfident, how can anyone else become convinced of its merits?)

2. When a venture source asks you what business you're in, he wants a clear, concise answer. Answers like, "I'm in the people business," or "I'm in the business of making money," or "Actually, I'm in six businesses," all sidestep the question. They're cute answers for cocktail parties, but they don't raise money. An example of a crisp and articulate answer might be, "We manufacture specialized equipment for a growing segment of the telecommunications industry," and go on from there. This seems like an easy question, but it's also an easy question to get tripped up on if you're not ready. Please see my comments in Chapter 3 (under the heading "What Business Am I In?") for further amplification of this point.

3. This is the trickiest question of the three. If you say, "No one," it's sort of like saying, "You're the first person I've ever kissed." It's a flattering answer, but is it credible? Of course, there's a way to turn that question around to make "no one" a credible answer, and I'll get to that in a minute. The other answer is "Yes, I showed it to so and so." Then the venture capitalist will undoubtedly respond, "Well, what did so and so say?" And you will probably say, "He's thinking about it." Then the venture capitalist will probably respond (and this is the kiss of death), "If so and so says yes, come back and we'll talk." An alternate answer is, "Yes, I showed it to so and so, and he turned it down," but if you're going to give an answer like that, you're asking not to get financed. Who wants to invest in the rejects of others?

The best answer (unless the answer "no one" is actually true) is "I went to so and so for advice, and he liked the plan but said he was oversubscribed (or another credible nondestructive reason) in my industry, so he referred me to you." That is the only answer that is both credible and positive.

YOUR BOARD OF DIRECTORS

The first question a venture capitalist asks when looking at a plan is "Who are the people?" And the answer is easy to find. _____ is the president, _____ is the treasurer, and _____ is the controller. If their names are known and they have good reputations, that's all to the good. But what if their names aren't known? The selling job just becomes that much harder. That is, unless the venture capitalist can find a strong board of directors, or consultants or investors he does know. It's nice to do business with successful people who are familiar.

Very often, an entrepreneur will neglect to build a board of directors. That can only hurt when it comes time for financing. A good board doesn't just happen, but if you're going to invest the time and energy (not to mention money) it takes to write a good plan, it pays to take the time and trouble to build a good board. I seldom see a plan that's an 11 that doesn't have a great board of directors. And while a good board doesn't necessarily make a good company, it certainly won't hurt. The recognition factor of a few names on a board will go a long way toward influencing a venture capitalist to finance someone who comes without any other built-in recommendations. The same holds for consultants and investors.

RAISING CAPITAL

When Is the Best time to Raise Capital?

The best time to sell is immediately after you've sold, and the best time to raise capital is immediately after you've raised capital—in other words, when you don't need it. This is Mancuso's Law of Small Business. The theory behind this phenomenon was developed by Dr. Leon Festinger of Columbia University, and it is known as the theory of cognitive dissonance. Cognitive means awareness, and dissonance means stress, so in other words, the theory is based on the awareness of internal stress.

Every individual who makes a difficult decision, including investment decisions, suffers from cognitive dissonance. When the stress reaches an intolerable level, the individual will take action to reduce it, returning himself to a level of equilibrium. And there's no more difficult and stressful decision than whether or not to invest in a small business.

What actions does an individual take to reduce stress? Let me use the common example of the automobile buyer. Assume that you are torn between purchasing one of three different mid-sized cars. On a free Saturday, you go first to the Ford dealership, then across the street to the Chevy dealer, and finally, down the street to the Plymouth dealer. Because you are a value-conscious buyer, you compare the features and prices of each car. But after these comparisons, you are still undecided as to which is the best value. After a week of pouring over all of the brochures, the only thing you are sure of is that you want to hurry up and get this process over with. So you finally decide to make a commitment—you go with the dealer you trust the most. For you, the whole decision-making process has been difficult and stressful.

This process occurs every day, and since millions of new cars are sold annually, many of us have experienced it. Everyone claims to have gotten a "good deal." I don't know of anyone who has ever admitted to making a bad deal as a result of this process.

This decision is known as a "stress decision" and the purchaser's dissonance is very high. When you bring the car home as the new owner, you take the following steps to reduce that dissonance and to justify the purchase.

1. You may inadvertently choose to leave the car in your driveway, rather than putting it in the garage. Or, you may drive it around and park it where it will be conspicuous to your peers.
2. The night you bring the car home, you will undoubtably read the owner's manual and begin to search out new information on the car you have chosen. (You will then misplace the manual and never read it again.)
3. You will become extremely receptive to television, newspaper, and magazine advertising about the car you just purchased. The car will be the single most exciting thing in your life for a short period of time, and you will ignore all other automobile ads for other cars. You will continually discover new reasons that your chosen automobile was a brilliant choice.

Because automobile companies are aware that you suffer from dissonance, they even go so far as to send you a personal letter from their headquarters (usually the president) congratulating you on your wise choice. Later they will even request your help by sending you a questionnaire about the process that went into selecting the car. There are easier and less expensive ways for automobile companies to learn this statistic information, but this technique allows the individual to vent any residual dissonance he may suffer from.

The message is simple. The best time to sell is immediately after you've sold, and the best time to make a sales call is immediately after you've made a sale. In the same way, the best time to raise money is when you don't need it or after you've just received money. This concept is built on Dr. Leon Festinger's theory of cognitive dissonance, and more importantly, it works. Mancuso's primary law of small business is: The only time to raise capital is when you don't need it!

THE ENTREPRENEURIAL MODEL FOR RAISING CAPITAL

The process of raising capital generally requires a specific sequence of actions. I call them the "Six-Step Process." Understanding this process can really improve your chances for success.

Step 1:   Locating Sources
Step 2:   The Approach
Step 3:   Qualifying the Source
Step 4:   Presenting the Business Plan
Step 5:   Handling Objections
Step 6:   Gaining the Commitment

Step 1: Locating Sources.   Without a doubt, prospecting is the hardest part of raising capital. Once you find the right person, your business plan will do most of the talking. This first step should occupy about ½ of the entire time used to prepare and present a business plan. Most entrepreneurs fail to do this step well and, consequently, fail at raising capital.

Step 2: The Approach.   During the approach, two things must occur. First, you should seek to reduce tension in your relationship with the venture source. While it may at times seem like an adversarial relationship, it is important to remember that your goal is to make money *together*. Second, the entrepreneur should simultaneously be building a degree of task tension. As relationship tension is reduced, a reciprocal concern about building up the task at hand should occur. The venture source needs to invest capital, and you need to raise capital. Fulfilling your mutual needs is the task you must accomplish *together*.

Step 3: Qualifying the Source.   This is also known as the "Hot Button," and it focuses on the reason that the venture source *will* eventually wish to be included in the deal. Every situation has its salient features and attributes. Certain benefits among the features will be more important to individual capital sources than others. Not everyone invests in the same deal for the same reasons. In fact, the same plan is likely to be supported by different people for different reasons. Which button is going to be the one to press in order to raise money? What is it that this source needs? These questions can only be answered through a careful study of the venture source's portfolio and needs. (See the section called "Twelve Questions to Ask a Venture Source.")

Step 4: Presenting the Plan.   This is the step entrepreneurs handle best. They are so familiar with their product, having lived with it night and day, that they can always make a convincing presentation. The principal issue to stress in a business plan presentation is benefits:

> What is the perceived value of your product vs. what your product actually does?
> What are its features?
> Why will everyone need your product or service?
> What will it replace?
> What is it most similar to?
> What will happen to your customers if they don't buy your product or service?

Step 5: Handling Objections.   There will always be objections or attempts to postpone the investment with a discussion of the weakness of your plan or your product. How should you handle these objections? I suggest this very simple technique, which I call the "Feel, Felt, Found Method." It works like this: When an objection is raised, don't disagree with it. Don't be negative. Whatever you do, make sure you respond to the objection in a sincere way. Empathize with it, legitimize it, then introduce new information to counter the objection.

Never counter an objection without first saying something to the effect of, "I understand how you *feel* about that. In fact, you're not the first person to bring this point up; I even *felt* that way initially. However, this is not going to be a problem because . . . ." In order to raise capital, you must be both patient and persistent.

The first two steps are to agree with his objection, and the third step changes his mind. The new information should be introduced something like this: "I'm going to show you some new information that we've just completed that should set your mind at ease." Usually you say "we found". . . . Remember, a venture source is never wrong. Occasionally they are only partially informed, but they are never wrong. Your job is to have all the facts at hand so you can turn the objection around—make a *no* into a *yes*.

Step 6: Gaining the Commitment.   This has traditionally been viewed as the most difficult step in raising capital. But this just isn't so. The most difficult steps are locating, then qualifying the source—finding the "Hot Button." If locating and qualifying the source, the approach, and the presentation are handled properly, then gaining the commitment will be the easiest and least stressful step in the entire process. And to gain a commitment, you may want to create an opportunity to close on an objection. To do this you must first sense what the venture source's prime objection is, then lead him to it, and by using the "Feel, Felt, Found Method," turn it around.

Frequently, an entrepreneur comes to enjoy the raising capital process so much that he will talk himself right past the close. In other words, he will continue presenting the plan when he should be making the deal. Don't be afraid to close early, because one of the things a venture source is investing in is your enthusiasm. Finally, remember that raising capital is the art of reaching an agreement. It is a process of building trust and confidence. Much of an entrepreneur's skill involves being able to listen while maintaining the inner desire to perform. Mastering the art of raising capital insures the opportunity to perform.

As a rule of thumb, you should be doing the most talking in the begining of the six-step process, asking questions, and learning. The venture source should do most of the talking near the end of the presentation. Too often this mode of talking and listening is reversed.

chapter 3

How to Write an 11

More than anything, raising capital is the art of success, and a venture capitalist's most important skill is the ability to recognize success in its early stages. But success is a funny thing because the people who want it right away seldom get it, and the people who get it are usually working so hard that they hardly notice it (at least not at first). Textron's founder, Royal Little, who's still going strong at age 89, attributes his success to two things: "Patience and persistence." Those two traits will serve you well in the business plan process as well. A statement I always liked about entrepreneurship is that it is 1% inspiration and 99% perspiration.

The entrepreneur's job is to demonstrate his success in a way that a venture capitalist will understand it. That's why the Six-Step Process is so important. By striking just the right balance between patience and persistence, it may not make the process of raising capital any easier, but it will make it more efficient. Don't think an efficient presentation will be lost on a venture capitalist.

PROSPECTING

I've said it before and I'll say it again: Prospecting is the hardest part of preparing a business plan. As much as 50% of your time should be spent prospecting. One of the biggest mistakes an entrepreneur can make is to write a terrific plan, then spend his time showing it to the wrong venture sources. It's demoralizing, and it will just wear you down. Not only do you have to match yourself to your business, you have to match your business to your financial source.

For most entrepreneurs, this is a big revelation. When I've mentioned in seminars that an entrepreneur should spend at least three months prospecting, I've gotten looks that said the audience thought I was crazy. "What am I supposed to do," I've been asked more than once, "spend three months walking up and down Wall Street?" No, Wall Street has nothing to do with it. The time you spend prospecting shouldn't be spent prospecting for venture capitalists, but instead, prospecting for entrepreneurs. This is a very novel concept, but it works.

Start out by studying Stanley Pratt's *Guide to Venture Capital Sources* (see Appendix) for the venture sources who are investing in your industry plus several of the guidebooks and directories (I like David Silver's *Who's Who in Venture Capital*). Once you have all of the names and addresses, you should call or write to each one you have determined would be a good potential investor and ask for a list of their portfolio of investments. For simplicity's sake, let's say you select Fred Adler (at Adler & Company) in New York. He's a technology investor, and let's say you've got a software deal that you think is just right for him. The first thing you do is to take a look at his investments. You discover that he's already got investments in seven software companies. Your next step is to get the names of those seven entrepreneurs. You then pick out the ones closest to you and start calling them. Introduce yourself and say something like, "I'm an entrepreneur down here in Tampa and I noticed that your operation was right up in St. Pete. I'm putting together a business plan and I thought you might be able to look it over and give me a few tips. I know you've been successful raising money, and maybe you could give me a few pointers that would help polish the plan. Do you work on Saturdays? Maybe I could drop it by Saturday morning and you could have a look at it."

You drop it off on Saturday. A week later you call him back and say, "Hi. I wonder if I could drop by next Saturday so we can talk about the problems I'm having putting the finishing touches on my plan." Pretty soon, this entrepreneur is involved. You see, entrepreneurs love to get those kinds of phone calls; they love to help each other out. And I'll tell you a secret: Everything you've heard about entrepreneurs being ornery and independent is true, but there's a certain camaraderie betweeen entrepreneurs—a linkage.

Now you have this entrepreneur involved—one of Fred Adler's portfolio investments. He's going to see Adler periodically and he's going to mention, "A funny thing happened to me, Fred. So and so who works over at so and so came over and I gave him a hand with his business plan. He's got a neat idea." A couple of months later he sees him again and says, "Fred, you remember so and so who worked at so and so? He left so and so and now he's working full time on the deal." A little later, he speaks to Adler and says, "You remember so and so? Well he's got the prototype finished, and it's working pretty well. I think it's a pretty good deal." So Adler says, "Why don't you give me the guy's phone number?"

All of this started because you phoned the entrepreneur. And if you're smart enough, you might say something like, "I see you have a board of directors." That's usually all you have to say, and when you put *your* board together, he'll be one of your key linkage people.

How many people do you do this with? In my example, it took only one phone call to get the ball rolling. In reality, you may have to speak to several different entrepreneurs. As I said, this may take three or more months, but the contacts you make will be invaluable.

I'd like to say I invented this technique myself, but I didn't. The way I discovered it was by asking venture capitalists where they got their leads. More than half of the time their answer was that leads come from their existing portfolio companies. More than half! It's a common sense thing, but you'd be surprised at how many entrepreneurs never think of it. After all, the financial source obviously has confidence in the people he invests in and trusts their judgment. Not only that, this experienced entrepreneur is multilingual. He knows how to speak your language, and he also knows how to speak the financial language. This is very important because you may need him to act as an interpreter.

You may ask, "Aren't entrepreneurs concerned about creating competition for themselves—especially if they're in the same field?" Well, they may be, but most of the time, they'll be willing to help. Furthermore, if a business is *so* similar to yours that the entrepreneur turns you down, his venture capitalist wouldn't be able to do the deal anyway because in the long run, before a venture capitalist invests in a company, he clears it with portfolio companies in the same field.

The concept is to call the entrepreneur, not the venture capitalist. The venture source gets thousands of calls. You'll be somewhat unique because the entrepreneur gets much less attention. Then again, he just could be flattered to hear from you.

THE APPROACH

Now you're ready for the approach. Whether you come in with an introduction from another entrepreneur or not, you will need to know some common tips. The first tip, believe it or not, is called "Hiding the Business Plan."

Some entrepreneurs walk into an office business-plan-first. Then they lay it down on the venture capitalist's desk as though it were the Bible. The venture capitalist then picks it up, looks it over quickly, and starts off the conversation with tough, sometimes impossible, questions. Before they even get a chance to get warmed up, they've blown the presentation. The venture capitalist does all the initial talking, and they are at an immediate disadvantage.

I say, keep the plan behind your back (or in your briefcase), and begin the conversation with something like, "I've looked over the investment patterns of several venture capital firms and think you are the logical choice for our deal because a, b, c, and d." You run off a list. This kills two birds with one stone—two big birds. First, you've bypassed the tricky question, "Who else have you shown the plan to," and second, the venture capitalist is now involved (by association) in the preparation of the document.

By showing him you've done your homework, you immediately get his attention. You're not just hunting and pecking like the guys who parade through his office on a regular basis. You've gotten the relationship off the ground on the right foot, and when he shows the deal to his partners, he's more likely to champion your cause. Remember the analogy earlier about emotional investment decisions: The analogy of buying a dress is right on!

THE "HOT BUTTON"

What usually happens when an entrepreneur arrives at a venture capitalist's office is that he leads with his business plan—plunks it down on the desk, then plays dodgeball for the next hour. That's a game where you stand in the middle of a circle and they throw balls at you. Venture capitalists are experts at the game. Just when you think you've ducked and dodged every ball, they'll let you have it from out of nowhere.

The problem is that you can't play dodgeball with a venture capitalist for more than a couple of minutes. Sooner or later he's going to ask you questions like, "What business are you in?" "How are you going to capture a significant market share?" and "If your company drops dead tomorrow, will the world still be OK?" These are the kinds of questions that seem simple enough, but they can get you in a lot of trouble if you aren't fully prepared to handle them.

You think you've brought him the greatest thing since sliced bread, but he knows twenty ways of saying, "So what?" And he won't give you any chance to rest. Just when you think you can give him a good answer to one question, he asks you another, and another. The venture source expects every question to be answered when he asks it, and the more you think you're being bombarded, the more impatient he gets. You're thinking, "If I could just answer these one at a time, if I could just get out of the circle and they'd stop throwing balls at me, I'd be OK." So the trick is to be prepared—not just to answer his questions, but to ask some of your own. The best way to get out of the circle for awhile is to put him in it. The person who's in control is the person asking the questions. And it's your job to be in control, so I've included a list of twelve questions you might want to use. Armed with these questions, you're going to stand up a hell of a lot better, and you're going to stand a lot better chance of finding his "Hot Button." Once you've found it, you want to push it.

LIST OF QUESTIONS TO ASK A VENTURE CAPITALIST

1. Ask for a list of his past investments and for the names and addresses of the entrepreneurs.
2. Ask about his most successful investments and the reasons for their success.
3. Ask about his most unsuccessful investments and the reasons they went bad.
4. Ask about the nature of his venture capital funds: SBIC or nonSBIC.
5. Ask about the length of partnership maturity.
6. Ask how long he's been in business.
7. Ask about the depth of his pockets—how far he will go to support an investment.
8. Ask about the decision-making process within his firm.
9. Ask about access to limited partners.
10. Ask him why you should deal with him.
11. Ask about the venture firm he likes to team up with.
12. Ask him what type of investor he will be: Active, Passive, Leader, or Follower.

Remember, in the first interview, the venture capitalist is trying to find out what makes you tick. If you want to do business with him, you're going to want to find out what makes him tick, as well. So these questions will accomplish two things. First, they'll let him know you're an inquisitive, take-charge guy. Second, they'll help you draw him out. If, for instance, you ask him why a particular investment went bad, and he begins to list the problems with genuine regret, you might want to concentrate on how your company will avoid those problems. Furthermore, you might want to solicit his advice on how to avoid other problems of that nature that might crop up. That's his "Hot Button." He wants an investment that will make what he learned from past investments pay off.

PRESENTING THE PLAN

When you finally do hand over your plan, the venture source will glance at it briefly and begin his preliminary comments. No matter how good you think your plan is, he's not going to look at it and say, "This is the greatest plan I've ever seen!" so don't go in looking for praise. It's highly likely that his remarks will be critical, and even if they aren't, they'll seem that way. Don't panic. Even if it seems like an avalanche of objections, bear in mind that Digital Equipment Corporation (DEC) was turned down by everyone before American Research & Development (AR&D) in Boston decided to take a $70,000 chance on them. That might not seem like much now, but at the time it made all the difference. And Fred Adler didn't put $25,000 into Data General until all of the other established venture capitalists had turned down the deal. These are two of the best venture capital deals of all time and they almost didn't happen, so don't expect results in the first twenty minutes.

HANDLING OBJECTIONS

Raising capital is the art of reducing risks, not the art of selling dreams. And it's likely that most of the objections you hear will come in the form of questions, and most of these questions will be concerned, directly or indirectly, with reducing the level of risk. Therefore, you should answer each question carefully with the goal of reducing the risk to zero.

Here are some examples of the typical objections you might hear. "You've assembled a great team for research, but you've no controller. Smitty here has got a management background, but you really need a financial man for a controller." Or, "According to your plan, John Q. is an engineer, but you've got him set up as your marketing director." Running a small company is never easy, and raising capital is like a trial by fire. At this point, you may want to say, "Hey, we're a small company; we can't afford . . . ."

I've even seen it happen that after the third or fourth objection, the entrepreneur says, "Hey, I don't want your money." But you don't walk into a venture capitalist's office to get your ego stroked; you're there to raise money. So just be patient. As an entrepreneur, you're going to have to be part alchemist; that is, you're going to have to know how to turn lead into gold. In other words, you need to take the objection and turn it around—make it work for you. What I recommend is the "Feel, Felt, Found Technique."

Feel, Felt, Found Technique

First you say, "I understand how you feel."

What I'm doing here is taking a sales technique that has worked for years and applying it to raise capital. What this technique does is to differentiate between the product feature and the customer benefit. For instance, every hardware store in the world sells quarter-inch drill bits, but what their customers buy are quarter-inch holes. IBM claims that its factories produce accounts receivable and payable systems, but its field sales force sells management information systems. Or, as Charles Revson, founder of Revlon, once said, "In our factory we make cosmetics. In the store we sell hope." Now, I'll show you how to put this technique to work for you.

When the venture capitalist objects to John Q. as your marketing director, the first thing you should do is to agree. Say something like, "I know exactly how you feel. It's very uncommon that an engineering person is also a skilled marketing person. I had the same reaction you did when my partner suggested him. But . . ." And here's where you supply the missing pieces of information.

I've said it before, but it's worth saying again. A venture capitalist is never wrong, he's simply not completely informed. So here's where you supply the information that puts a fix on the big picture. "But, John Q.'s been on the team for six months now, and just listen to what we *found* out he's accomplished. He already has a purchase order from Intel, and we worked on Intel for two and a half years and came up empty. Not only that, he's written a purchase order from General Mills with advance payment-in-full. He's also instituted the first sales/cost control system in our history. He's a very methodical person, not at all flamboyant. And what we've *found* is . . ." Do you get the picture? You take the objection and spin it around. That's the raising capital game. Very often, a venture capitalist will challenge your plan, as much to get a chance to watch you think on your feet as to find out how a problem might be resolved.

GAINING THE COMMITMENT

If a venture capitalist is genuinely interested in your deal, you should be able to get him to say so. Conversely, if he's not interested, it won't do either of you any good to end the meeting with a maybe. Maybe's don't meet payrolls.

If you've done all your homework to this point—if you've boiled down the venture capital firms to the top 3 to 5 for your kind of deal—then this is really the moment of truth. You want the venture capitalist to look over your business plan, look back at you, and say, "You've got a deal." Well it doesn't happen that way. No venture capitalist is going to say *yes* at the first meeting, but if you're really lucky, he might say *no*. Why do I say that? Because nine times out of ten, the venture capitalist is going to say *maybe*. So if you try like hell to get him to say *no* to the deal and he won't do it, maybe you're a step closer to being financed. Venture sources are experts at using the word *maybe*. It's their favorite word.

Remember, as much as you've practiced holding the business plan behind your back and saying, "Don't worry about it, it's in the plan," he's got more practice saying *maybe*. That's why the realistic thing to do is to go for the *no*. *Maybe* sounds like *maybe so* to you, but it means *probably not*, and you don't want to hang up your deal on false hopes. Once you get the *no*, you can gather information for your visit to the next venture capitalist with my ten questions, "What to do When a Venture Capitalist Turns You Down."

Armed with the information you've gathered at your first meeting, you should go into the next venture capitalist's office with the same intention: to get a *no*. You go through the whole song and dance again (maybe with a little more polish this time), and you go for the *no*. And it may be a little harder to get this time. The point is that you're probably not there to get money for next year; you want it next month or next week. *Maybe* means, "Maybe I'll tell you *no* next month."

You visit your three or four most likely venture capitalists, and if you can't get them to say, "We don't want the deal," then it becomes a waiting game. Chances are that if they're going to finance you, they won't hang you up so long that they endanger the company. If they're not . . . well, that's why you've tried to get the *no*'s. If your best bets turn down the deal, there's probably something wrong with it. Then you're back to the drawing board. Maybe

WHAT TO DO WHEN A VENTURE CAPITALIST
TURNS YOU DOWN: TEN QUESTIONS

1. *Confirm the Decision*: "That means you do not wish to participate at this time?"
2. *Sell for the Future*: "Can we count you in for a second round of financing, after we've completed the first?"
3. *Find Out Why You Were Rejected*: "Why do you choose not to participate in this deal?" (Timing? Fit? All filled up?)
4. *Ask for Advice*: "If you were in my position, how would you proceed?"
5. *Ask for Suggestions*: "Can you suggest a source who invests in this kind of deal?"
6. *Get the Name*: "Whom should I speak to when I'm there?"
7. *Find Out Why*: "Why do you suggest this firm, and why do you think this is the best person to speak to there?"
8. *Work on an Introduction*: "Who would be the best person to introduce me?"
9. *Develop a Reasonable Excuse*: "Can I tell him that your decision to turn us down was based on _____?"
10. *Know Your Referral*: "What will you tell him when he calls?"

it's your plan, maybe it's your people, or maybe it's your product. Try to find out what they don't like about it, then rework it and bring it back. Don't start picking out venture capitalist firms at random, trying to sell them the plan that you couldn't sell your best bets, because it's just going to mean more time and more frustration. If your best bets don't want the deal, then 999,999 chances out of a million, the firms that you've already ruled out won't want it either.

What do you do? If you really believe in your plan and you need money right away, you may have to go for debt. If you can wait, you go back and work on your plan some more. You use everything you've learned from everyone you've talked to, and you try to make it that much better. Those are my suggestions for what to do when you don't get financed (and not everybody will). When you *do* get financed—and my technique has raised hundreds of millions of dollars—then the hard work begins.

Remember, only the best business plans (10's and 11's) raise venture capital. The others **raise capital** that has to be paid back (debt) or must be internally generated.

WHAT BUSINESS AM I IN?

How to Establish Corporate Strategy

No one knows for sure what makes one corporate strategy work and others fail. It is known that those companies that succeed have better strategies than those that fail. It's not known whether the strategy causes success or the success results from the strategy. Consequently, it is difficult to offer reliable advice about setting corporate strategy in entrepreneurial ventures. More practical advice is possible about ineffective strategies.

While setting strategy, the leader must assimilate the many variables that interact simultaneously while developing a strategy. Strategy is a function reserved only for the Chief Executive Officer of a small company. The top guy is the lead dog in the sled pack, and he exchanges an unobtrusive view of what's in front for a willingness to establish the course.

A computer will never lose in competition to the world's greatest human checker player—it will at least draw with the most talented checker-playing human beings. In other words, the computer has the capacity to assimilate the finite number of moves in a checker game, and it is programmed to always win or at least draw. It can never lose. The best a human can achieve against a computer in checkers is a draw. This is not so in the more complex game of chess.

A master chess player can best a computer almost consistently—not an average chess player, mind you, but a master chess player. The reason the computer cannot outthink a master chess player is two-fold: 1) The computer can't handle within its memory the capacity a human being can handle within its memory. In other words, a person's brain can store and access more data of a useful nature than the computer's memory. 2) A computer must handle decisions on a step-by-step incremental or digital basis, whereas an individual can decide upon a strategy that encompasses a wide range or series of moves (analog), and the master chess player can beat the computer in most chess games.

Effective management of small business requires a clear and concise answer to the question, "What business are you in?" This single question has been most difficult to resolve for all business people, for small as well as large businesses. The answer is elusive, and the pace of internal or external changes is a small enterprise requires an endless examination of this question. This question is the full-time focus of most presidents and executives. Its answer is the zenith of intellectual achievement for any leader or chief executive officer. All but a handful of leaders answer it ineffectively and thereby fail at this most fundamental level of conceptualization. According to Mr. Peter Drucker, a management expert, all companies that answer this question properly eventually succeed.

"What business am I in?" is the question that establishes the mission of any organization. An effective answer requires a definite, accurate, meaningful statement of an organization's goals, objectives, and purposes. The question is a bit circular and jelly-like, but it lies at the heart of leadership-related activities in a profit-seeking business. A complete answer requires a comprehensive analysis of the strengths and weaknesses of the firm, combined with an appreciation of the firm's future needs within a changing marketplace. This issue was originally articulated by Peter Drucker in the mid-fifties in his classic book, *The Practice of Management*, and has become one of the most popular subjects for modern management.

While "What business am I in?" might also be a casual thought for a lost shopper, it has another more crucial focus. The answer to this central question separates good from bad management. It's a circular question that never ends, much like the individual's counterpart, "Who am I?" The strategy of selecting the right business to be in is only part of the right answer. To be a success requires more. The right answer must be followed up with winning tactics and execution to achieve management success. Tactics and strategy must interplay to properly answer the question, "What business am I in?"

Comparing tactics with strategy, it can be said the strategy employed determines whether one wins or loses a war. The tactics for a single battle determine the outcome of the battle, not necessarily the war. Definition from *Webster's New Collegiate Dictionary*:

STRATEGY: from the Greek, meaning *generalship*; The science and art of employing the political, economic, psychological and military forces of a nation or a group of nations to afford the maximum support to adopted policies in peace or war. The science and art of military command exercised to meet the enemy in combat under advantageous conditions. A careful plan or method. The art of devising plans toward a goal.

This last statement in the definition about goals best suits our purpose. It relates well to running entrepreneurial ventures. Now, in Webster's definition of *tactics,* we find that again it is a word derived from the Greek.

TACTICS: The art and science of disposing and maneuvering forces in combat. The art and science of employing available means to accomplish an end. A system or mode of procedure.

Notice how *tactics* differs from *strategies.*

The objectives of all dedicated employees should be to analyze all situations thoroughly, anticipate all problems prior to their occurrence, have answers for these problems, and move swiftly to solve these problems when called upon. However, when you are up to your ass in alligators, it is difficult to remind yourself that your initial objective was to drain the swamp.

Notice the difference between strategies and tactics in this often quoted phrase. It's catchy the way they interrelate in the story because each individual can relate to the story of draining the swamp, which is the long term objective. But the alligators of life tend to get in the way. That's why some entrepreneurs are successful, and some are not.

In the year 378, the Roman Emperor Valens and 40,000 Roman legionnaires were slain in battle by an inferior force of Goths led by Fritigem. On the field of Mars near Adrianople, these Romans fell victim to an opponent who developed and implemented a superior plan of battle. The demise of the empire was foretold as adversaries began outfoxing and outfighting the theretofore immovable Romans.

The consequences of mismanagement for presidents of small companies can be equally disastrous. A poorly managed small company can actually cease to exist if it performs poorly, whereas its larger competitors do not face such frightening consequences. Without a doubt, the issues that separate success and failure for small companies focus on small business strategy.

Examples

Let's look at some "for instances" on the same basis. How about soft drinks? In the late 1920s the leading manufacturer of soft drinks was a Boston-based company known as Moxie. They had a larger market share than Coca-Cola. Moxie determined their critical skill to be marketing herb-like soft drinks. Coca-Cola determined their critical skill to be supplying a variety of soft drinks, not unusual herb-like drinks. Today, Moxie has moved its business south and is still selling a few million dollars worth of this unusual drink, while Coca-Cola is an international giant. Why couldn't Moxie capture that market before Coca-Cola even had a chance to get off the ground? Why didn't they properly answer the elusive question, "What business am I in?"

"The problem with the railroad industry is that it defined its mission too narrowly," claims Professor Theodore Leavitt of the Harvard Business School. Rather than answering the popular question, "What business am I in?" by the single word, "railroad," a sounder strategic choice would have been built around the phrase, "the transportation industry." What has placed the railroads in trouble is their narrow view of the business they're in. The railroad business, per se, offered a rather bleak future. In turn, the transportation industry (which encompasses all modes of transportation) offered a much brighter future.

The same issue, although not articulated by Dr. Leavitt in the article, can be highlighted for other industries that have failed in strategic decisions. Another is the U.S. typewriter industry in the early and mid-fifties. It defined its business by the machine and by its corporate name as well, such as Royal *Typewriter*, Underwood *Typewritter*, Olivetti *Typewriter*. They undoubtedly would answer the question, "What business am I in?" with the single word, "typewriter." Notice the parallel with the railroad industry? Both had the narrow interpretation of their business spelled out in their name—*Typewriter* and *Railroad*.

Yet if they had chosen the broader interpretation in response to the same query, they would have offered the phrase, "We are in the office equipment business." In fact, they might even have said, "We are in the international business machines business." It's interesting in hindsight to examine the sales success of the large dominant supplier today in the international business machine business, which, if you're unaware, is known as IBM. The sales of IBM today dwarf the sales of the entire typewriter industry. However, in the early 1950s this was not the case.

How to establish corporate strategy is as elusive as finding a needle on a sandy beach. It just seems to slip through your fingers.

A business's success in the marketplace depends on total commitment to marketing—on whether the organization is entirely imbued with the marketing concept or whether it views its marketing as an entity separate and independent of the other divisions. Commitment to a marketing orientation must permeate the organizational whole, from the very top through every major division.

Too often, the concept of marketing has been limited to the sole endeavor of selling. Though selling is an integral part of total marketing, it does not encompass the whole of the marketing concept. The essence of marketing in an entrepreneurial venture is evidenced in five major areas of endeavor. To fulfill and utilize the marketing concept to serve the needs of the company and, in turn, increase the sales of the company, a marketing organization must be willing to do the following:

1. Define its market areas.
2. Research customer needs and wants.
3. Develop and redevelop product and/or service to meet the demand.
4. Recruit, select, and train manpower to deliver the product or service.
5. Develop its sales approach and advertising support.

A man seldom begins a journey unless he first knows his desired destination. If he is a careful traveler, he has planned his route, his stops, his time of arrival, and how much it will cost to get there. If you don't know where you are going, any road will take you there. The lead dog in a sled dog pack exchanges an unobtrusive view for a willingness to set the course. When the lead dog has a marketing orientation, the sled dog pack can run swiftly to its destination.

chapter 4

What Is
a Business Plan?

HOW TO PREPARE A BUSINESS PLAN

A document written to raise money for a growing company is known as a *business plan*. The most popular types are written for entrepreneurial companies seeking a private placement of funds from venture capital sources. Internal venture management teams of larger companies also write business plans. Although these venture plans seldom circulate to external private placement sources, they do progress upward within the organization for approval by corporate management.

Modest differences exist between the entrepreneurial plan and internal venture group plan. The major difference rests in the enterprise's risk and reward structure and not in the reading or writing of the document. The objectives of both types of plan are the same—launching a new business or expanding a promising small business. The ultimate responsibility for success or failure in one case rests with an entrepreneur/venture capitalist and in the other with a manager/vice president. But no matter what its origin, the document that consummates the financing is called the business plan. In both cases, the document must be thorough and well done to be successful in securing new capital.

The vast majority of business plans are prepared by entrepreneurs seeking venture capital. New venture groups within large companies are expanding their activities, but they do not approach the number of existing small companies seeking the same goal. As a comparison, there are about 14 million small businesses in the U.S., while only several thousand larger companies exist in the country. In addition, start-up companies, which still appear despite current depressed economic conditions, require a special breed of entrepreneurial business plan. This third category of brand new companies is the least common source of business plans.

The term *business plan* is the more formal name for the document; however, many within the financial and legal communities prefer the nickname *deal*. Although the latter is crude and a bit harsh, it does have shock value, which makes it a realistic and descriptive phrase. Some financiers carry this nicknaming one step further and compare the fund-raising process to the television program "Let's Make a Deal." In any case, the word *deal*, which embodies the excitement of the chase, becomes *business plan* when the chase is successfully completed.

The Business Plan*

Why should you go to the trouble of creating a written business plan? There are three major reasons.

1. The process of putting a business plan together, including the thought put in before beginning to write it, forces you to take an *objective, critical, unemotional* look at your business project in its entirety.
2. The finished product—your business plan—is an operating tool which, properly used, will help you manage your business and work toward its success.
3. The completed business plan is the means for communicating your ideas to others and provides the basis for your financing proposal.

The importance of planning cannot be overemphasized. By taking an objective look at your business, you can identify areas of weakness and strength, pinpoint needs you might otherwise overlook, spot problems before they arise, and begin planning how you can best achieve your business goals. As an operating tool, your business plan helps you to establish reasonable objectives and figure out how to best accomplish them. It also helps you red-flag problems as they arise and aids you in identifying their source, thus suggesting ways to solve them. It may even help you avoid some problems altogether.

In order for it to work, it is important that *you* do as much of the work as possible. A professionally prepared business plan won't do you any good if you don't understand it thoroughly. This understanding comes from being involved with its development from the very start.

No business plan, no matter how carefully constructed and no matter how thoroughly understood, will be of any use at all unless you use it. Going into business is rough—over half of all new businesses fail within the first two years of operation; over 90% fail within the first ten years. A major reason for

*Copyright permission granted by Andy Bangs of Upstart Publishing, Portsmith, NH 03801. Excerpted from the book *The Business Planning Guide*, Osgood and Bangs. Reprinted with permission.

failure is lack of planning. The best way to enhance your chances of success is to plan and follow through on your planning.

Use your plan. Don't put it in the bottom drawer of your desk and forget all about it.

Your business plan can help you avoid going into a business venture that is doomed to failure. If your proposed venture is marginal at best, the business plan will show you why and may help you avoid paying the high tuition of business failure. It is far cheaper not to begin an ill-fated business than to learn by experience what your business plan could have taught you at a cost of several hours of concentrated work.

Finally, your business plan provides the information needed by others to evaluate your venture, especially if you will need to seek outside financing. A thorough business plan automatically becomes a complete financing proposal that will meet the requirements of most lenders.

Preparing a Business Plan for Lenders or Investors*

This is a true story. In the late 1960s a sightless entrepreneur raised $2 million at a luncheon with the partners of one of New York's most prestigious investment banking firms. The purpose was to launch a new company whose objective was to merge computer technology and education to solve social problems. I don't mean the partners of the investment banking firm set off after lunch to raise $2 million. I mean that following the dessert, the entrepreneur left the luncheon with a certified check for $2 million in his hands. Nothing in the annals of venture capital has happened before or since, so don't hold your breath until happens again!

The late 1960s were fascinating times on Wall Street. Venture capital could be raised for any purpose via a public offering. The stock price of any new company from 1967 to mid-1969 went up. One prospectus from that era described the background of a man and his wife, each about 23 years of age, who intended to use the proceeds of the public offering to identify and promote a new business. The prospectus, or business plan, provided no more information than that. The public poured millions of dollars into small underwritings to launch companies whose names they did not know. Little or no due diligence was performed by the brokerage firms that were underwriting these new issues. Today, when most of the new companies of the late 1960s and their underwriters are out of business and the public is reluctant to return to a stock market that cost so dearly, the process of launching a new company is considerably different.

As the 1960s passed into the early 1970s, private venture capital firms became the primary source of start-up and expansion capital. The new issue

---

*Reprinted with permission from A. David Silver, *Up Front Financing,* John Wiley & Sons, Inc., New York, 1982.

public market was laid to rest. For example, in 1974, the only new issue I can remember was that of a small firm whose business was liquidating brokerage firms. Between 1975 and 1976 there were a handful of new issues and in 1977 and 1978 perhaps twenty. The few private venture capitalists, beaten about their wallets by the stock market's decline, began to demand substantially more information from entrepreneurs about their objectives, the costs of achieving those objectives, and myriad other details. In addition, someone had to take the blame for the huge portfolio losses. Rather than blaming themselves for their Koros, Ubris, and Até, as would the good Spartans carrying their dead on their shields, the venture capitalists of the early 1970s pinned the blame on the entrepreneurs. They told them, in effect: "I'll finance your company, but I have to own most of the stock and I must have voting control of the board." This did not encourage new company formation, although a few interesting enterprises were launched between 1973–1975, which will be discussed later. The primary effect of this attitude was to reduce the number of new companies launched in the early 1970s, shrink the number of venture capitalists, and usher in competitive government programs to assist in new company formation. For specifics, see *Up Front Financing* by A. David Silver, published by John Wiley & Sons, Inc., New York, 1982.

The venture capital industry is new, immature, and seemingly in perpetual transition. This industry is constantly trying to grasp and absorb the various changes that affect it. Entrepreneurs are not aware of this. All too frequently entrepreneurs think that a venture capitalist is J. P. Morgan or Jacob Schiff reincarnate: very wealthy, ultra-conservative, and poised to press a buzzer under the desk that will call in a runner with bags of cash to pour on the table for the entrepreneur to scoop up. Not true! Venture capitalists are intelligent young men and women seeking to simultaneously recommend to their investment committees the next Syntex, Polaroid, or Xerox and prevent erosion of capital in their fund through portfolio demise. Therefore, when an entrepreneur and a venture capitalist meet, the entrepreneur should bear in mind the following ideas:

a. The venture capitalist wishes that the information he or she is given by the entrepreneur is true.

b. The venture capitalist, if sold, must resell the idea to his or her investment committee and must be given the facts with which to do so.

c. The venture capitalist has 20 other situations on his or her desk, each competing for time and attention.

d. Venture capitalists make judgments about a new company's projections based on their recollection of past projections, both realized and unrealized.

The latter is a process similar to the description in Plato's *Republic* of the artisans in the cave chained in place all day staring at shadows. They are not permitted to turn around and see the shadowcaster; they can only stare straight ahead at the shadow. But they must form judgments about the shadowcasters based on the shadows.

Similarly, venture capitalists literally stare at projections all day, unable to see the actual future operating-statement numbers. If the projections remind the venture capitalist of the sales and earnings trend to Intel, City Investing, or Teledyne, he or she will be inclined to dig into the deal. If they evoke memories of Stirling Homex or Viatron, the venture capitalist will not be so inclined.

The uncertainty surrounding the entrepreneur is the ability to realize the projections. He or she may be merely a good projection maker and a lousy accomplisher. The venture capitalist does not know which. Herein lies a duel: The venture capitalist tries to attack the business assumptions on which the projections are based to determine their credibility, that is, the ability of the entrepreneur to make the projections come true. The entrepreneur jabs with upside potential. The venture capitalist counters with downside risk. The projections are dissected to their most minute ratio to try to see if the business plan has credibility. The battle lasts on into the night for day after day, until finally the seller and buyer become joined in their enthusiasm for the new business and have but to agree on a price on order to complete the funding.

This all sounds a bit romanticized, yet there is no denying that raising money is a battle in the war called Wealth. It is but an easy battle in a three-to-five-year war, and the entrepreneur has far less experience in fighting it than the venture capitalist. Knowing how to prepare a credible business plan helps put the two on equal footing.

THE FIVE-MINUTE READER

Business plans are comprehensive documents that often require several months to compile. Although they vary in length and complexity, the process of writing them requires the coordination of external legal, financial, and accounting assistance. In addition, the internal analysis of manufacturing, finance, and marketing must coincide with the external activities; this coordination adds to the time required for preparation. Spending $2,000 to $20,000 for outside services to prepare a business plan is typical. The preparer intuitively believes that the plan's thoroughness and sophistication reflect the enterprises's likelihood of success. Consequently, the tendency is to do the plan well and sometimes to do it and redo it.

Despite all this care during the preparation, most business plans are not read in detail from cover to cover. Although five weeks may have been required to compile it, potential investors will initially invest only *five minutes* in reading it. A venture capitalist who receives a dozen plans a day—hundreds annually—simply does not have enough time to read through each one. In fact, a leading venture capitalist at a large Boston bank claims he never reads any plan. "They all say the same thing and it's never true," he comments, "so I never read them."

In spite of this, you should not conclude that a business plan is unnecessary; it is essential to raising new money for internal or external entrepreneurs. The business person without a plan will be immediately conspicuous and will be turned away by a venture capitalist. This fact of financial life is unlikely to change: Even though the plan may not be read initially, the entrepreneur must write one, if for no other reason than to prove that he eventually can do it. It will be read from cover to cover if you are successful in writing it.

Multiple exposures are often given to a single business plan, one of the reasons hundreds of deals arrive at a single venture capitalist's office. An entrepreneur in dire need of funds will often mail the plan to a long list of venture capitalists. Such lists are available from several sources. This multiple exposure, frequently described as "shopping the deal," often seriously weakens rather than improves the chances of raising the needed capital. On the other hand, not showing the plan to anyone assures failure. A thin line exists beween exposure to too few or too many potential investors. Incidentally, the Security Exchange Commission (SEC) frowns on exposing a deal to more than 35 potential investors. This issue is in constant flux; first you must comply with the federal government's regulations for an offering, and second, you must comply with each state's so-called blue sky offering laws. Just as you'd guess, these two regulatory bodies (state and federal government) don't always have common laws. For instance, in Massachusetts, a deal can only be shown to 25 potential investors while the federal limit is 100 potential investors. Hence, both rules must be observed. Also, these rules vary depending upon the amount of money you seek. Lately, it's been significantly more attractive to raise less than $100,000 within any consecutive twelve-month period to avoid costly registration problems. Check with your lawyer on this issue because the guidelines are constantly changing.

The number of deals reviewed by a venture capitalist depends upon his or her reputation, which in turn depends upon past success. Currently, about one thousand venture capital firms exist in the United States, and a little better than one-half are also SBICs, small business investment companies regulated by the federal Small Business Administration (SBA). The number of successes contained within a single venture capital portfolio seldom exceeds one in ten, or, in baseball language, a batting average of .100.

GOING PUBLIC

If you're thinking of taking your company public while the window is still wide open, you'll have to comply with both federal and state securities laws and invest considerable time and money to make it happen. The chart on

Table of Certain Federal Securities Offering Alternatives

	RULE 504	RULE 505	RULE 506	SECTION 4(2)*
Limitation on Amount Sold	$500,000	$5,000,000	None	None
Limitation of No. of Offerees	No Limit	No Limit	No Limit	No specific numerical limit, but cannot rise to level of public offering
Limitation of No. of Purchasers	No Limit	35 nonaccredited purchasers. Unlimited number of accredited purchasers	35 nonaccredited purchasers. Unlimited number of accredited purchasers	No specific numerical limit, but cannot rise to level of public offering
Qualifications for Purchasers or Offerees	None	None	All nonaccredited purchasers must be sophisticated	All offerees and purchasers must be sophisticated and/or must be able to bear the economic risk
Prohibition on Advertising and General Solicitation	Yes, except for certain state-registered offerings	Yes	Yes	Yes
Mandatory Disclosure	None specified	None specified if all investors accredited. If nonaccredited investors, disclosure requirements vary	None specified if all investors accredited. If nonaccredited investors, disclosure requirements vary	None specified, but must furnish or make available same kind of information as registration would provide
Financial Statement Requirements	None specified	Yes, but requirements vary		None specified, but see box immediately above
Limitations on Issuer	Not available to 1934 Act reporting companies or investment companies	Not available to investment companies or issuers disqualified under certain provisions of Reg. A	None	None
1934 Act Reporting Obligations Triggered	Not unless 500 or more shareholders and $3,000,000 or more in total assets	Not unless 500 or more shareholders and $3,000,000 or more in total assets	Not unless 500 or more shareholders and $3,000,000 or more in total assets	Not unless 500 or more shareholders and $3,000,000 or more in total assets
SEC Filings	Yes, Notices	Yes, Notices	Yes, Notices	No
Resale Restrictions	Yes, except for certain state-registered offerings	Yes	Yes	Yes

*There is considerable uncertainty concerning the precise factors requisite to the availability of the Section 4(2) exemption, and there are numerous, sometimes conflicting, court decisions interpreting that exemption. Accordingly, the factors specified in this column of the table should be viewed with some caution.

Table of Certain Federal Securities Offering Alternatives (continued)

SECTION 4(6)	RULE 147	REG. A	FORM S-18
$5,000,000	None	$1,500,000	$5,000,000
No Limit	No Limit	No Limit	No Limit
No Limit	No Limit	No Limit	No Limit
All purchasers must be accredited investors	All offerees and purchasers must be residents of single state	None	None
Yes	No	No	No
None Specified	None Specified	Yes	Yes
None Specified	None Specified	Unaudited financial statements for two fiscal years	Audited financial statements for two fiscal years
None	Must be organized and doing business in state where securities offered and sold	Unavailable for sale of oil or gas or mineral rights and to investment companies	Unavailable to investment companies, insurance companies and 1934 Act reporting companies
Not unless 500 or more shareholders and $3,000,000 or more in total assets	Not unless 500 or more shareholders and $3,000,000 or more in total assets	Not unless 500 or more shareholders and $3,000,000 or more in total assets	Yes, but reporting obligations reduced for first year
Yes, Notices	No	Yes, Offering Statement	Yes, Registration Statement
Yes	Yes, out-of-state resales prohibited for nine months.	No	No

pages 48-49 highlights some of your options. The chart is taken from the excellent 60-page booklet, *A Businessman's Guide to Capital-Raising Under the Securities Laws,* by Michael M. Coleman and Irving P. Seldin. It offers a valuable appendix which deals with the new and popular "Regulaton D" and "Form S-18." The booklet is available from Packard Press, 1528 Walnut Street, Suite 2020, Philadelphia, Pennsylvania 19102 (215-236-2000).

A typical million dollar venture portfolio might be invested in ten companies. Although only one winner is the average, the typical portfolio would have five businesses that are essentially bankrupt; two or three marginal firms with little real potential; and one or two firms with a chance to become big winners. The pattern reveals the dangers of the venture business and demonstrates the crucial nature of a single winner.

A venture capitalist heading up the largest bank-owned Small Business Investment Company (SBIC) in Boston believes the batting average is a poor measure of a venture capitalist's performance. "The batting average which is so often quoted by academicians," claims this venture capitalist, "mixes up the singles, doubles, and home runs. A better average would be the slugging average, or, in baseball terms, an average that weights the home run and triple more than the single and double." In either case, he argues that the ultimate criterion is always based on a Return on Investment (ROI) analysis. For instance, the typical venture source previously mentioned, with 10 investments of $100,00 each, will have committed $1 million to its portfolio. If all the investments eventually turn sour save one, the batting average will be .100. However, if the one success produces a $2 million gain on the original $100,000 investment, or a 20 times return, the slugging average would be calculated as 2:1 or $2 million returned on the $1 million invested. This, according to one of the venture capitalists in Boston, accounts for the confusion in analyzing the industry. One success could actually count much higher than a grand slam home run.

Writing for a Five-Minute Reader

The primary problem in writing a business plan is making it comprehensive and shaping it for the reader for whom it is intended—the prospective investor with five minutes to read it. The entrepreneur should accept the inevitable: A potential investor will initially invest only five minutes to read a plan; therefore, the plan should be adapted to this time span.

Many authors concerned with the writing of business plans focus on checklists, blank sample forms, and tables of contents. As guides, they help catch items that might be overlooked because they force a full and balanced consideration of the many intertwined issues. In the appendixes of this book are a number of actual tables of contents of business plans, as well as an actual business plan that secured bank debt for a solar industries business in New

Hampshire. Excerpts of a business plan, a table of contents from a typical plan, or a checklist can be useful guides and are strongly encouraged.

A central message of how-to-write-a-plan advice is that you should tailor the document to meet the needs and desires of the potential investors. This sound advice does not mean that you should exaggerate, lie, or inflate the sales projections. It does mean that you should emphasize items of special interest for a specific potential investor. In some cases, a business plan is written in modular form, the appropriate modules being combined to appeal to the characteristics of the investor. A single plan rarely suffices for all possible uses. However, every plan eventually has its moment and is given a once-over lightly.

Insight into what happens to a plan when it finally reaches the top of the pile is scarce. What happens during the five minutes the venture capitalist examines the plan? How is it read? How is it analyzed? An understanding of the reading and interpretation process may help to direct the writing style and the focus of the plan. On the basis of field research involving several dozen venture capitalists and several hundred entrepreneurs, I have concluded that all knowledgeable investors use the precious five minutes of reading time in about the same way.

chapter 5

How a Business Plan Is Read

In order to determine how a business plan is analyzed, I conducted in-depth interviews over the past three years with two dozen venture capitalists and twice as many others (including bankers, lawyers, accountants, and consultants) in the financial community. The reading process is naturally a private affair between the company and the money source. Each source prides itself in the sophistication it has developed for analyzing investment opportunities. I spent several days actually observing several venture sources; and, as an investor in several entrepreneurial companies, I have read hundreds of business plans.

Almost everyone, the study revealed, analyzed the plans in the same way; the initial five-minute reading is a good average, if all the plans that are never read are excluded. The following steps are typical of the reading process (less than a minute is invested in each step):

Step 1. Determine the characteristics of company and industry.
Step 2. Determine the terms of the deal.
Step 3. Read the latest balance sheet.
Step 4. Determine the caliber of the people in the deal.
Step 5. Determine what is different about this deal.
Step 6. Give the plan a once-over lightly.

DETERMINE THE CHARACTERISTICS OF COMPANY AND INDUSTRY

Each venture capitalist has preferred areas for investment. Some like high technology and others like low technology; some others computers; others like consumer goods; and still others prefer publishing. A single venture capitalist is seldom at ease in every industry, just as a single entrepreneur cannot manage with equal skill in diverse industries. The venture capitalist's area of expertise is developed over the years and is based upon past successes; success in a particular industry will cause him to be receptive to deals in the same industry. Consequently, many of the potential investors may never read a business plan beyond Step 1, regardless of the terms of the deal, if they have little interest in the industry.

Consequently, it is well worth your time to be careful in selecting the venture capitalist who will read and analyze your plan. Several good venture capital guidebooks exist that not only identify venture capital sources but highlight their industry preferences. These are listed in the appendix.

Every potential investor also factors the current glamour of the specific industry into the analysis. Are there any larger publicly traded companies in the same industry? If so, how high is the stock price earning multiple (P/E ratio) of these firms? Or, better yet, is there a larger company that is extremely successful in this industry? How well has it done? Companies find it easier to raise funds when another company has pioneered successfully. For example, in the computer industry, the Data General Corporation could point to Digital Equipment Corporation; in the consumer goods industry, many smaller companies have pointed to Avon Products or Alberto-Culver. A specialty chemical company that eventually failed, Lanewood Laboratories, Inc. raised $500,000 based on a business plan that pointed to Lestoil. The B.L.T. Company in the appendix, the carwash gas station, successfully raised over $1 million just after Robo-Wash went public with an initial offering. However, B.L.T. went bellyflop in less than two years.

Industry glamour rises and falls much like the length of women's skirts. Ten years ago, the glamour field was electronics, followed by franchising, and then by computers. Currently, the glamour field is energy, and tomorrow it will be genetic engineering. Despite the obvious problems with financial fads, everyone accepts them as a reality. They exist and they do make a difference; if one's industry is momentarily glamourous, one's chances of securing funds suddenly increase.

The reason for the glamour is important. Investors must hope to get out of their investments eventually. They must become liquid again to be able to invest in the next business, as that is their business. So, determining the salability (glamour) of an industry before investing is crucial. Otherwise, no other financial source will buy out their investments and they will be locked into a business.

After the potential investor examines and evaluates the industry, he or she will quickly categorize the company within the industry. The potential investor will determine the following six facts about the company.

1. Annual sales for the past twelve months
2. Profit or loss for last year
3. Number of employees

4. Share of market
5. Degree of technology
6. Geographic location of facilities

The fundamental value of carefully highlighting these items in a front page summary of the business plan is that it saves time.

Depending upon his or her interpretation of these facts, the investor will soon be able to determine whether the company matches the venture capitalist's profile of an ideal investment. Is it too large or small? Is it too far away? There are numerous acceptable reasons for not making the investment. Seldom, if ever, is a venture capitalist faulted for the investments not made. More often and more intense is the criticism of the investments he or she actually selected. The sequence in Step 1 is first to check the industry, then to check the company.

DETERMINE THE TERMS OF THE DEAL

How much of a company is being "sold for what price" are the terms of the deal. The peripheral issue is the form (debt or equity) of the deal being offered. Many venture firms strongly prefer convertible debt (or debt with warrants) to a straight equity deal. Their profit-seeking structure may require the venture firm to generate annual income to pay current overhead in addition to the capital gains expected from the capital portfolio. Naturally, these firms would prefer interest-bearing debt to help cover this overhead, and a few of them will discourage deals that do not satisfy this basic requirement. In these cases, form is not a peripheral issue; but in the majority of cases the more substantive issue of "how much for how much" is of more concern.

Accordingly, a well-done business plan informs the reader of the following financial items on the first page. Other items should also be included in this summary, such as number of employees, geographic location, types of products, annual sales, and profits.

A. Percentage of company being sold (after dilution)
B. Total price for this percentage of the company (per share figures also included)
C. Minimum investment (number of investors sought)
D. Total valuation (after the placement) being placed on the company
E. Terms of the investment:

1. common stock
2. preferred stock
3. debt with warrants
4. convertible debentures
5. subordinated convertible debt
6. straight debt

Following is a more complete explanation of these last six terms.

1. Common Stock: Common stock is the term used to describe the documents that represent the value on the books of the business. When the funds are initially put into a company, common stock is known as capital stock. These certificates of common stock describe the ownership of the company.

2. Preferred Stock: This is a special category of stock which, in some ways, is preferred or treated better than simple common stock. Most of the time, preferred stock has certain advantages, such as guaranteed dividends or prior rights in a liquidation, and it is a separate category above common stock.

3. Debt with Warrants: The debt of a company is simply an obligation to repay a certain amount of money over a certain period of time at an agreed-upon rate. In the simplest terms, it's a loan. Some loans are risky, and a high interest rate is not enough to make the loan financially attractive. Hence, stock warrants are attached to the debt to sweeten the attractiveness of the investment. Warrants are the right or privilege to buy shares of common stock at a fixed price within a specified time period. If the price of the common stock rose above the predetermined stock warrant price within the time period, the holder of the warrant could opt to exercise the warrant. If, for instance, the warrant was at $3 per share and the stock was trading at $5 per share, a holder of 1,000 warrants could buy stock from the company for $3,000 and supposedly resell the same stock for $5,000, less appropriate commissions. Hence, a warrant is like a stock option and it has some value. The value is only realized after the warrants are exercised and the stock is sold.

About ten years later, State Mutual had received full payment for its loan, exercised the warrants on the company, and sold the stock in the public market. Rumor has it that this conservative life insurance company realized about $12 million in turn for making this loan. The McDonald's Corporation was the most successful of all of State Mutual's investments.

A classical example of a debt with warrants type of investment occurred in the mid-1960s. Fred Fideli of the Worcester-based firm, State Mutual Life Assurance Company, traveled to Chicago in order to evaluate a growing chain of hamburger stands. Although only 100 units were operating at this time, after personally visiting about 75 of the chains, Fideli offered a loan of $750,000 with an interest rate of 7½% to this business now headed up by the famous entrepreneur, Ray Kroc. In addition, to sweeten the financial attractiveness of this loan, Fideli obtained warrants to purchase 10% of the common stock of the chain.

About ten years later, State Mutual had received full payment for its loan, exercised the warrants on the company, and sold the stock in the public market. Rumor has it that this conservative life insurance company realized about $12 million in turn for making this loan. The McDonald's Corporation was the most successful of all of State Mutual's investments.

4. Convertible Debentures: A debenture is a loan and it is a type of debt. The convertible feature allows the debt holder to choose whether or not to convert the remaining outstanding debt into stock. For instance, a five year note for $500,000 at 10% simple annual interest, payable monthly, is a form of debt.

The convertible feature would add the possibility that the note holder could convert any remaining debt into common stock at a specific price. Consequently, when and if it becomes attractive, a note holder could trade in the remainder of the debt for common stock at a predetermined price. The difference between this technique and debt with warrants is simple. Under convertible debts, the note holder might not retrieve all the loan before purchasing the stock. In the case of debt with warrants, all of the debts must be repaid and, in addition, the note holder is given warrants that he may or may not exercise. Consequently, most venture capitalists prefer a debt with warrants rather than convertible debt.

5. Subordinated Convertible Debt: This is a special class of debt. The adjective *subordinated* refers to the ranking in event of liquidation of this debt as compared to other forms of debt. Subordinated debt is usually senior to any equity but subordinated to any other debt, especially bank borrowing. In case of bankruptcy or liquidation, subordinated debt is paid after all other debts, usually including trade payables, are satisfied. The stockholders are traditionally the only group of investors with lower priority than holders of subordinated debts. The convertible feature remains the same as described in 4 above. The difference between 4, convertible debenture, and 5, subordinated convertible debentures, is only that 5, subordinated convertible debentures, is also subordinated to other debt.

Following is a common possible ranking of rights in a bankruptcy.

1. Certain IRS liens
2. Secured creditors
3. Unsecured creditors (trade payables)
4. Subordinated debt
5. Stockholders

6. Straight Debt: This is simply a loan or debenture: an obligation to pay back an amount of borrowed funds at an agreed-upon rate over an agreed-upon period. There are two basic forms of straight debt: secured and unsecured. Secured debt is further backed up by an asset that is pledged to guarantee the payment of the debt. In the event of default, the secured lender would seize the pledged asset to recover the outstanding debt. A house mortgage is a good example of secured debt. Any debt without an asset pledged as collateral is considered unsecured debt.

This information is most helpful if it is presented both clearly and quickly to the potential investor. There is a considerable amount of detail and intricacies in every business plan, and the terms mentioned only cover a few points of interest.

Unfortunately, many deals do not spell out these financial details plainly. The short time invested by a venture capitalist in looking over the plan is spent digging out these pieces of needed information. If they were clearly stated at the beginning, potential investors could spend more time analyzing the plan's more positive selling features (such as the product literature). A summary sheet saves everyone's time and increases an interested reader's enthusiasm.

Finally, after the terms are known, the follow-up analysis focuses on these related issues; depending upon the specifics, the following may also be included in the summary.

How does the price per share of this placement compare with the founder's price per share?

Are the founders reinvesting in this placement?

What was the value of the company at the last placement and why has it changed?

How will the new funds be used; and, more specifically, will they be used to repay old debts or to undertake new activities that, in turn, will increase profitably?

READ THE LATEST BALANCE SHEET

A current balance sheet is usually located at the end of the written business plan, just before the appendix and future estimates of (*pro forma*) cash flow and income statements. The most current balance sheet is often the first page of the financial exhibits; and often it is also the ONLY financial page glanced at during an initial reading of a business plan. This historical document exposes the company's history, whereas most other financial documents in the appendix describe the company's future hopes.

Much preferred to any pro forma analysis is a one-minute process for interpreting the balance sheet and income statement. (Merrill, Lynch, Pierce, Fenner & Smith publishes a free twenty-four page brochure, *How to Read a Financial Report,* which contains greater detail on the same subject. Call any of their local offices to receive this free brochure.) The following four-step process, which is used to read a balance sheet from the top down, offers most of the financial information needed to make a quick evaluation of the deal:

A—Determine liquidity

B—Determine debt/equity structure

C—Examine net worth

D—Examine assets and liabilities

A—Determine Liquidity

Check working capital or current ratio, each of which measures about the same thing. Working capital is equal to current assets minus current liabilities, while the current ratio is current assets divided by current liabilities. Below is a typical balance sheet illustrating these relationships.

Cash	$ 50,000
Accounts Receivable	200,000
Inventories	+ 250,000
Total Current Assets	$500,000
Accounts payable	$250,000
Notes payable (within one year)	75,000
Accrued expenses payable	100,000
Federal income tax payable	+ 25,000
Total Current Liabilities	$450,000

Working Capital = $50,000 ($500,000 − $450,000)
Current ratio = 1.1 ($500,000/$450,000)

A firm's working capital should be positive while the current ratio should be greater than 1 (those two statements say the same thing in different words). A current ratio closer to 2 indicates a more financially stable company. A company with less than a positive $100,000 of working capital will be tight on cash. A quick check will determine the firm's payroll; and then relating payroll to cash (or working capital) will place the firm's needs for cash in a better perspective. For instance, if the firm above needs $100,000 per month for payroll, its cash is only two weeks of payroll and its working capital is only half a month of payroll. This analysis indicates the firm's need for cash and is a fair indication of how well they are doing.

B—Determine Long-Term Debt/Equity Structure

It is important to remember that the debt/equity ratio is equal to total debt divided by total equity. The ratio reveals how much credit a debt source (such as a bank) has already extended to the company. In addition, it offers insight into the remaining borrowing power of the company. A 400 debt/equity ratio, where a lender advances three dollars for every equity dollar, is a ballpark upper limit for this ratio. Seldom will debt sources advance three long term debt dollars for every equity dollar in a small company. Consequently a debt/equity ratio of 3:1 is rare, while a ratio of 1:1 usually indicates the company has some borrowing power remaining.

The numerator usually consists of long term debt, such as bonds or mortgages, and never includes current liabilities (due within one year), such as accounts payable. The denominator is tangible net worth or owner's equity at the time of the placement. This is not to be confused with the initial investment of the owners, which may have been made some time ago. Many times, small companies have unusually high (larger than one) debt/equity ratios. This often indicates that outside assets other than those on the company's balance sheet are securing the debt. A wealthy owner may have countersigned the bank note or pledged an asset in order to obtain more debt. The debt/equity ratio often uncovers this discrepancy. In the following example, the debt/equity ratio is ⅔.

C—Examine Net Worth

The potential investor extracts from the balance sheet the amount of money initially invested in the firm, which is the initial capitalization provided by the founders. The cumulative profits (or losses) that are contained within retained earnings offer another benchmark of the company's success to date. These two items added together algebraically determine a company's current net worth. Below is a typical balance sheet:

Long term debt (current portion that is due this year is shown under current liabilities)	$100,000	Line 1
Capital stock (initial capitalization)	+ 250,000	Line 2
Retained earnings (profit or loss to date)	(100,000)	Line 3
*Owner's equity (combines capitalization and retained earnings)	150,000	Line 4

*Owner's equity is what is initially put in to start the company plus or minus the earnings to date, which is equal to Line 2 + Line 3.

$$\frac{\text{Line 1}}{\text{Line 2} \pm \text{Line 3}} = \frac{\text{Debt}}{\text{Equity}} = \frac{\$100}{\$150} = .667 = \frac{2}{3}$$

A prospective investor interprets this information by noting that the founders began the company with $250,000 and that they have lost $100,000 since its inception. The company has a long term interest-bearing note that was probably awarded when the company was founded and was based upon the initial capital of $250,000. A further check to determine what, if anything, is offered as security for the long term debt would follow by examining the footnotes to the balance sheet. However, due to the losses to date, the company probably has little remaining borrowing power. The investor will make a quick check to determine which assets (accounts receivable, inventory, and fixed assets) are pledged to secure any of the debt. Free and unencumbered assets would indicate more borrowing power.

Remember the debt to worth ratio is only one factor to consider in determining a business's borrowing power. There are three other issues of concern to any lending source. First and foremost is the ability to repay the loan. This vital element is a function of the two other variables mentioned:

(a) the strength of any personal endorsements, and (b) the profitability of a business enterprise.

As a rule of thumb, a debt source will allow the following amounts of debt shown in column 2 to be secured against the assets shown in column 1.

COLUMN 1	COLUMN 2	
Asset as It Appears on Balance Sheet	Percentage of Balance Sheet Value That Can Be Borrowed Against	
Cash or marketable securities	100%	
Accounts receivable	75–85%	of those under 90 days
Inventory	20–30%	(Percentage will depend on market value, not on book value)
Fixed assets	75%	(Percentage will depend on market value, not on book value)

D—Examine Assets and Liabilities

A potential investor will quickly check to be sure all assets are real (tangible); and then he or she will check liabilities to verify that debt is owed to outsiders, not to insiders (such as notes to stockholders). This determination also hinges on the reputation of the accounting firm that prepared the financial statement. An unaudited, company-generated financial statement is seldom even interpreted, since the investor needs some independent assurances that the financial reporting is accurate. Without this assurance, investors will undoubtedly pass over the deal, at least at the initial reading.

By examining the asset categories, investors check to be sure soft assets (such as good will, patents or trade secrets, formulas or capitalized research and development) are not large or unreasonable. For some unexplained reasons, small companies often choose to capitalize research and development (R & D) or organizational expenses rather than write off these expenses during the period in which they occur. This practice is frowned upon by all potential investors because it distorts the balance sheet, impairs future earnings, and is a sure sign of danger. If this "asset" is large, it can dampen an investor's interest. Furthermore, entrepreneurs and friends and relatives of entrepreneurs often choose to make their initial investment in small companies as debt rather than equity. This makes these founders feel more secure because it offers some protection in the event of bankruptcy. By making a quick check, a potential investor uncovers the identity of the company's creditors and the amount of debt.

This four-step process (A through D) usually takes less than one minute of reading time from beginning to end. In the initial reading of the business plan, potential investors are not probing the balance sheet in depth but are searching for red flags. Before an investment is consummated, the balance sheet, income statement, and pro formas will be analyzed in considerable detail. However, during the first glance, the balance sheet analysis and a quick look to determine the magnitude of last year's sales from the profit-and-loss statement are the extent of the financial investigation. The balance sheet, along with a magnitude of sales, provides sufficient data to judge whether or not a more detailed financial investigation is warranted.

DETERMINING THE CALIBER OF THE PEOPLE IN THE DEAL

This step, most venture capitalists claim, is the single most important aspect of the business plan. A potential investor begins by examining the founders, board of directors, current investors, outside professionals (accountants, lawyers, bankers, consultants, directors) in hopes of uncovering a familiar name. The reputation and "quality" of the team are the issues in this measure. Unfortunately, this is a subjective area, and, as such, is open to a wide range of individual interpretations; what is good to some is not so good to others. Because it is subjective, opinions and assessments fluctuate dramatically.

Potential investors usually know someone associated with the company (at least they will know someone who knows someone), and this person will set the tone for the whole deal, regardless of his affiliations with the company. Even if he is only a small investor, the company loses its identity and the business plan becomes known as "John Smith's deal" around the office. These known insiders become the links for further information sought by the potential investors.

Consequently, the reputation of *all* the individuals surrounding the business is of serious concern in securing additional funds. For start-up deals or for situations where the company is unknown to the potential investors, a number of questions are asked in order to determine management's abilities. This format is about the same for both internal and external businesses. However, internal venture teams are greatly assisted when the project directors are highly regarded by corporate management. Many times this *golden boy syndrome* becomes the crucial variable in approving new corporate funds. Here are the issues.

> What is the track record of founders and managers, including where they worked and how well they performed in the past? Without a doubt, this is the single most significant ingredient when assessing management's abilities.
>
> How much balance and experience does the inner management team possess? How long have the members worked together, and what is the degree of balance among marketing, finance, and manufacturing represented by the operating managers?
>
> Who is the financial man (or bank or accountant), and what are his credentials? Potential investors much prefer a deal with one strong full-time financial type.

He speaks their language and is more at home with money than products. Potential investors like to envision this financial type as a caretaker for any newly arrived funds.

DETERMINE WHAT IS DIFFERENT ABOUT THIS DEAL

This difference is the eventual pivotal issue on whether or not a specific venture capital firm chooses to invest. The same holds true for obtaining headquarters approval for internal venture management teams in larger companies.

Is there an unusual feature in the product? Does the company have a patent, an unusual technology, or a significant lead over competition? Is this a company whose critical skill rests in marketing, manufacturing, or finance? Does the company's strength match the skills needed to succeed in this industry? Or is there an imbalance? What is different about this company, and how much better is its product? The answers to these questions are the investor's chief concerns.

Does the company have the potential to open up a whole new industry, such as Polaroid, Xerox, IBM, Digital Equipment Corporation, McDonald's, or Hewlett-Packard did? Or is this a modest idea with limited future growth? A venture capitalist needs a return of greater than ten times his or her investment just to stay even (one in ten succeed). He or she is seldom intrigued with companies that hold a marginal advantage over competing firms or products. In essence, this is what Rooser Reeves has called the Unique Selling Proposition (U.S.P.)! Good ideas or products that are better than others attract capital. Marginal improvements do not possess enough potential to offset the risks inherent in a new business venture.

Give the Plan a Once-Over Lightly

After this analysis, the final minute is usually spent thumbing through the business plan. A casual look at product literature, graphs, unusual exhibits, samples, letters of recommendation, and letters of intent is the purpose of this last check. Seldom, if ever, are new opinions formed during the final minute. However, the fact that everyone engages in this leafing through process supports the argument for unusual enclosures. A product pasted on a page, a letter with a meaningful letterhead, or an unusual chart or two can be helpful in maintaining interest. Although enclosures will not make the big difference in the final analysis, an eye-catching enclosure can extend the readership of a business plan.

After this final step, the analysis is over and the investors decide whether to obtain more information or to return the plan. Ninety-nine times out of a hundred, the deal is turned down. A few investors make phone calls at this stage, and then reject the deal after a detail or two is confirmed. But it is important to remember that deals are actually turned down during the first reading even though the act of formal rejections is postponed a few additional days.

THE PLAN PACKAGE

Most entrepreneurs assume that a positive relationship exists between time invested in reading the plan and the likelihood of obtaining capital. "If they would only read my plan," mumbles the unsuccessful entrepreneur, "They would be chasing me instead of vice versa." With this goal in mind, and assuming that the product is only as good as the package, business plans are often dressed in their Sunday best, in leatherbound jackets sometimes costing over ten dollars each.

In research with several dozen venture capitalists, I conducted some small tests to determine the method used to select a single business plan from a group of 5 to 10. Several deals were randomly placed on a table and the investors were asked to examine only the covers of the business plans before selecting which of the half dozen plans they would read first. The plans that received the most initial attention were not the ones with pretty covers; instead, the company name was more crucial. Next in importance was the geographical location of the company. The third element was the thickness of the plan; the shorter plans received more attention.

In these tests, nothing else was revealed about any of the business plans other than what appeared on the cover. The position of the deals on the tables was random, and I observed each venture capitalist as he or she glanced over the deals. I have ranked the variables in descending order of importance.

1. Company name
2. Geographic location
3. Length of business plan
4. Quality of cover

The next question I explored was, "How can an entrepreneur increase the likelihood that a capitalist will read a business plan once past the cover?" Should the entrepreneur send it along in installments with the final chapter first, or should he or she send along a summary? In my research, I concluded that summaries and "miniplans" are not effective documents. A teaser summary that is not an integral part of the plan only delays the eventual reading of the entire plan, and the teaser is often vague or incomplete. It is much better to have the entire document available to each and every potential investor and highlight the plan with a succinct and informative summary page as the first page of the business plan.

Two additional variables were uncovered that help to determine a plan's eventual reading, and, to a lesser extent, the likelihood that a venture capitalist will make an investment. The first is the method of dispatching the plan. The second is the *preselling*, which precedes the plan. Months may be spent preparing the plan, but only a few minutes are spent deciding how to deliver it. The naive entrepreneur follows the suicidal path of a blind mass mailing. Armed with a directory and helped by a secretary, the plan is mailed with a form letter to a sampling from the directory. This wastes everyone's time and the entrepreneur's money, because this procedure never works.

Another bad approach for the entreprenuer is to make a personal visit with the business plan tucked under his arm. This humble, straightforward approach is like going to a doctor as an unreferred patient. Everyone asks, "Who sent you?" The key man is often away from his office or unable to see the visitor, who then begins to feel like an intruder.

The best method of delivering a business plan is through a third party. Unless the entrepreneur is already established and successful, a third-party referral adds credence to the plan, and as a result, increases the likelihood that it will be read. Anyone from the following groups is acceptable as long as the reputation and liaison with the venture capitalist are positive (it need not be the same person for each potential investor): Consultants, bankers, lawyers, accountants, or other entrepreneurs.

The second level of improvement—a good job on *preselling*—is invaluable. If the potential investors are told about the exciting company six months before the plan arrives and then about current developments each month for the intervening six months, they will be more receptive to reading the plan when it finally arrives. *After all, the best time to raise money is when it isn't needed.* The same holds for arousing potential investor interest. A well-managed company planning to expand will invest time in such preselling often and early. The preselling is as important as any aspect of the process.

The same person should both presell and eventually deliver the plan. With the company name and address and location clearly spelled out on the cover page, it should be hand-carried by a mutual friend to a select group of venture capitalists.

If the process is depressing, always remember that the two most successful venture capital deals in the Northeast were turned down a number of times before receiving a "yes." In 1958, Digital Equipment Corporation (DEC) finally convinced American Research & Development to invest about $70,000. Rumor has it that the investment today is worth over $500 million.

A spin-off from DEC occurred in 1968 when three engineers in their twenties approached Fred Adler, a New York attorney, who agreed to a modest investment in a struggling new company known as Data General Corporation. It is rumored that the four principals each made in excess of $10 million within four years of launching this venture. The rewards are high for those who play and win. Unfortunately, those who play lose most of the time, and plans of this type significantly outnumber the winners.

Explaining the format for reading a business plan suggests that the document's preparations should be based on the process that will inevitably be used to read and interpret the plan. Whether the writer is an internal or external entrepreneur, it is his responsibility to put the company's best foot forward once the business is underway. Thus, a well done business plan will be tailored to the reader.

The definition of a "good" business plan is one that raises money; a "bad" plan does not attract investors. It is that simple; but the entrepreneur must remember that the terms "good plan" and "good business" are not synonymous. A good plan may raise money, but the business may still fail. However, a bad plan almost always means business failure. In order to succeed in reaching the more crucial objectives of a profitable business, a good plan plus a good business is required.

The five-minute process is so cold in concept that it may seriously alienate many business people. The business becomes part of life and the plan becomes the essence of the business. Hence, to add a degree of warmth and a bit more understanding to the central aspect of small business, actual business plans should be interpreted against the above process.

While dealing in this abstract area remember a quotation that links entrepreneurs and venture capitalists:

The men who manage men manage the men who manage things, *but* the men who manage money manage the men who manage men.

PECKING ORDER	EASE OF HANDLING	
	Venture Capitalist	*Entrepreneur*
1. Money	High	Low
2. Men	Medium	Medium
3. Things	Low	High

chapter 6

Writing a Business Plan

CHECKLIST OF NECESSARY INFORMATION MADE PRIOR TO WRITING

The business plan is such a personal document that actual hard advice on its proper preparation is like giving any extremely personal counsel. Usually this type of guidance is not specific enough to be of applied value. Yet there are some common, helpful ideas that can and should be embodied in a business plan.

The most important first stage of development for a business plan is the development of the table of contents. This should be done before any serious writing occurs. The process of then subdividing the actual writing of each module that appears in the table of contents is an extremely common practice. Although subdividing is an efficient and reasonable practice, any plan that is developed by the modular approach runs the risk of appearing pieced together. Naturally, this nonintegrated business plan risks the substantial danger of lacking an overall thrust.

The purpose of writing a business plan is to raise capital by the direct sale of securities to one or more private investors. The transaction is exempt from registration with the Securities and Exchange Commission (SEC), provided that it conforms to certain SEC established laws. Very often a business plan does not seek to sell equity but rather to arrange for long term debt financing.

In many cases, particularly in the past few years, the condition of the public stock market prohibits companies from securing new financing through an initial sale of of common stock. In the late 1960s, it was not uncommon to have several thousand small companies *go public;* but the early and middle 1970s were years when this figure fell from several thousand to 14 or

16 per year. In those lean years, the only viable alternative was the long term debt market. These facts give some indication of why the development of the business plan should be integrated with the needs of the financial markets.

To offer guidance in writing a business plan, a typical table of contents follows.

A.1 History of the Company

A.2 Business Summary

A.3 Manufacturing Plan

A.4 Production and Personnel Plan

A.5 Products and Services

A.6 Marketing and Sales

A.7 Competition

A.8 Research and Development

A.9 Management

A.10 Financial Reports Supplied by the Company and Accompanying Explanations, Footnotes

A.11 Capitalization or Equity Structure

A.12 Capitalization or Debt Structure

HISTORY OF THE COMPANY

A. Date and place, including state of incorporation as well as preincorporation organizational structure.

B. Founding shareholders and directors.

C. Important changes in the structure of the company, its management, or its ownership. Set forth predecessor companies, subsidiaries, and divisions in an easy to understand manner.

D. Company's major successes or achievements in the field to date.

BUSINESS SUMMARY

A. Principal products or services.

B. Describe the unique features of the business and the products. Compare these objectively with the competition. Give specific goals on annual sales growth and profits and relate to actual past performance.

C. Detailed breakdown of sales or services for the current year and for the past five years. Indicate the cost of goods sold and the pretax profit by product line for all products or services that contribute more than 10% in pretax profits.

D. Breakdown of sales by industries, including the U.S. (military versus nonmilitary) and export.

E. Product brandnames, price ranges, and quality.

F. Capital goods versus consumer goods. How cyclical or seasonal?

G. Describe patents, trademarks, and other trade advantages, such as geographic or labor advantages. List expiration dates, if any, and impact on sales, profits, and marketing strategy.

H. Give the statistical record of the industry or subindustry in which company operates, with an evaluation of its prospects.

I. Maturity of the product line. Discuss the problems of technological obsolescence and product line, and the problems of competition.

J. Describe any technological trends or potentialities within the business environment that might be favorable or unfavorable to the company.

MANUFACTURING PLAN

A. Fill in data below.

1. Plant location
2. Square feet
3. Number of floors
4. Type of construction
5. Acres of land
6. Owned or leased
7. Lease value
8. Annual rent expires

B. Describe levels of current operations. Estimate the capacity and the current percentage utilization of plant and equipment.

C. List auto equipment, including delivery trucks, number of vehicles, and whether rented or owned. What are the lease arrangements?

D. Describe the company's depreciation policies. How are they accounting for wear on their assets? Over what time period and at what rate are these assets being depreciated?

E. What manufacturing and/or office equipment is leased?

F. Condition and description of plant equipment (enclose evaluation if possible):

1. List major equipment
2. Condition
3. Location
4. Owned or leased
5. Value estimate

G. Is the plant layout efficient? Describe.

H. What is the general housekeeping condition?

I. Is the operation job-shop or mass-production oriented? Do they build custom products per individual jobs or is it a mass-produced product that can be manufactured under large cost-efficient methods and inventoried?

J. Incremental increase in space and equipment required for $1 million increase in sales. For each major increment of expansion in revenue, is an equal, more, or less increment necessary in facilities, people, and equipment?

K. Logic for plant location(s).

L. What future capital expenditures for plant and machinery are planned? How will they be financed?

N. Any sale of assets planned—on what basis, cash or deferred payments?

O. Number of shifts being worked daily. Percentage of overtime. Breakdown by departments. Economics of a two- or three-shift schedule.

PRODUCTION AND PERSONNEL PLAN

A. Brief description of manufacturing operation.

B. Number of personnel (breakdown by functions).

C. Union affiliation. State address and representative.

D. Strike history.

E. Turnover and morale.

F. Labor market (description of important skills) and competition for labor.

G. Percentage of labor content in cost of goods sold by product.

H. Fringe benefits provided and their cost percentage to wages.

I. Does the company rate itself as a low-cost, high-cost, or average-cost employer? What is the unemployment rate based upon the business's past hiring and firing practice charged to the company by the state government?

J. Steps being taken to improve production methods.

K. Are competent people assigned to production planning?

L. Describe quality control procedures.

M. Unit costs versus production levels, detailing fixed and variable costs.

PRODUCTS OR SERVICES

A. Principal suppliers; location; product; volume; officers dealt with.

B. A brief description of significant materials and supplies, including availability. Are the storage and material handling facilities adequate?

C. Are purchase economies available? Are purchase discounts available?

D. Are make-or-buy decisions made?

E. What is the average inventory turnover within the company's industry? Explain any deviations for your firm.

F. Does the finished inventory have a shelf-life?

G. Methods of inventory valuation.

H. Current inventory status of distributors and ultimate users.

MARKETING AND SALES

A. Describe the market. History, size, trend, and your product's position in the market. Identify sources of estimates and assumptions.

B. Is the market at the take-off stage? Project the market back five years and forward five years.

C. Where are the products sold, and who is the essential end user?

D. Are the products sold by salaried or commissioned sales force, by distributors, by brokers, or . . . ?

E. Are accounts receivables sold, discounted, or pledged? If so, to whom, at what discount, with or without recourse, and so forth? If receivables are pledged to a loaning source, either the lender or the borrower actually receives the cash. If they are discounted, the lender gives a percentage of the receivables at the moment they are pledged as collateral. Resource means that the lender can recover any bad debt on an uncollectable receivable from the borrower, thus lowering the lender's risk.

F. Number of customers or active accounts, and the amount of accounts receivable due over 90 days.

G. How many customers make up 80% of the sales? Please list.

1. Principal customers
2. Location
3. Product
4. Volume
5. Percent of company's sales
6. Officer dealt with

H. Describe any special relationships with customers.

I. Describe pricing policies with respect to all product lines. How sensitive are prices to costs?

J. Current backlog and current shippable backlog. The shippable backlog can be shipped and billed immediately upon completing the manufacturing of the product.

K. How many purchase orders are on hand at present (dollar amount)?

L. Warranties on present products (enclose copies).

M. Advertising: annual budget and media used (enclose recent copy).

N. Is business seasonal? If so, explain peaks in production, sales, and so forth.

O. Selling costs as a percentage of revenues. How will these vary with more or less sales volume?

P. Customer primary motivation to purchase your product: price, delivery time, performance, and so forth.

Q. Are any proposed government regulations expected to affect your market?

COMPETITION

A. List major competition, location, sales earnings, percent of market and strengths and weaknesses.

B. Nature of competition: cut-throat or permissive; poorly or well financed.

C. Competitive advantages; disadvantages. Be specific.

D. Is new competition entering the field?

E. Compare your company's prices with those of the competition.

F. Share of the business you receive by market area.

G. Describe service arrangements and service experience.

H. Describe advertising and promotional efforts. Discuss the importance of brand names and trademarks.

I. Independent firms, publications, or outside agencies that have evaluated your firm against competitors.

J. Effects of regulatory agencies, including government.

RESEARCH AND DEVELOPMENT

A. Amount of percentage of sales spent per annum in the past five years and projected. Compare with competitors. Detail any capitalized R & D costs.

B. Number of employees in this area. Advanced college degrees.

C. Detail product developments and R & D that is not related to specific products or services, which is basically research and not development.

D. Percent of current sales generated by past R & D.

E. State any new field your firm contemplates entering: Is it complementary to the present product or service line?

F. List any outside consulting R & D relationships, such as firms, universities, individuals, and so forth; and state the percentage of total R & D budget let to outside sources.

G. Funding and its consistency from government sources.

MANAGEMENT

A. Is an organization chart included?

B. Are résumés included?

C. Are references included?

D. Have credit and personal investigation checks been performed?

E. Analysis of reputation, capabilities, and attitude. Analysis of team: one-man show, executive turnover, morale.

F. Profit consciousness: Is there an on-going profit improvement plan? An executive incentive program?

G. Innovative ability. Be specific. How is creativity fostered?

H. Schedule of past, current, and proposed salaries and other compensation for each member of management and/or owners, including bonuses, fee arrangements, profit sharing, and so forth. Please list.

   1. Key personnel
   2. Annual salary
   3. Bonuses, fees, and so forth

I. If a stock option or other management incentive plan is in effect, provide an outline.

J. How are salary increases for management controlled?

K. Directors—other than officers and employees: Please list.

   1. Name and identity
   2. Compensation
   3. Shares of stock owned
   4. Common or preferred

L. Life insurance on officers (amount and company).

M. Enclose any contract or proposed contract between the firm and any member of management, any stockholder, or any outside consultant.

FINANCIAL REPORTS SUPPLIED BY THE COMPANY AND EXPLANATIONS

A. Reports

   1. Audited annual reports for the past five years, including balance sheets, profit and loss statements, and statements of sources and applications of funds.

2. Current financial reports, with officer's statements as to material changes in condition.
3. Pro forma balance sheets giving the effect of the proposed financing on a quarterly basis for two years.
4. Month-by-month projections of profit and loss, cash receipts, and disbursements for the two-year period.
5. Yearly projections of revenues and earnings for five years.
6. Analysis of sales by markets, products, and profits.
7. Record of the industry or subindustry in which the company operates to contrast with the performance of the specific business.

B. Describe accounting principles regarding depreciation, R & D, taxes, inventories, and so forth.
C. Are the tax returns of the company and its subsidiaries for the past five years included?
D. If the business is seasonal, explain its cycle and relate it to the company's financial needs.
E. Discuss the aging of accounts receivable and accounts payable.
F. List the losses from bad debts over the past five years.
G. Describe the trend and give percentages for the following:

1. Sales, increases or decreases
2. Cost of goods sold
3. Overhead, fixed and variable
4. Selling expenses
5. Research and development
6. Taxes
7. Pretax and after-tax profit margins
8. Return on total capital, including long term debt
9. Return on total equity
10. Industry trends in each of the above areas

H. Does the balance sheet contain hidden or undervalued assets or liabilities?
I. Discuss any nonrecurring items of income or expense in recent financial statements.
J. Describe the company's profit improvement plan.
K. What years' tax returns have been audited?
L. Are all taxes paid?
M. Are there any disputes between the company and any taxing authority?

CAPTIALIZATION: EQUITY

A. Total shares authorized: Common_____Preferred_____
B. Total shares outstanding: Common_____Preferred_____
C. Describe principal terms, including voting rights, dividend payments, conversion features, and so forth for each class of stock.
D. If a private company, list all shareholders. If a public company, list all shareholders who directly or indirectly control more than 5% of the outstanding voting stock.

1. Name and identity
2. Consideration for shares
3. Number and class of shares
4. Percentage owned of outstanding stock

E. If any of the shareholders listed in D are not members of the company's management, describe their motivation for becoming shareholders.

F. If individuals or entities who might be considered founders, promoters, or insiders under any law are no longer shareholders, describe the reason for their withdrawal from the business.

G. Provide a chronological list of sales of stock, stating prices, terms, number of buyers, and their names.

H. Describe any other transactions involving the principal shareholders and the company—such as those involving real estate, equipment leases or sales, loans to or from shareholders, and voting trusts.

CAPITALIZATION: DEBT

A. Principal bank. Name of officer handling account.
B. List the following for each long term debt obligation.

1. Lender and contact
2. Total amount
3. Initial date
4. Length of term
5. Sinking fund
6. Date of maturity
7. Security or collateral

C. Are seasonal loans required? What was the largest amount borrowed in each of the past two years? Minimum?

D. Amounts of current lines of credit, and with whom.

E. Describe all contingent liabilities.

F. Debt to equity ratio: for company; for industry.

G. What guarantees are currently required by lenders?

SOURCES OF INFORMATION ON PREPARING A BUSINESS PLAN

1. Small Business Reporter, P.O. Box 37000, Bank of America, San Francisco, CA, 94120 (Tel: 415-622-2491). $2.00 per copy. The "Business Operations" series is helpful for general information on running a business. Titles include: *Operating Your Own Business, Small Business Success, How to Buy or Sell a Business, Financing Small Business, Personnel for the Small Business, Steps to Starting a Business.* Other series are "Business Profiles," which cover specific small businesses and "Professional Management" for doctors, dentists, veterinarians.

small businesses and "Professional Management" for doctors, dentists, veterinarians.

2. One of the finest pieces of information for understanding financial statements is offered free of charge by the world's largest securities firm, Merrill Lynch Pierce Fenner & Smith. This 24-page red book, entitled "Understanding Financial Statements," is so good it is often used as a free handout in graduate level college finance courses. It offers an understanding of the three basic financial tools.

1. Balance Sheet
2. Cash Flow Statement
3. Profit & Loss Statement

I suggest you call your local Merrill Lynch office, which can be found in your local telephone directory.

3. Several excellent articles on developing a business plan are contained within the books offered by the most professional source of venture capital information, Capital Publishing Company. These books provide some of the articles on the business plan that are truly excellent and tips that are practical and worthwhile. Write:

The Center for Entrepreneurial Management, Inc.
83 Spring St.
New York, NY 10012
212-925-7304

4. The Small Business Administration offers several excellent pamphlets on writing a business plan. These are very inexpensive and surprisingly good. They even offer further information on where to obtain further information on writing a business plan. I'd suggest your local SBA field office for current information.

Small Marketeer Aid # 153
Business Plan for the Small Service Firm
24 pages

Small Marketeer Aid # 150
Business Plan for Retailer
24 pages

Management Aid for Small Manufacturers # 218
Business Plan for Small Manufacturers
22 pages

A new center was established in February 1978 to speed up the delivery process of SBA pamphlets. All requests to this high speed center should be on SBA Form 115A, which is a list of available SBA publications. Form 115A can be requested from the center. Write:

The Small Business Administration (SBA)
Box 15434
Fort Worth, Texas 76119

Nationwide toll free number is 800-433-7272. In Texas call 800-792-8901. The telephone recording service is available 24 hours per day, seven days a week.

5. The Center for Entrepreneurial Management puts out a list including the following publications on business plan preparation:

How to Prepare and Present a Business Plan. Joseph Mancuso, 300 pages. Contains what you need to know to make your plan perfect. Includes three actual plans.

How to Write a Business Plan that Rates an 11 (on a Scale of 1 to 10). Four one-hour cassettes recorded live at one of Joseph Mancuso's recent live seminars on the subject. A complement to the business plan books, the tapes include questions from the audience.

Business Planning Guide. Osgood & Bangs. 107 pages, 1980. How to prepare and present a business plan in workbook format. A very popular book in 8½ × 11″ format.

Business Plan Series. 2 books, 1 set of 4 audio tapes.

To obtain the complete list with prices, write to:

The Center for Entrepreneurial Management
83 Spring Street
New York, NY 10012
(212) 975-7304

chapter 7

The Entrepreneur's Life Cycle

Having a business of your own is not too different from having a child. You experience many of the same emotions and problems. And, as with a child, starting one is half the fun. However, only being a business starter is less than one-half of the job. The hard part is to make a business successful. As I pointed out earlier, a successful business plan alone is not sufficient to insure a profitable business. A successful plan plus a sound entrepreneurial team are the basic cornerstones for a successful business enterprise.

All successful small businesses start with an idea and proceed through the classic entrepreneur's life cycle. Following is a life cycle for entrepreneurs.

Stage I	The entrepreneur's early development
Stage II	The idea stage
Stage III	The start-up problem
Stage IV	The venture financing
Stage V	The growth crisis
Stage VI	The maturity crisis
Stage VII	The impossible transition

One of the interesting aspects of small business is the team built around the entrepreneur. A talented entrepreneur recognizes that the central fact of management is *accomplishing tasks through other people*. An ineffective entrepreneur tries to do everything himself. This raises the classic issue of delegating, which is often contrary to the entrepreneur's natural tendencies.

The vast majority of successful small companies were built around an entrepreneur team and not a single entrepreneur. In fact, partnerships are an increasingly effective method of balancing each entrepreneur's strengths and weaknesses to produce a well-balanced top management team.

Some of the most successful companies were launched by two equal partners who complement one another. Rolls and Royce, the founders of the prestigious British motor car company bearing their names, were totally opposite in philosphies and lifestyles. One was Mr. Inside and the other Mr. Outside, but together they were an effective entrepreneurial team. The same holds for the largest consumer goods company, Proctor & Gamble. David Packard and William Hewlett of Hewlett-Packard electronics fame in California are another example. In discount retailing it was Two Guys from Harrison who started the revolution, not one individual.

The team allows balance and strength to exist in the enterprise. The stronger the team, the more powerful the company. It's the synergistic concept of 2 plus 2 being equal to 5.

Franklin Delano Roosevelt summed up the process this way. "I'm not the smartest fellow in the world, but I can sure pick smart colleagues." He claimed: "Because I'm not so smart, I have to surround myself with real talent." The entrepreneur who can adopt this same philosophy will select the following members of the team:

1. Partners
2. Lawyers
3. Advertising Agencies
4. Accountants
5. Bankers
6. Board of Directors—Angels
7. Consultants
8. Manufacturer's Representatives
9. The Controller

Following is a commentary on the roles of these team members. Along with a sound business plan, a team of professionals adds the final ingredient to mixing up a profitable business enterprise.

BUILDING AN ENTREPRENEURIAL TEAM

Partners

A partner can be a blessing or a curse. Whether you take one or more into your business venture depends on your needs for additional depth in management, marketing, technology, or financing.

Selecting your business partners is not much different from choosing your spouse, and it should be done with the same care. More, perhaps, because the wrong partner can put the entire venture in jeopardy. Marriages are relatively easy to start. A marriage license and a blood test only cost a few dollars. If one fails, you can try again. In business it's not so easy.

I advise finding a partner whose talents complement your own, but whose business philosophy, personality, and background differ. The most successful companies are formed with two partners whose combined abilities give depth to the enterprise, and whose different backgrounds serve as a buffer against excesses of any kind. You both may disagree and you both may have conflicts, but usually they are over business issues rather than personalities. A good marketing/financial man is an ideal partner for a strong production/engineering type, but two optimists or two pessimists can kill a business before it has a chance to get off the ground. The outside and inside philosophy has also been applied to David Packard, former Secretary of Defense (Mr. Outside) and to his equally talented, but less outgoing partner, William Hewlett (Mr. Inside).

Once you have selected your partner, you should immediately agree to disagree. From my experience in mediating between partners, I never become concerned about disagreements. They are akin to fights between alley cats: After all the scrapping, the only result seems to be more cats. The success of a partnership depends on arriving at sensible decisions through cooperation and equal participation.

Every partnership should have a *godfather*. Not the kind made famous in Mario Puzo's recent novel about the underworld, but one who is trusted and respected by both partners and who can serve as a mediator to help resolve conflicts. This helps unstick the sticky problems in the 50–50 partnerships.

This godfather should be unbiased; he should have little or no vested interest in the company. He can be a business acquaintance, a friend, a college professor, or someone respected in the technology of your business. Bring him into the picture right at the beginning and keep him abreast of what goes on so he can understand the causes of any problems.

If you're lucky and if the situation is very unusual, you may never require him to do more than settle minor disputes or serve as a sounding board for new ideas. If worst comes to worst, however, and you must dissolve the partnership, the godfather may be the only one who can keep the pieces together long enough for the company to gain its equilibrium and survive. Remember, nothing lasts forever. But the business, if it survives at all, will most likely outlive the partnership.

Lawyers

How to Form Your Corporation Without a Lawyer for Under $50 (and imitations by dozens of other writers), a book written by Ted Nicholas and published by Enterprise Publishing Co., Wilmington, Delaware, 1971, seems to imply that incorporating a small business can be a homemade process. I don't disagree. It can be done cheaper on your own, but I suggest that the first step in the starting-a-business game is to see a lawyer. Not just so he or she can incorporate the business to avoid the legal disadvantages in a proprietorship, but to begin a long relationship. Selecting a proprietorship as the form of your new business can leave you and your assets exposed to law suits by unsatisfied creditors. Using a corporate format will strongly discourage unsecured creditors from suing any individual management member to collect unsecured, unpaid corporate bills. However, the corporate form of organization will seldom protect an individual from repaying secured bank debt, as almost all banks require a small business person to sign two ways—first, as the president of the corporation and second, as an individual. Hence, secured creditors, such as banks, receive payment of either the corporation or the individual responsible for the management of the business. Unsecured creditors, traditionally known as the accounts payable, are legally discouraged from pursuing any management individual to collect unsecured debts. This level of legal protection for a corporation is not available to a sole proprietor, and often the small business person is responsible for all debts, secured and unsecured. It's not the money you save that counts, but the headaches you avoid by having competent legal advice from the beginning. I say step one in the start-a-business-process is to see a good lawyer. You can still buy Ted Nicholas's book, but I would not recommend any homemade legal advice.

The lawyer is one of the critical elements in any business. He or she is a full-fledged team member and many times captains the team. Hence, he or she must be well qualified. I'd suggest going into the city to select your lawyer and choosing a young one who specializes in the Securities and Exchange Commission (SEC), which regulates security markets, or a corporate specialist at one of the prestigious law firms. Your lawyer will know how to take companies public, how to set up tax shield stock plans, and how to keep all the liabilities to a minimum. One good lawyer is worth a dozen bad ones; a good lawyer is a critical player on your management team.

Advertising Agencies

Most entrepreneurs tend to avoid advertising agencies or they put off hiring one until they hit an impasse in their marketing plans. Then it may be too late. I believe in finding a good, small (no more than ten people) agency early.

With advertising agencies, unlike law firms or public accounting firms, the largest is not always the best for the small businessperson. With a small agency, you'll get the attention—and probably plenty of it—of the top person.

The agency is often a junior member of the team but they should be selected early. An integrated corporate communications concept for letterheads, business cards, envelopes, and logos will establish a corporate identity that blends well together. It makes a big difference when all communication is well coordinated from the beginning. It avoids the embarrassment of not looking professional or of not being taken seriously.

Once you've found the right advertising agency, give them their head. Don't tell them what colors *you* like. Be candid and honest and give them all the information you can about your product and your markets—but don't impose your artistic talents. The more you give them, the more they'll be able to give you.

When it comes to agency compensation, please don't rely on the old 15% of the media costs method. This old method of compensating for agency efforts was very simple but it is now antiquated. Most approved media will allow an accredited agency to deduct a 15% discount very much like the airlines allow a travel agency a 7% discount. Hence, an advertising agency that annually placed $100,000 of media billing for a client would be indirectly compensated by paying the various media $85,000 while billing the client the published rates of $100,000. First of all, it's impossible for an agency to work profitably on a straight commission basis unless your media expenditures are considerable. Remember, they're in business to make a profit, too. Furthermore, it tends to create a conflict of interest for the agency, since it is to their advantage if your advertising dollars go into a commissionable media. The best course for your company may be direct mail or some other noncommissionable medium. Do you want the agency working for your company or for the commissionable media? There is a possible conflict between what is good for the media and what is good for the client. An agency that is singularly reimbursed for commission media, print or electronic, may be unreceptive to designing brochures or trade literature because the printing commissions may be less than the earned discount from the commissionable media. An estimate of the annual advertising budget should be the foundation for determining an agency's compensation. This allows a fuller, fairer choice of the optimal allocations between commissionable and noncommissionable activities.

The most practical and fairest method of agency compensation is a monthly retainer fee that amounts to about 10% more than the commissions they would receive on annual forecasted commissionable media expenditures. This method eliminates the conflict of interest and lets the agency worry about what's best for you, not about what's best for them.

Accountants

Another person you'll want to get on board at the earliest moment is a top-flight certified public accountant (CPA). Numbers are the language of business management, and intelligent decisions require an understanding of the quantitative factors involved.

If you have hopes for expansion or for going public, line up one of the big accounting firms. A merely adequate accountant is suicide. A big, well-known firm immediately lends credibility to your numbers; and, when the time comes for that public offering, three years of audited statements from one of the big names adds plenty of status. Don't worry about a big firm being too expensive. Most of them have separate divisions for small businesses. They'll install a one-write check system (which can save hours of work and improve your accuracy) and an accounts-payable voucher register (so you'll know who owes you money), and set up all the necessary systems to help you avoid unnecessary false starts.

Next, introduce your lawyer and your accountant to your banker. There will be plenty of decisions where their functions overlap, so they should know one another from the outset.

Bankers

Pick a banker, not a bank. If he is with a large bank, or a bank with a captive small business investment company (SBIC), so much the better. Many bankers are really venture capitalists in disguise and they can be sources of valuable financial assistance.

Here again, forget the big titles and pick a young loan officer or assistant vice president, then gain his confidence. Supply him or her with detailed pro forma cash flow projections to show what your cash needs will be. Simply stated, this is a cash plan that estimates the future incoming cash and subtracts the estimated future cash needs of the business. The difference will be the estimated future cash needs (or excess cash) generated by the business. Then meet or exceed your projections. Getting financial aid will be easy from then on.

In working with your friendly banker you'll soon learn that he or she expects you to countersign your company's bank debt personally. Don't let it throw you. It's the only way he or she has to certify your numbers and your confidence in what you're doing. But don't take this responsibility lightly, either. It's easy for you to be overly optimistic and that can get you into a lot of trouble. Before you sign that note, take a good, hard look at those figures again. That signature on the back of the note isn't an autograph—unless you become very, very famous. The countersignature on a bank note means that you, as an individual, are personally responsible for the debts. In the event that the business goes into bankruptcy and is unable to meet the financial obligation that bears your countersignature, the lender can seek the difference between what is collected and what is owed from you as the countersigner of the debt.

If you have inventory and/or receivables, you may be able to avoid the countersignature; or you may at least be able to limit your personal vulnerability by assigning them to the bank. I like the concept of limited personal guarantee and banks are more receptive to a limited guarantee than to no guarantee at all. It usually is reasonable grounds upon which a compromise can be established.

If the worst happens and the bank has to go after your security, it is better that the bank secures the company's inventory, not your wife's diamond ring. Some states protect your home from creditors or bankers trying to collect against a bankrupt company under the Homestead Act. The Homestead Act originated years ago to protect farmers who often lost their farms when they were unable to meet the payments for large farm equipment. The states individually passed legislation in the 1800s that protected a person's primary residence from creditors other than the principal mortgage holder. But to gain this level of additional legal protection, a short two-page document must be filed prior to any seizure attempts by creditors. It's all very complicated, very legal, and it varies from state to state. But all of these issues point out the reason you selected a good lawyer first. Ask your lawyer how to do it; that's why lawyers are paid so well.

Board of Directors

There is no doubt that the most crucial single personification of an entrepreneur's management team is the board of directors. A board of directors is charged with establishing policy-level decisions. A well-balanced board of directors adds depth to a small, understaffed enterprise. When the board is composed of respected business advisors who meet periodically and debate policy and develop corporate strategies, then the company is operating on a solid foundation.

Unfortunately, too many small businesses do not have actual boards of directors. The entrepreneur who is concerned with day-to-day activities often ignores the potential advantages of establishing a balanced board of directors. The board of directors is often comprised of a wife and father who never influence business issues. They are rubber stamps in the true sense of the word.

Whether to choose accountants, lawyers, bankers, or others to serve on the board of directors is a puzzle with no single answer. Rather, the answer depends on the other talents of the individuals and on the needs of the company. The only group who consistently offers a universal appeal as board members is a group affectionately labeled "angels." These seasoned investors/businessmen are often the nucleus of a good working board of directors.

Angels are hard to find, but they do exist. They're those marvelous people who descend from the heavens just to invest in small companies. No, they're not supernaturals. Usually they are just successful, wealthy businessmen, who, instead of putting their money in the stock market, investing in a mutual fund, or buying savings bonds, invest a portion of their wealth in young businesses.

This is the best sort of investor/director. Such an individual usually joins the team at the founding level and stays with the company until it makes a public offering. Often he makes useful contacts for the company. When more money is needed, he is usually the first to step forward. Most angels have invested between $100,000 and $200,000 in several small businesses, keeping their stake in each venture below $50,000. They are likely to be the only nonemployee investors in the companies. To top it off, they're usually the salt of the earth: nice people—but smart. As venture capitalists, they don't value their advice as highly as a professional venture capitalist, even though it's usually better; they don't value their money as highly as a professional venture capitalist, because they don't have large fixed costs for offices and the like. Compared to doctor and lawyer money, angels are seldom nervous or irrational over business problems because they grew up in business, not in law or medicine. If you can find one (in a city the size of Boston there are probably only 100 angels), you can't go wrong by bringing him into the financing arrangements. Then go the extra step to involve him in a balanced board of directors who meet monthly and debate business policies vigorously.

Management Consultants

Entrepreneurs, more than most businesspeople, rely on other people—such as professional management consultants, college professors, other company presidents, or anyone else who can intelligently offer advice and objectivity.

These people serve as sounding boards for the entrepreneur's ideas and help him or her weigh alternatives before making the final decision. In other fields—such as government, the military, and even sports—these sounding boards exist internally in the form of staff assistants.

Since small businesses can't afford droves of staff assistants, they have to rely on external sources, and this leads to the emergence of professional management consultants for small businesses. The management consultant (M.C.) is usually a person with a broad range of knowledge in the management of businesses, and he or she applies that experience to your problems in order to guide you in the right direction. Ultimately, the decision is always yours, but the M.C. plays a vital role in helping you see flaws and correct them before you implement the plan. The M.C. is often the source for new creative concepts, too.

In order to demonstrate the emergence of the management consultant, I counted the number of consulting firms listed in the Yellow Pages in various cities and noted their increase over the years. The results are shown in the table below. Apparently there is no other means to prove this point, as neither the government nor any association compiles statistics on the number of management consulting firms by city. I believe the data demonstrates the growth, and thereby the value, of the service.

NUMBER OF MANAGEMENT CONSULTANT FIRMS IN YELLOW PAGES BY YEAR									
City	1951	1960	1963	1964	1965	1969	1970	1974	1976	1983
Boston	17	60				178			365	420
Chicago					268		449			
Los Angeles		112			225		337	340		700
Philadelphia					108		158			
Washington, D.C.				111					401	400

Strangely enough, many small businesses use the services of management consultants successfully. They can often provide the frosting on the cake but should never be over-extended to provide the cake. That's the job of the entrepreneur. This is often confusing or misunderstood by a struggling businessperson who is unsure of the economic return from a small business consultant. If the business succeeds, it's because of the entrepreneur, not the adviser. The same if it fails. The consultant only provides help, guidance, and assistance, and he or she is never the pivotal difference between success and failure in a small growing enterprise. That's the job of the entrepreneur.

Manufacturer's Representatives

Manufacturer's representatives or reps are the mainstay of the sales force of most small businesses. They are independent businesspeople, entrepreneurs in their own right, peddling the merchandise of several manufacturers rather than just one.

Reps don't add to a company's fixed costs. They're paid on a commission basis according to what they sell. Because of this, a small company can afford to maintain a respectable sales force without incurring large, fixed overhead costs.

The rep is also a valuable source of industry intelligence. He or she is a kind of mercenary soldier, stomping through the industrial mud as a commissioned member of several armies. If anyone knows what's going on, the rep does. He or she's the sage of his or her industry.

When you latch onto a good rep (there are some poor ones), hold onto him or her—even when it's time to hire an inside person. Many companies make special arrangements with best reps to keep them on. It's good for the company; and it's good for the rep, who lives in fear of selling him- or herself out of a good line. If a rep performs too well in a territory, many small companies get confused and suddenly believe that the best alternative would be to fire the rep and hire a direct salaried person. A manufacturer may eventually decide that a certain territory is lucrative enough to support a full-time company employee. This cost efficient decision will occur at different levels for different companies and products. A cost efficient decision is elusive in practice but easily explained in theory. It's elusive because the opening assumption usually proves to be misleading. The question is, given the same sales in both cases, when is an independent, commissioned agent less expensive than a salaried full-time company salesman? The pivotal assumption (remember *assume* derives from the Greek, meaning ass of u and me) is underlined. The answer is, when less commissions are paid to the agents than salary that would have been paid to the salesperson, for a given level of sales. Whenever the crossing point occurs for a sales territory, it is commonly thought to be more cost efficient to replace the commissioned agent with a salaried employee. But watch out for the *assumptions*.

It is useful to clarify this issue in the early stages of business growth, for many small companies begin with manufacturer's representatives and eventually shift to full-time company paid salespeople. The issue is, "What are the trade-offs in making these decisions?" There are both qualitative and quantitative reasons to prefer one type of sales force to another.

The qualitative advantages of each are listed below.

MANUFACTURER'S REPRESENTATIVES

1. A commissioned agent who receives compensation only when he or she sells something.
2. Usually the representative firm has a number of persons covering a single territory instead of just one person.
3. A manufacturer's representative also sells the products for other manufacturers and this can help him or her in merchandising complementary products.
4. The nature of their specialization makes them knowledgeable about their territory and their customers.
5. The marketing effort by a team of experienced reps is usually more efficient than a headquarters-directed effort at identifying and merchandising key accounts.

COMPANY SALESPERSON

1. Loyalty undoubtedly rests with the single employer and is not scattered among many manufacturers.
2. Willing to invest effort to develop new products or to maintain service to customers, both of which may be less income productive than pursuing other activities.
3. More efficient above a certain sales volume.
4. Able to develop better inside managers by having them initially perform at field sales.
5. Able to control sales activities better.

The Controller

Show me a successful small company with great growth potential and I'll show you a company with a talented financial person keeping his or her thumb on the cash flow—the company controller. This is the person who passes on all company expenditures. This person's also the one who manages to get the quarterly audit done, in spite of last quarter's foolish mistakes.

When given the chance, he or she will vote *no* 80% of the time. He or she frustrates everyone with pessimism, and is accused of throwing cold water on every good idea. Production doesn't like the controller because he or she refuses to sign purchase orders. Sales doesn't like him because he or she gives them a hard time about expense reports.

The controller is never popular, but he or she is the one person in the company who can provide the balance it needs. With him or her, there's temperance. Without him or her, there could be a drunken spending spree that might cripple a small, young company or one growing old. This financial genius, along with the first mate, are the two most crucial picks in your draft of management talent. Let's call them the first two rounds of the draft, or the number one and two draft picks.

Entrepreneurs often make fatal mistakes in selecting the financial specialist. This is especially true of the Boston Route 128 technical types. Typically, they are unfamiliar with finance, as compared to their extensive engineering and technical knowledge. Hence, in selecting the financial genius, they often rely on those with college degrees rather than on those with proven experience on the job.

Consequently, technical entrepreneurs hire business school MBAs (Masters in Business Administration) the way some large firms hire minority groups. It's the thing to do—especially if those hired are finance majors. Entrepreneurs tend to be infatuated with the MBA—the brash kid in his late twenties who knows all the answers and all the words, like *game plan* and *M.B.O.*—Management by Objectives, a managing technique made famous by Mr. Peter Drucker.

The trouble with most of today's business school graduates is that they have more answers than there are questions, just as there are more horses' asses than there are horses. It may sound strange, but too many solutions can create a problem. Furthermore, it's claimed they get too much money and change jobs too often.

In my experience with MBAs in small business, I have found that they spend most of their time analyzing their employer and the company. The ones who excel in small business management are running their own companies. They won't work for entrepreneurs; they *are* entrepreneurs. Think twice before you offer an unusually high salary for a would-be soothsayer.

If you must hire one of the new MBAs, try to find one who is in his or her second or third job. A little experience under the belt could do you a lot of good. A person with an MBA in finance or marketing who is looking for his or her third job and who has some small company experience could be the right medicine for your company. This is especially true for retail businesses because of the unique nature of retailing. In retailing, it's often best to wait until the MBA is past the age of 40, regardless of the number of previous jobs. A certain maturity plus an MBA is extremely powerful medicine, even for a certain sick business.

chapter 8

Capital: Where It Is and How to Get It

VENTURE CAPITAL TIPS

One of the leading investment bankers of Santa Fe, New Mexico, David Silver, who is also a columnist for *Venture Magazine,* claims all financial forecasts look like a hockey stick. That is, they start out flat and suddenly take a sharp steep upward slope one or two years in the future. Silver further claims there are only three crucial ingredients in a business plan. Silver's perspective is from the eyes of a venture capital investor, and he claims all successful plans contain these three ingredients in the following order.

A. Big market
B. Good product
C. Good management team

He likes to tell the story of one of the most successful venture capital investments ever to illustrate his message. This investment wasn't in some high technology esoteric product but, rather, in a service business. The rule of thumb has always been that a service business is not a good candidate for a venture capital investment. But, in this exciting story, a 28-year-old up-shot known as Freddie Smith proved everybody wrong as he raised $94 million to launch Federal Express. Better yet, according to Silver, Smith was able to maintain 4% of the business while providing less than 1% of the capital. (He invested just about $1 million).

One of the venture capital sources who invested in Federal Express tells an affectionate Freddie Smith story. It goes like this.

Four people were stranded on an island in the Pacific when a group of leaflets descended from the sky announcing that the island was to be annihilated in five minutes by a nuclear blast. Looking dejected, one of the inhabitants, an older man, walked into the bushes to enjoy his last bottle of wine. Two of the other inhabitants, a young couple, also went into the bushes to spend their last five minutes alone. Freddie Smith was the fourth person on the island and he immediately dove into the vast Pacific ocean. The other three people eventually emerged from the bushes and they watched Freddie diving and swimming in the ocean. Finally one of them shouted, "What are you doing?" Freddie ignored them but shouted over his shoulder, "I've got five minutes to learn to swim underwater, please don't bother me now."

They say that the original founders of Federal Express so believed in the venture and Freddie Smith that they all hocked their watches just to make payrolls!

In 1980 there were private (nonSBIC) venture capital firms with an average portfolio of $30 million each. Just ten years ago there were only three venture funds that were private. So, the success of past venture investments, such as Federal Express, has spawned a renewed interest in venture capital investing.

What does a venture capitalist look for? According to Silver they have several goals. First, they seek a minimum of five times on their money. In practice, they are often able to turn their money four times in three years, which is a 45% annual return on investment (R.O.I.). To make an investment, they want to know the five answers to these five questions.

1. How much can I make?
2. How much can I lose?
3. How do I get out of the deal?
4. Who is in the deal?
5. Who says the product and the people are any good?

The 400 or so nonprivate small investment companies (SBICs) firms and the 150 Minority Enterprise Small Business Investment Companies (MESBICs) have an average of about $10,000 of capital to invest. In 1981, more venture capital was available in more funds than ever in the history of the venture capital industry. A record of $900 million of new capital was committed to the venture industry in 1980. Private venture firms received $657 million of this, a figure four times greater than 1979 and greater than any previous single year. Of the $657 million, $42 million in private capital was raised by Small Business Investment Corporations in 1979 and $17 million was raised by Minority Enterprise Small Business Investment Corporations. Since 44 SBICs and 31 MESBICs were licensed in 1980, these totals are not surprising. This total of 75 new firms is the highest number of new licensees since 1964. (Incidentally, these new SBICs combined brought a total of $61,372,723 into the venture capital industry.)

The industry now boasts a total of approximately $4.5 billion in venture capital broken out in the following way.

Independent venture firms	$1.8 billion
SBICs, MESBIC's	1.4 billion
Corporations	1.3 billion
Total	4.5 billion

Watch the growth of the venture capital industry as another 30 groups, many headed by experienced venture capitalists, attempt to raise another $600 million in 1982, which would bring the total capital available to over $5 billion in 1982.

While the philosophy of venture capital is similar throughout the United States, there are several regional differences which might be useful to know before making your final selection. Here is the regional focus of venture capitalists around the United States.

South: (Texas) The emphasis is on "who are your people?"

East: (New York) The emphasis is on "who do you know?"

Midwest: (Chicago) The emphasis is on "who do you work for?"

West: (California) The emphasis is on "what's your package?"

The only axiom that seems to hold no matter what part of the country you are from is a very simple but very true expression. "Speak Yiddish but dress British when raising money."

For the very reasonable cost of one dollar, you can obtain all the information you ever wanted to know about SBICs (including the names and addresses of those closest to you) by sending for the directory of SBIC.

National Association of Small Business
Investment Companies (NASBIC)
618 Washington Bldg.
Washington, DC 20005
(202-638-3411)

BREAKEVEN

A breakeven analysis is a critical calculation for every small business. Rather than calculating how much your firm would make if it obtained an estimated sales volume, a more meaningful analysis determines at which sales volume your firm will break even. The other statistic is really pie-in-the-sky because the estimated sales volume is very questionable. Don't assume a sales volume and determine your profits; do it in reverse; determine the sales volume necessary for your firm to break even. Above the breakeven, the firm makes money; below, it loses money. A breakeven point, then, is a level of sales volume over some period of time. An example would be: "My firm broke even on $10,000 a week in sales."

$$\text{T.C.} = \text{V.C.} + \text{F.C.}$$

Total costs = variable costs plus fixed costs*

T.C. = Total costs = All costs to operate the business over a specified time period.

V.C. = Variable costs = Those costs which vary directly with the number of products manufactured. Sometimes called direct costs, they typically include material and labor costs plus a percentage of the overhead costs.

F.C. = Fixed costs = Costs which do not vary with the number of products produced. Also known as indirect costs, these costs typically include executive salaries, rent, insurance, and are considered fixed over a relevant range of production.

B.E. = Breakeven point = Where total costs are equal to total revenues.

Here is an example for a plant which produces only one product.

A. The fixed costs are $100,000 per year. These costs include:

lights and power and phones (utilities),
rent,
insurance,
administrative salaries.

These costs are fixed over 20,000 units to 40,000 units manufactured annually.

B. The variable costs over the 20,000–40,000 unit range are:

$2.00 material
$3.00 labor
$1.00 overhead (50% of material)
$6.00 per unit.

C. Sale price per unit is $10.00

Note: A word of caution. In a small business, there is no such item as a truly fixed cost. No costs are fixed forever. Insurance can be cancelled, executives can be fired and rent can be renegotiated. Hence, a fixed cost should be thought of as a fixed cost only over a period of time or over a finite range of production.

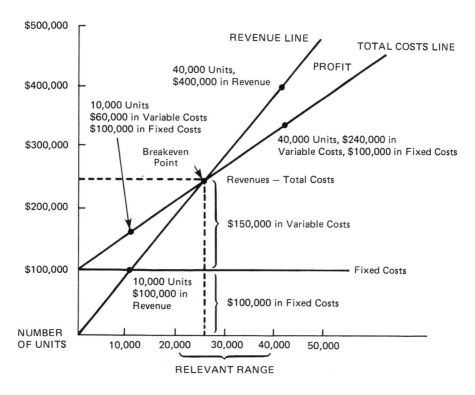

$500,000 ⊢

REVENUE LINE

TOTAL COSTS LINE

$400,000 ⊢

40,000 Units,
$400,000 in Revenue

PROFIT

10,000 Units
$60,000 in Variable Costs
$100,000 in Fixed Costs

$300,000 ⊢

40,000 Units, $240,000 in
Variable Costs, $100,000 in Fixed Costs

Breakeven
Point

Revenues — Total Costs

$200,000 ⊢

$150,000 in Variable Costs

$100,000 ⊢

Fixed Costs

10,000 Units
$100,000 in
Revenue

$100,000 in Fixed Costs

NUMBER
OF UNITS

10,000   20,000   30,000   40,000   50,000

RELEVANT RANGE

A BREAKEVEN CHART REVENUE = $10/UNIT FIXED COSTS = $100,000
VARIABLE COSTS = $6/UNIT

Creation of the Breakeven Chart

A breakeven chart (also known in more optimistic circles as a *profit* graph) translates the three known facts into linear terms: The fixed costs of $100,000, the variable costs of $6 per unit, and the sales price of $10 per unit.

The fixed costs line is horizontal because the fixed costs are $100,000 regardless of production volumes. To determine the revenue line, calculate that at 10,000 units the revenue is $100,000 (10,000 × $10) and that at 40,000 units it will be $400,000, and draw a line through those two points. From the revenue line, you can determine the revenue if you know the number of units or the number of units if you know the revenue.

The total costs line is determined by calculating what the variable costs would be at any two volumes, adding the $100,000 in fixed costs to each of these numbers, and drawing a line through the two points. The total costs at 10,00 units are $160,000 (10,000 × $6 = $60,000 + $100,000), and at 40,000 units the total costs are $340,000. The total costs line through these two points shows the total costs at different volumes.

When you have drawn the fixed costs, revenue, the total costs lines, you see the breakeven point is 25,000, which is the intersection of the revenue and total costs lines. At volumes greater than 25,000, there will be profit since revenues will be greater than total costs.

The Breakeven Formula

Although the breakeven chart is probably the most useful means of visualizing breakeven analysis, the following formula provides the same information.

$$\text{Breakeven} = \frac{\text{Fixed Costs}}{(\text{Revenue/Unit} - \text{Variable Costs/Units})}$$

Using the figures from the example, there is a breakdown equal to $100,000 ÷ ($10 − $6) = 25,000 units. Being able to determine the specific breakdown point is handy, but the main value of breakeven analysis comes in applying the concept to evaluate a variety of business problems.

Pricing Decisions

A common business problem is estimating the effects of raising or lowering a product's price. How many more would need to be sold to maintain the profit level if you lowered the price a dollar? How many fewer would need to be sold to maintain that profit level if you raised the price a dollar? A rough estimate can be quickly made by drawing new revenue lines on the breakeven chart. If you do draw new revenue lines on the chart in the figure, you will confirm the finding that if the price is raised a dollar, the breakeven point drops from 25,000 to 20,000 units. If you lower the price a dollar, the breakeven jumps to 33,333 units. As you change the revenue line, you will also see how much the profits rise and fall with other price changes.

Breakeven is a valuable tool, but only one of many useful tools for analyzing your business. Breakeven oversimplifies decision. While the advantage is that it makes it easier to comprehend difficult small business issues, it also has some disadvantages. The assumptions are its disadvantages and some of them are listed here.

1. All fixed costs are not really fixed, even over the relevant unit range. They can and do vary.
2. A changing product mix can change the breakeven. The assumption that one plant produces one product can be misleading.

3. Costs do not vary directly with production. Material or labor costs often vary even over very narrow ranges.
4. Selling price is seldom fixed.
5. Inventory costs are seldom calculated within a breakeven and these costs can be large.

As a final tool in *understanding* pricing decisions, the following formula can also be helpful for determining prices.

S.P. = T.C. + P.
S.P. = Selling Price = Per unit selling price
T.C. = Total Costs = Variable costs plus fixed costs per unit.
P. = Profit = Profit per unit.

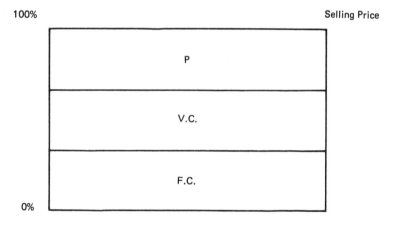

A further understanding of this breakeven calculation can be gained by comprehending a concept known as contribution analysis. Contribution is a difficult concept in practice but easy in theory. Any revenue above the variable costs for a product can *contribute* to fixed costs plus profit.

As the example above, with

S.P. = $10.00 per unit
V.C. = $6.00 per unit

$$\text{F.C.} \div 40{,}000 \text{ units} = \frac{\$100{,}000 \text{ F.C.}}{40{,}000 \text{ units}} = \$2.50 \text{ per unit}$$

Profit = S.P. − T.C.
        = $10.00 − ($6.00 + 2.50)
Profit = $1.50/unit

Hence at 40,000 units, the firm will show a per unit profit of $1.50 per unit.

The crucial question in a contribution analysis usually occurs when cutomers suddenly announce they will pay $9.00 for your 40,001st unit of production. Take it or leave it.

The classical school that discounts the contribution type of analysis suggests you refuse the order. The contribution school claims, if this is your only choice, take the order for the 40,001st unit at $9.00 as you will still be making 50 cents of profit [$1.50 − ($9.00 − $8.50)].

In fact, the contribution school further argues, on this rare example, that any revenue above the level of variable costs would be better to accept than to reject. For instance, a price of $6.01 per unit would be the lowest price where the order for the 40,001st unit should be accepted. At this level, the sale produces one cent to be contributed to profit and fixed costs. The decision, in the final analysis, will depend on other variables as well. But the purpose of this exercise is to outline the rationale of contribution analysis for use in your final decision making.

UNUSUAL SOURCES OF CAPITAL

Lending institutions prefer to loan money against collateral because they retain the option of liquidating the collateral to repay the loan. Following is the rule of thumb for what can be loaned against different forms of collateral from the balance sheet of an entrepreneurial venture.

In practice, the actual ratios are even more pronounced. In other words, banks prefer not to lend against inventory as contrasted to lending against receivables. In turn, easily liquidated fixed assets are the most attractive type of collateral (automobiles) and they usually command both a high percentage of their lendable market value as well as a subsequently lower interest rate.

A lender is basically unsure of an inventory's value until it is converted to cash by being sold. That's the underlying reason that lenders shy away from accepting inventory or certain types of fixed assets as collateral for a loan. Thus, the role of T.H.E. Insurance Company is to write an insurance policy to protect a lender against bankruptcy. Insurance companies essentially appraise the collateral asset and insure to repossess it from a lender at the assessed rates.

Rather than the insurance policy paying off at death, the policy is paid upon default in the loan. Here's how it works.

1. T.H.E. appraises the assets to be pledged, including both inventory and fixed assets.
2. T.H.E. then issues an insurance policy for the amount of their appraisal.
3. The company hands this policy over to the lender and then borrows 100 percent of the value of the policy in a loan.

4. If the company defaults, T.H.E. takes title to the collateral and sells it. The lender is paid in full using T.H.E.'s credit and capital to be reimbursed.

What Does All This Insurance Protection Cost?

1. Appraisal fee: minimum amount $1000. This is for the appraisal and it is 1% of the appraised value of the collateral plus out-of-pocket (travel) expenses.
2. A 2% add-on interest rate on the outstanding loan balance, not on the full appraisal of the collateral. The premium interest rate of 2% is charged only on what's borrowed or what is at risk.

The value of T.H.E. policy allows more capital to be secured from existing lenders. On the one hand, a lender typically allows only 10% of inventory value to be used as loan collateral. With a policy the inventory allowed as collateral might be above 50% of its value, depending upon T.H.E.'s assessment. This arrangement often allows a two or three times greater amount to be loaned against an asset.

Often an asset or inventory can be borrowed against when it was given zero valuation by a bank because of the T.H.E. formula. On a theoretical basis, the lending interest rate can be reduced if you can convince the lender of the merits and security of the guarantee. In effect, given the policy, the lender should advance funds on T.H.E.'s credit, not the credit of your entrepreneurial venture.

	Percentage to be Loaned Against
Accounts Receivable	75%–80% under 90 days
Inventory	10%–20%
Fixed Assets	70%–80% market value

In practice, you are seldom ever able to negotiate a lower bank interest rate by securing a T.H.E. guarantee and, in total, you are paying 5–6% above prime rate for this type of lending. If your entrepreneurial venture can service debt, write to Mr. Ed Shifman, Vice President, T.H.E. Insurance Company, 80 Bent Street, Cambridge, MA 02141, (617) 494-5300.

ENTREPRENEURIAL BANK BORROWING

There is a small but developing trend that may be of interest to entrepreneurs currently searching for a new banking relationship. Recently two major changes have occurred in the overall United States banking structure that have created some measurable differences between banks. The first of these changes is foreign banks doing business in the United States. In 1972, when the Federal Reserve started keeping statistics on such issues, there were 52 foreign banks with 100 offices in the United States. By mid-1978, the number of foreign banks had more than doubled to 123 and they operated 268 offices. The assets of these foreign-owned United States-based banks have grown more than four times during the five-year period, and today their assets are over $100 billion. The second change is the two-tier prime rate structure now being charged to small business. But more about that in a minute.

Why are these foreign banks expanding in the United States? There are two basic answers: the relative devaluation of the United States dollar and the ability of these banks to avoid United States banking regulations. Because of these factors, these banks have generally been taking a more aggressive posture toward loans to entrepreneurial ventures. This is not true for every banker at every bank, but it is true as a generality. So, if you're considering a banking relationship, why not consider Britain's Barclay Bank, or the Bank of Montreal, or any of the host of Japanese, Swiss, or French banks?

These foreign-owned banks are allowed to open branches outside their countries (U.S. banks are not) and they often have offices in the major cities of the country. They are seldom located in small towns, much preferring the New York or Los Angeles type of city. This ability to operate across counties can also be a feature for your company if they operate in the same cities where branches of your business are located. Besides this benefit, these banks are not required to tie up a portion of their assets with the Federal Reserve System because they most often choose to operate under state banking regulations. These two fundamental reasons allow these banks the slight tendency to be more aggressive in securing new business. Hence, it may prove to be to your advantage to do business with them.

Further, with this expansion continuing, I would predict a major overhaul in United States banking restrictions to allow United States banks to compete on more favorable terms with these foreign banks. Hence, if this happens, this opportunity for more aggressive banking will prove to be available only for a moment in time.

There are the obvious advantages of doing business with a foreign-based bank, if your entrepreneurial venture business happens to sell or buy from the host country. For the bank nearest you, consult the Yellow Pages of the largest city near you.

The second major change was triggered by the heroes of small business at The Mellon National Bank in Pittsburgh, Pennsylvania. They began offering small businesses a borrowing rate below the prime rate. They did this during money shortages (now) to help entrepreneurs, and they deserve pioneering recognition! For an up-to-date list of banks who offer a revised two-tier lending rate, write to Chief Counsel for Advocacy, Small Business Administration, 1441 L St. N.W., Washington, DC 20416, (202)653-6881 or (800)368-5855.

WHERE ARE THE HIDDEN SOURCES OF CAPITAL?

Turn-Around Technique

One of the most interesting problems in small business is turning around unsuccessful companies. A condensed story of how Mr. Bill Frustajer, the founder of several highly successful businesses, and his consulting team turned around the H.S. Scott Hi-Fi Company in Maynard, Massachusetts serves a point. H.S. Scott is one of the leading quality manufacturers of stereo equipment in the United States. Some years ago they ran into terrible price competition from foreign suppliers, mainly Japanese, and the company was teetering on the verge of bankruptcy. Payroll had been paid intermittently, bills were overdue, and the large Boston-based State Street Bank had closed in. Bill Frustajer's first chore was to discover any sources of short term cash. Cash would stay-off the creditors and pay past due payroll to keep the employees working. The technique he used was to uncover a heretofore undiscovered asset. Three years previously, the earnings of the company had been sufficient to warrant the company paying income taxes of $1,200,000 on that year's profits. The losses the last two years had been staggering, but profits were respectable the preceding year. Bill Frustajer rewrote his financial statements and filed IRS form 1139 in order to go back and get a tax refund against those assets. A tax loss can be either carried forward for five years or back for three years. Below is a simplified statement of the company's performance.

	SIMPLIFIED PROFIT AND LOSS			
	1971	*1972*	*1973*	*1974*
Sales	$12,000,000	$13,000,000	$14,000,000	$12,000,000
Profit before taxes	2,400,000	(250,000)	(2,700,000)	
Taxes	1,200,000	—	—	
Profit after taxes	1,200,000	(250,000)	(2,700,000)	

While this statement is simplified to demonstrate the example, income taxes are not due until April 15th of the following year for a company with a calendar year end. Consequently, by filing an amended set of financial statements and tax returns plus IRS form 1139, he was able to obtain a tax refund for the taxes paid in 1971. In the H.S. Scott case mentioned, although these are not the actual numbers, the tax refund saved the day and in turn, the company.

Actually, the turn-around time on receiving an IRS rebate is too long (months) to ordinarily save a faltering business. So Bill pledged this refund to the bank along with the documents filed to secure the IRS refund and was able to borrow against this asset, thereby shrinking the processing time to receive the needed cash infusion. He received the funds in less than a month.

Hidden assets don't always appear on financial statements in plain view. Examples of other hidden assets are foreign rights to products, licensing arrangements, patents, and goodwill.

Farmers Home Loan

The SBA is supposedly the government agency charged with helping the entrepreneur, but in practice, other federal agencies also provide a great deal of help. The FmHa is the loan program of the Farmers Home Administration, which offers guaranteed loans to growing businesses. Unlike the SBA's program with a $500,000 ceiling, the FmHa loan program has no ceiling. In fact, loans have ranged from $7,000 to $33 million with an average of about $900,000.

The FmHa loan gives preference to distressed areas and rural communities of less than 25,000 inhabitants. It will loan money for any worthwhile business purpose. The minimum equity requirement is 10% and, if your venture can be shown to be job-creating, your loan has a greater chance of approval. Unlike the SBA, you do not have to prove to be an unbankable company to secure a FmHa loan. The loans are for fairly long terms, thirty years for construction, fifteen years for equipment, and seven years for working capital. The interest rate is about the same as can be negotiated with a bank, but the FmHa has a one-time fee that is calculated by multiplying 1% of the principal loan amount by the percentage of the guarantee. Even given the one-time fee, the good standing of the United States government stands behind the guaranteed portions of the loan, and the interest rate eventually negotiated often affects these favorable considerations. Why not write the FmHa in care of the (USDA) United States Department of Agriculture, Washington, DC 20250, or look in your nearest largest city Yellow Pages for one of the 1800 county offices. Look under United States Government—Agriculture.

SBA's BUSINESS LOAN PROGRAMS

Sources: Other SBA Nonbank Lenders

Money Store Investment Corporation, Springfield, NJ, (201) 467-9000. Offers SBA Guaranteed Loans in branch locations in 12 states.

Merrill Lynch Small Business Lending Company, New York, NY, (212) 637-7455. Loan program functions nationwide.

Allied Lending Corporation, Washington, DC, (202) 331-1112. SBA guaranteed loans for the Washington area.

NIS Capital Funding Corporation, White Plains, NY, (914) 428-8600. Provides SBA guaranteed loans locally.

Independence Mortgage Company, Inc., Odessa, TX, (915) 333-5814. SBA guaranteed loans for the Odessa area.

The First Commercial Credit Corporation, Los Angeles, CA, (213) 937-0860. Provides SBA loans in Los Angeles.

ITT Small Business Finance Corporation, Minneapolis, MN, (612) 540-8509. Offers SBA loans on a national basis. (This is a subsidiary of International Telephone & Telegraph Finance Corporation.)

Under a congressional mandate, the United States Small Business Administration (SBA) assists the nation's small businesses through a number of programs and efforts. SBA helps new or growing businesses meet their financial needs, counsels small firms with problems, offers special assistance to minority and women-owned businesses, helps small businesses to secure government contracts, and acts as a special advocate for small business with other federal agencies, with states, and within the private sector.

Basic Types of SBA Loans

SBA loan proceeds can be used for working capital, purchase of inventory, equipment, and supplies, or for building construction and expansion. The SBA offers two basic types of business loans.

1. Loans made by private lenders, usually banks, and guaranteed by SBA. SBA *bank guaranteed loans* are tied to funds appropriated by Congress. The amount of loans that SBA can guarantee is much larger than funds appropriated for direct loans. Thus, the majority of SBA loans is of the guaranteed type. By law, SBA can guarantee up to 90% of a loan made by a bank or other private lender.

2. Loans made directly by the agency. Monies for *direct loans* also come from funds appropriated specifically by Congress for this purpose. Those direct loan monies are limited, however, and demand invariably exceeds supply. In addition, in recent years the SBA has approved an increasingly larger share of its direct loans for small firms that have unusual difficulty raising funds in the private market—that is, firms headed by women, handicapped persons, and representatives of socially and economically disadvantaged groups.

In general, direct SBA loans carry interest rates lower than those in the private financial markets. They are available only to applicants unable to secure private financing or an SBA-guaranteed or participation loan.

SBA also offers special *economic opportunity* loans for socially and economically disadvantaged persons (mostly representing minorities). These loans help small firms adversely affected by government regulations. Loans are also made to small firms engaged in manufacturing, selling, installing, servicing, or developing specific energy measures. Local development companies obtain loans for projects aiding small business in urban or rural communities.

The SBA licenses, regulates, and financially helps private firms called *Small Business Investment Companies* (SBICs), which supply equity capital and regular loans to small firms with unusual growth potential. Details concerning special loan programs can be obtained from any SBA office.

Even with its varied programs, the SBA cannot assist all the small businesses, or all the persons interested in starting a small firm. Agency funds and personnel are limited. Therefore, in recent years, the SBA—as a small business advocate—has increased its liaison and cooperation with the private sector. The primary aim is to widen assistance and make more funds available to the millions of small entrepreneurs in the country. The nation's banks have been made more aware of the advantages of participating in SBA guaranteed loans and have been urged to respond through their own loan programs to small business needs and wants. The SBA has instituted a special arrangement with a number of certified banks to cut down on red tape and paperwork in SBA guaranteed loans. Other companies have been organized as SBA nonbank lenders and can make small business loans guaranteed by the Agency.

This approach, involving greater cooperation with the private financial markets and putting the Agency more and more into a role of a *wholesaler,* will be emphasized in the months and years ahead. The private lender will be more and more the *retailer* of small business lending, while SBA takes on the role of *wholesaler.*

Who Is Eligible for an SBA Loan?

By law, the Agency may not make or guarantee a loan if a business can obtain funds on reasonable terms from a bank or other private source. A borrower therefore must first seek private financing before applying to the SBA. This means that a person first must apply to a bank or other lending institution for a loan. In a city of over 200,000 population, a person must be turned down by two banks before applying for an SBA loan.

A company must be independently owned and operated, not dominant in its field and must meet certain standards of size in terms of employees or annual receipts. Loans cannot be made to speculative businesses, newspapers, or businesses engaged in gambling.

Applicants for loans also must agree to comply with SBA regulations stating that there will be no discrimination in employment or services to the public based on race, color, religion, national origin, sex, or marital status.

What Is a Small Business?

At present, eligibility for loans varies by industry and SBA program. For business loans, the general size standard eligibility requirements are as follows:

Manufacturing—Number of employees may range up to 1,500 depending on the industry in which the applicant is primarily engaged.

Wholesaling—Yearly sales must not be over $9.5 to $22 million, depending on the industry.

Services—Annual receipts not exceeding $2 million to $8 million, depending on the industry in which the applicant is primarily engaged.

Retailing—Annual sales or receipts not exceeding $2 to $7.5 million, depending on the industry.

Construction—General construction: average annual receipts not exceeding $9.5 million for the three most recently completed fiscal years.

Special Trade Construction—Average annual receipts not exceeding $1 to $2 million for the three most recently completed fiscal years, depending on the industry.

Agriculture—Annual receipts not exceeding $1 million.

What Are the Credit Requirements?

A loan applicant must:

1. Be of good character.
2. Show ability to operate a business successfully.
3. Have enough capital in an existing firm so that with an SBA loan the business can operate on a sound financial basis.
4. Show that the proposed loan is of such sound value or so secured as to assure repayment.
5. Show that the past earnings record and future prospects of the firm indicate ability to repay the loan and other fixed debt, if any, out of profits.
6. Be able to provide, from personal resources, sufficient funds to have a reasonable amount at stake to withstand possible losses, particularly during the early stages of a new venture.

How Much Can a Person Borrow?

Loans made directly by SBA have a maximum of $150,000. The bank guaranteed loan program permits the Agency to guarantee up to 90% of a loan, or a maximum of $500,000, whichever is less. (Legislation is pending in Congress to increase this figure to $750,000.)

Economic opportunity loans are limited to $100,000 under each type of lending program. Handicapped assistance loans have a limit of $350,000 under the guaranteed program. A handicapped assistance loan made directly by SBA is limited to $100,000. Energy loans carry a ceiling of $500,000 for the guaranteed type and $350,000 for direct or immediate participation types.

Loans to businesses affected by federal legislation, regulation, or actions have no statutory maximum. The amount of economic injury is the governing factor. Small companies are eligible if they are displaced as a result of government action, or adversely affected by occupational safety and health legislation, strategic arms limitation actions, air and water pollution control legislation, military base closings, or emergency energy shortage situations.

Local Development Company loans carry a maximum of $500,000.

Terms of SBA Loans

Regular business loans generally have a maximum of ten years. Working capital loans are limited to seven years. Loans that include construction or acquisition of real estate have a 20-year maximum.

The SBA regularly sets a maximum allowable interest rate that banks can charge on guaranteed loans. Interest rates on direct loans and the SBA's share of an immediate participation loan are tied to the cost of money to the federal government and adjusted periodically.

Economic opportunity loans carry a maturity of 15 years. Handicapped assistance loans carry a 15-year maturity. The interest rate is 3% for SBA's share of a handicapped assistance loan.

Displaced business loans and other loans to alleviate economic injury resulting from federal legislation or other action have maturities of 30 years and carry the same interest rates as direct loans. Emergency energy shortage economic injury loans are subject to these same terms.

Collateral

One or more of the following may be acceptable security for a loan.

1. A mortgage on land, a building, and/or equipment
2. Assignment of warehouse receipts for marketable merchandise
3. A mortgage on chattels
4. Guarantees or personal endorsements, and in some instances, assignments of current receivables

Note: A new standard definition of a small business has been proposed based on a single measurement of size—total number of employees per firm. SBA field offices can advise firms which standard applies to them, if this proposal is formally adopted.

Note: When neither private financing nor a loan guarantee is available, SBA may provide loan funds on an *immediate participation* basis with a bank. The bank disburses part of the loan, at market interest rates, and the balance of the loan is disbursed directly by the SBA, at a lower interest rate. The SBA's share of an immediate participation loan may not exceed $150,000.

How to Apply for a SBA Loan

Those already in business should:

1. Prepare a current financial statement (balance sheet) listing all assets and all liabilities of the business.
2. Have an earnings (profit and loss) statement for the current period to the date of the balance sheet.
3. Prepare a current personal financial statement of the owner, or each partner or stockholder owning 20% or more of the corporate stock in the business.
4. List collateral to be offered as security for the loan, with an estimate of the present market value of each item.
5. State the amount of the loan requested and exact purposes for which it can be used.
6. Take the foregoing material to your banker. Ask for a direct bank loan and if you are declined, ask the bank to make the loan under the SBA's Loan Guarantee Plan or Immediate Participation Plan. If the bank is interested in an SBA guaranteed or participation loan, ask the banker to contact the SBA for discussion of your application. In most cases of guaranteed or participation loans, the SBA will deal directly with the bank.
7. If a guaranteed or a participation loan is not available, write or visit the nearest SBA office. The SBA has 110 field offices that often send loan officers to visit many smaller cities as the need is indicated. To speed matters, make your financial information available when you first write or visit the SBA.

Those wanting to start a business should:

1. Describe the type of business you plan to establish.
2. Describe your experience and management capabilities.
3. Prepare an estimate of how much you or others have to invest in the business and how much you will need to borrow.
4. Prepare a current financial statement (balance sheet) listing all personal assets and all liabilities.
5. Prepare a detailed projection of earnings for the first year the business will operate.
6. List collateral to be offered as security for the loan, indicating your estimate of the present market value of each item.
7. Follow steps 6 and 7 for those already in business.

chapter 9

Facts About Small Business and the U.S. Small Business Administration*

FACTS ABOUT SMALL BUSINESS

Small Business in General

There are an estimated 14.4 million businesses in the U.S. Of this total, 3.4 million are farms and 11 million are nonfarm businesses. Of the nonfarm businesses, 10.8 million (8.2%) are considered "small" by the SBA's loan application size standards. Approximately 99% of the 3.4 million farms are considered small businesses by the Agency's size standards.

The number of small businesses in the U.S. has increased annually in most of the last 30 years. New business incorporations increased by 10% in 1979, to 524,565 from 478,019 in 1978. Incorporations increased by 16% in 1977 and decreased by 3% in 1974 (Dun & Bradstreet statistics).

Business failures (bankruptcies and discontinuances for other reasons) increased by 14% in 1979, to 7,564 from 6,619 in 1978. Nearly 55% of failures (bankruptcies or closures with losses for creditors) among small businesses occur within their first 5 years of operation. 92% of all business failures are a direct result of poor management.

Estimates for 1976 (the latest year available) indicate small business produces 39% of the Gross National Product (GNP). (For these statistics, a small business is defined in Internal Revenue Service data as one with 0 to 499 employees.)

Approximately 62% of nonfarm businesses have annual sales or receipts

*Reprinted from the U.S. Small Business Administration, Public Communications Division, February 1981.

of less than $25,000. Eighty-two percent have sales or receipts of less than $100,000 and 98% have sales or receipts of less than $1 million (IRS data, 1975).

Small businesses account for nearly $8 of every $10 earned by construction firms (excludes farms).

Small businesses account for nearly $7 of every $10 in sales made by retailers and wholesalers (excludes farms).

Small nonfarm businesses account for nearly $6 of every $10 of receipts in the service industries.

Small nonfarm business provides 58% of U.S. business employment.

Small business directly or indirectly provides the livelihood of over 100 million Americans.

One-third of all small nonfarm businesses are in the service industries.

Nearly ¼ of all nonfarm small businesses are in retail trade.

Seventy-five percent of all U.S. businesses are sole proprietorships, and virtually all of these are small businesses.

Nearly 80% of all U.S. nonfarm businesses employ fewer than 10 people.

The small business sector of the economy creates more jobs than any other: Between 1969 and 1976, 16 million new jobs were created. One million of these jobs were created by the 1,000 largest corporations. Three million of the new jobs were in state and local governments. The remaining 12 million were created by small business.

> 66% of the total jobs generated between 1969 and 1976 were in firms with 20 or fewer employees.
>
> 77% were in firms with 50 or fewer employees.
>
> 82% were in firms with 100 or fewer employees.
>
> 87% were in firms with 500 or fewer employees.
>
> 13% were in firms with over 500 employees.
>
> —(David Birch, *The Job Generation Process*)

Minority-Owned Small Businesses

(Except where noted, the Census Bureau figures are for 1972, the latest year available).

561,000 businesses are owned by members of minority groups (black Americans, Hispanic Americans, American Indians, Asian Americans, Eskimos, and Aleuts), according to 1977 data. Members of minority groups own 4.4% of all businesses.

In 1977, black Americans owned 231,000 businesses, compared with 194,986 in 1972.

Hispanic Americans owned 220,000 businesses in 1977.

Asian Americans, American Indians, and members of all other minority groups owned 111,000 businesses in 1977.

Nearly all minority-owned businesses are small businesses.

Gross receipts for minority businesses were $26.4 billion in 1977.

63% of minority-owned nonfarm firms are in the retail and service industries.

80% of minority-owned firms have no employees.

Women-Owned Small Businesses (Data for 1977)

Women own 702,000 businesses. A Department of Commerce survey in 1977 used the following definition of a woman-owned business: "A woman-owned business is one in which the sole owner is a woman or *one half or more* of the partners is a woman, or 50% or more of the stock in a corporation is owned by a woman or women." SBA defines a woman-owned business as: "A woman-owned business is one that is at least 51% owned, controlled, and operated by a woman or women. 'Controlled' is defined as 'exercising the authority to make policy decisions,' and 'operated' is defined as 'actively involved in the day-to-day management of the business.'" This definition was changed from 50% in March, 1979.

Gross annual receipts for women-owned businesses were $41.5 billion. This represented 6.6% of all U.S. business receipts, excluding those of large corporations.

Nearly all women-owned businesses are small businesses.

75.8% of women-owned businesses are sole proprietorships. They accounted for 22.8%, or $9.5 billion, of the gross annual receipts generated by women-owned businesses.

23.9% of women-owned businesses have employees. 70.4% of the women-owned businesses that do have employees have fewer than 5 employees.

Average gross annual receipts for women-owned businesses without employees were $11,800. Average gross annual receipts for women-owned businesses with employees were $209,000.

8.4% of women-owned businesses were corporations that accounted for 46%, or $19 billion, of all gross annual receipts generated by women-owned businesses.

15.9% of women-owned businesses were partnerships that accounted for 31.2%, or $13 billion, of all gross annual receipts generated by women-owned businesses.

75% of all women-owned businesses were in the services and retail trade industries. These firms accounted for 74% of the gross annual receipts generated by women-owned businesses.

FACTS ABOUT SMALL BUSINESS AND THE U.S. SMALL BUSINESS ADMINISTRATION

SBA in General

The U.S. Small Business Administration is an Executive Branch agency of the Federal Government. The head of the Agency—the Administrator—reports directly to the President. SBA was created on July 30, 1953 to provide broad assistance to small businesses.

The Agency's government antecedents were:

The Reconstruction Finance Corporation (1932–1957)
The Smaller War Plants Corporation (1942–1947)
The Small Defense Plants Administration (1951–1953)

SBA has 110 offices in 100 cities throughout the U.S. This includes 10 Regional Offices, 63 District Offices, 18 Branch Offices, and 19 Post-of-Duty Stations.

On September 30, 1979, SBA had 4,372 permanent employees. A year earlier, the Agency had 4,402 permanent employees. In 1969, SBA had 4,099 permanent employees.

SBA's operating expenses for FY (fiscal year) 1979 were $192.2 million ($171.5 million for the Agency's regular assistance programs and $20.7 million for the disaster loan program). The Agency's FY 1978 operating expenses were $176 million ($146.3 million for the regular programs and $29.7 million for the disaster program).

Small Business Size Standards

On March 11, 1980, SBA proposed a new set of small business size standards. These standards would be based on a firm's average number of employees for the preceding twelve months and would vary by industry. The merits of these standards are still being discussed. Until a new set of size standards is adopted officially by the Agency, the following small business size measurements apply to firms seeking SBA assistance.

Finance

Interest Rates. SBA sets maximum allowable interest rates for guaranteed and immediate participation loans and for lines of credit. Rates are based on a continuous survey of the market for fixed income securities, both federal and

Size Standards (Maximums)

A. FOR LOANS	ANNUAL RECEIPTS MAXIMUM
Services	*$2–$8 million
Retail	*$2–$7.5 million
Wholesale	*9.5–$22 million
General Construction	*$9.5 million
Farming and Related Activities	*$1 million
	AVERAGE EMPLOYMENT MAXIMUM
Manufacturing	*250 to 1,500

B. FOR PROCUREMENT	ANNUAL RECEIPTS MAXIMUM
Services	*$2–$9 million
General Construction	*$12 million
	AVERAGE EMPLOYMENT MAXIMUM
Manufacturing	*500 to 1,500

C. FOR SBIC ASSISTANCE	
All Industries	NET WORTH MAXIMUM
	$6 million
	AVERAGE NET INCOME
	(after taxes) maximum
	$2 million for the preceding two years

D. FOR SURETY BONDS	ANNUAL RECEIPTS MAXIMUM
All Industries	$3.5 million

*Varies by industry
Note: A and C standards increase 25% if a firm operates in an area of high unemployment, as defined by the Labor Department.

private, and on the prevailing rate for loans as determined by SBA field personnel.

Interest rates on SBA direct loans are based on a formula that considers the cost of money to the federal government.

The interest rates are reviewed quarterly and adjusted at that time and at other periods if adjustment is warranted.

A variable interest rate is also permitted if it is agreed to by both the borrower and the lender at the time a loan is made.

Business Loans. Total SBA financial assistance to businesses (loans, surety bonds, and Small Business Investment Company funds) has averaged $4.7 billion in recent years (excludes disaster loans to businesses).

The total number of all business and disaster loans was 107,112 for $4.9 billion in FY 1980.

Since it began and through September 30, 1980, SBA approved 1,251,096 loans of all kinds for $39.7 billion, and 413,982 business loans for

$26.2 billion. At the end of FY 1979, the Agency's loan portfolio contained 402,229 accounts outstanding valued at $13.4 billion. The cumulative loss rate on all disbursed business loans since SBA was started is 4.18%.

Thirty-nine percent of the Agency's business loans and 53% of the business dollar volume since the Agency's beginning occurred in the last five fiscal years.

FISCAL YEARS			
1979	30,176	Loans	$ 3.41 Billion
1978	31,727		3.31
1977	31,793		3.05
1976 Budget Transition Quarter	6,795		0.58
1976	26,078		2.07
1975	22,348		1.59
	148,917		$14.01 Billion

In SBA's first year of operation (FY 1954), 473 business loans were approved for $28 million.

In terms of business loans approved, FY 1973 was the record high year with 33,948 loans approved for $2.2 billion.

June of 1975 was the highest single business loan month in the Agency's history with 3,475 business loans approved for $248 million.

Private sector participation in FY 1979 business loans was $2.9 billion, decreasing from $3.0 billion in FY 1978. In FY 1977, this figure was $2.7 billion.

FY 1979 business loans made directly by SBA totalled 6,066 for $356 million. In FY 1978 the figures were 5,988 direct loans for $311 million and in FY 1977, 6,467 direct loans for $300 million.

Twenty-four percent of the FY 1979 business loans were used to create 7,328 businesses. In FY 1978, 30% of the business loans were used to create 9,657 new businesses.

Of SBA's 10 organizational regions throughout the country, Region 6 (Texas, New Mexico, Oklahoma, Arkansas, and Louisiana) approved the highest number of business loans in FY 1979; 4,342 loans for $470 million. Region 5 (Illinois, Ohio, Michigan, Indiana, Wisconsin, and Minnesota) approved the highest number of loan dollars: 4,090 loans for $556 million. In FY 1978, Region 6 approved the highest number of business loans for the highest dollar amount: 4,893 loans for $470 million.

Ninety-five percent of all SBA business loans are for one year or more.

The average maturity of SBA business loans is 8¾ years.

The current average size of a guaranty business loan is $85,000.

10,000 of the 15,000 banks in the U.S. (66%) participate in SBA loans.

Disaster Loans. 69,943 natural disaster loans for $1.2 billion were approved in FY 1980, compared with 69,413 loans for $1.4 billion in FY 1979.

Eighty-one percent of the natural disaster loan dollars went to businesses in FY 1979. In FY 1978, this figure was 86%.

The largest single natural disaster to which SBA has responded was Tropical Storm Agnes, which occurred in 1972 and was the most destructive storm in recorded U.S. history. SBA assistance for business owners, homeowners, renters, and nonprofit institutions victimized by Tropical Storm Agnes totalled 144,738 loans for $1.3 billion, a record high for any single disaster.

Since the beginning of the disaster program in 1953, SBA has made 837,114 disaster loans for $9.4 billion.

Surety Bonds. In FY 1979, there were 31,972 Surety Bond guarantees resulting in 18,071 contracts valued at $1.4 billion, a record high dollar figure. In FY 1978, there were 32,125 guarantees on 19,044 contracts for $1.4 billion

Detailed Chart of Business Loan Program For FY 1980 and FY 1979

LOAN PROGRAM	FY 1980		FY 1979	
	Number	Dollar Amount in Millions	Number	Dollar Amount in Millions
Regular Business	28,168	3,604	26,776	3,200
Disaster	69,943	1,202	69,413	1,400
Economic Opportunity	2,434	90.9	2,841	100.7
Economic Injury Disaster	1,138	78.5	980	49.3
State Development Co. Loans & Local Development Co.	476	79.2	479	79.7
Seasonal Line of Credit	Not Available		254	35.0
Handicapped Assistance	258	20.6	288	22.4
Contract Loan Program	Not Available		224	22.0
Displaced Business	155	35.8	80	15.1
Small Business Energy	183	27.2	108	14.4
Water Pollution Control	18	3.0	18	4.6
Economic Dislocation Disaster	1,422	56.6	88	4.5
Occupational Safety & Health Disaster	19	8.0	14	4.3
Air Pollution Control	26	6.5	11	3.6
Consumer Protection Disaster	7	1.7	6	1.7
Emergency Energy Shortage Economic Injury	24	2.1	5	1.0
Base Closing Economic Injury Disaster	14	1.3	5	0.5

and in FY 1977, 29,932 guarantees on 15,435 contracts for $1 billion. The Surety Bond Program has grown more than 1,387% since 1972, its first year of operation.

Investment (Data for FY 1979)

Small Business Investment Companies. There were 327 operating SBIC's licensed by SBA in 40 states, the District of Columbia, and Puerto Rico as of September 30, 1979. In FY 1978, there were 294 SBIC's operating in 38 states and Puerto Rico. SBIC's had $1.2 billion in assets. This compared to $1 billion in FY 1978.

SBIC's made 2,221 small business financings for $267.1 million, an increase from 2,097 financings for $232.2 million in FY 1978. Figures for FY 1977 and FY 1976 were: 1977—2,071 financings for $206 million; 1976—1,720 financings for $129 million.

Equity-type financings represented 52% of the dollars disbursed by the SBIC's. The remainder of the dollars were for debt financing. Outstanding SBIC loans and investments totalled $604.5 million.

Thirty-eight percent of SBIC financing involved new firms. Since the SBIC program was started in 1958, SBIC's have made more than 59,000 investments for $3.6 billion.

Procurement, Property Sales, and Technology Assistance (Data for FY 1979)

Total federal procurement was $82.4 billion. Prime contracting awards to small business were $19.6 billion, an increase of $435 million over FY 1978.

Small business set-aside contracts were $5.8 billion, 29.7% of the prime contracts awarded to small business. Subcontracting dollars awarded to small business were $10.7 billion, 43.4% of the total.

Total federal contracting dollars were $24.6 billion.

The Certificate of Competency Program resulted in the award of 425 COC's totaling nearly $105 million. This represented a savings of $8.8 million for the government.

8(a) Contracts to Firms Owned and Controlled by Socially and Economically Disadvantaged Persons. Since its first full year of operation (1969), the 8(a) Business Development Program has grown from 28 contracts valued at $8.9 million to over 22,097 contracts valued at nearly $4 billion through FY 1979.

Of the 1,583 companies receiving 8(a) contracts during FY 1979, approximately 36% were in the construction industry, 19% were in nonprofessional services, 36% were in professional services, and 9% were in manufacturing. There were 3,919 8(a) contracts for $1 billion issued in FY 1979. This was an increase from 3,409 contracts for $768.0 million in FY 1978. The number of firms assisted by the 8(a) program in FY 1979 was 1,593, an increase from 1,140 firms in FY 1978.

Property Sales Assistance. During Fiscal Year 1979, more than 2,800 individual sales of federal timber worth $1.3 billion were awarded to small businesses. These sales resulted in the purchase of 5.7 billion board feet of federal timber by small business. This was an increase from more than 2,700 sales for $951 million FY 1978.

Technology Assistance. In FY 1979, SBA's Technology Assistance Program helped approximately 2,500 small businesses utilize technology that had been developed by the federal government or by private industry at the expense of the government.

Procurement Automated Source System (Pass). PASS is a SBA-developed computerized data base of small firms interested in bidding on government contracting opportunities. The capabilities of small firms registered in the system are available when requests are made by federal procurement officers or private sector buyers. More than 35,000 small businesses were registered in the PASS system at the end of FY 1980.

At the end of FY 1979, direct terminal access to the data base was available at 30 locations at SBA, the Department of Energy, and other government departments. Additional terminals were added to the system in FY 1981.

Management Assistance (Data for FY 1979)

SBA's Management Assistance program reaches millions of individuals annually. Over 700,000 current or prospective small business owner/managers were counseled or trained. For FY 1978, this figure was 650,000. 229,000 businesses were provided sustained MA counseling.

1979 Detail:

Counseling—423,000 individuals

Training—284,000 individuals in 7,635 training units

Six million SBA Management Assistance publications were distributed to the public. In FY 1978, this figure was 5.5 million.

Highlight: 23 Business Basics self-study booklets on small business management subjects were distributed to more than 450,000 readers.

SCORE, the Service Corps of Retired Executives, was developed by SBA in 1964. ACE, the Active Corps of Executives, was developed by SBA in 1969 as an adjunct to SCORE. There are 12,000 SCORE/ACE volunteers in 365 chapters in 49 states, the District of Columbia, and Puerto Rico. SCORE/ACE volunteers counseled nearly 150,000 business men and women. Historically, SCORE/ACE volunteers have counseled over 730,000 small business firms.

The SBI (Small Business Institute) program was started by SBA in 1972 at 36 participating colleges and universities. Nearly 500 colleges and universities participate in the SBI program.

During FY 1979, 10,000 SBI graduate and undergraduate students and 2,000 SBI deans and professors counseled more than 8,000 current and prospective business owners.

There are 18 SBA-chartered Small Business Development Centers at the following universities.

The University of Georgia at Athens
The University of Missouri at St. Louis
The University of Nebraska at Omaha
The University of West Florida at Pensacola
Rutgers University
The University of Maine at Portland
The California State University at Chico
The California State Polytechnic University at Pomona
Howard University
The University of South Carolina at Columbia
The University of Wisconsin at Madison
St. Cloud State University at St. Cloud, Minnesota
The University of Arkansas at Little Rock
The University of Utah at Salt Lake City
Washington State University at Pullman
The University of Pennsylvania at Philadelphia

The SBDC program was started by the SBA in December, 1976. In FY 1980, SBDC's were established at the University of Alabama at Birmingham and the University of Massachusetts at Amherst.

In FY 1979, 160 firms were awarded "406" Call Contracts for a total of $11 million. In FY 1978, 83 such contracts were awarded for $8 million. Under the Call Contracting Program, SBA gives contracts to qualified firms and individuals so they can provide services (accounting, marketing, engineering, etc.) for other SBA clients.

Assistance to Members of Minority Groups (Data for FY 1979)

5,518 business loans for $428.3 million were approved for members of minority groups. In FY 1978, there were 6,118 loans for $401.6 million and in FY 1977, 6,180 loans for $352.3 million. The average size of an SBA minority business loan is $77,619.

Minority business men and women received 13% of the dollar value and 18% of the number of all SBA business loans. In FY 1978, they received 12% of the SBA loan dollars and 19% of the total number of loans.

Six percent of all SBA business loan dollars went to black Americans, 6% to Hispanic Americans, and 1% to members of other minority groups. In FY 1978, 5% of the loan dollars went to black Americans, 5% went to Hispanic Americans, and 2% went to members of other minority groups.

Financings to start new minority-owned businesses totalled 1,838 for $124 million. In FY 1978, there were 1,964 such financings for $112 million.

Minority business owners and homeowners received 4,878 disaster loans for $42 million, a decrease from 7,607 loans for $56 million in FY 1978. In FY 1977, disaster loans to members of minority groups totaled 2,001 for $31.8 million.

There are 110 "301(d)" Small Business Investment Companies licensed to assist members of minority groups in 29 states, the District of Columbia, and Puerto Rico. These companies are capitalized at $79.4 million. At the end of FY 1978, there were 86 such companies in 29 states, the District of Columbia, and Puerto Rico, capitalized at $61.9 million.

"301(d)" SBIC's made 467 financings for $33.7 million, an increase from 454 financings for $29.2 million in FY 1978. In FY 1977, there were 344 such financings for $13.6 million. Forty-three percent of the businesses financed by "301(d)" SBIC's were new firms. In FY 1978, 36% of the businesses financed were new businesses.

54,025 minority business men and women received SBA management counseling, compared with 47,957 in FY 1978 and 25,478 in FY 1977. 62,109 minority business men and women received SBA management training, compared with 55,671 in FY 1978 and 45,693 in FY 1977.

Business loans approved for minority women in FY 1979, FY 1978, and FY 1977 compared as follows:

	FY 1979*		FY 1978		FY 1977	
	Number	Dollars	Number	Dollars	Number	Dollars
Black Women	404	$22,794,846	442	$21,861,454	427	$19,439,170
Puerto Rican Women	93	$ 3,363,600	126	$ 3,658,500	102	$ 3,310,212
Other Hispanic Women	242	$15,132,100	277	$13,855,484	229	$10,645,800
American Indian Women	48	$ 3,433,300	48	$ 3,531,000	69	$ 3,605,626
Asian American Women	156	$12,921,683	162	$11,592,200	127	$ 7,512,271
Eskimo and Aleutian American Women	0	$ 0	4	$ 551,600	3	$ 183,000
Totals	943	$57,645,529	959	$55,050,238	857	$44,696,079

*SBA defines a women-owned business as "A woman-owned business is one which is at least 51% owned, controlled, and operated by a woman or women. 'Controlled' is defined as 'exercising the authority to make policy decisions,' and 'operated' is defined as 'actively involved in the day-to-day management of the business.'" This definition was changed from 50% in March, 1979.

Assistance to Women (Data for FY 1979)

61,109 women received SBA Management Assistance counseling, an increase over the 55,856 women counseled in FY 1978. In FY 1977, 19,806 women received this counseling.

130,026 women attended SBA-sponsored Management Assistance training conferences, seminars, and workshops, an increase from 122,109 in FY 1978.

4,817 business loans for $381 million were approved for women-owned businesses, a decrease from 5,699 loans for $444 million in FY 1978. In FY 1977, 4,665 loans for $325 million were approved for women-owned businesses.

Women in business received 16% of all SBA business loans approved and 11% of the business loan dollars. In FY 1978, women received 18% of the number of loans and 13% of the dollars. The average women's business enterprise loan size is $79,046.

SMALL BUSINESS ADVOCACY ISSUES

The Impact of Tight Credit Policies on Small Business

The debt-equity ratio for small firms tends to be greater than that for large firms, particularly in manufacturing, construction, and the distributive trades.

The percentage of short-term debt to total assets tends to be higher for smaller firms than for larger firms, and this percentage has been growing in recent years.

The ratio of indebtedness to banks to total indebtedness has been growing more rapidly for smaller manufacturers in recent years than for larger manufacturing firms.

Small Business and Regulatory and Reporting Paperwork

The small business community spends $12.7 billion a year when filling out required government forms and reports.

Small businesses file more than 305 million federal government forms a year totalling over 850 million pages containing over 7.3 billion questions.

About $10 billion of the total, small-business, $12.7-billion-paperwork expense is the result of federal reporting requirements. The balance is spent on state and local paperwork requirements.

One hundred-three federal agencies require small businesses to fill in one or more reports.

Forty-three percent of the federal forms are mandatory, 33% are voluntary, and 24% are required for small business to derive some benefit from federal programs.

Small Business and Government Competition

Small firms could gain more than $2 billion worth of business annually if the federal government produced less of its own goods and services and bought more from the marketplace. The federal government directly engages in more than 21,000 commercial and industrial activities at a taxpayer cost of at least $10 billion annually.

Small Business Innovation

Independent small business entrepreneurs have been responsible for more than half of all the product and service innovations developed in the United States since World War II.

A recent review of the leading 500 technological innovations in the United States between 1953 and 1973 showed that small firms (defined as those with up to 1,000 employees) produced four times as many innovations per research and development dollar as medium-sized firms (defined as those with 1,000 to 10,000 employees).

Nearly every major energy-related innovation in the past 100 years has been developed by small business, such as the electric car, the air conditioner, the gasoline engine, the electric light, petroleum cracking, gasoline, and transformers.

Of the seven major innovations in the areas of petroleum refining since 1945, all were developed by small business.

SMALL BUSINESS INVESTMENT CORPORATIONS

SBICs are government-backed, flexible financing devices for furnishing equity capital and long-term loan funds to enable small businesses to operate, grow, and modernize.

These companies are formed to operate under the regulations of the Small Business Investment Act once they have followed the simple steps to obtain an SBIC license. Recent changes in law and regulations offer new incentives to investors, who stand to gain from the government leverage funds and the tax advantages provided.

When SBICs were developed, they were visualized as potential sources of capital and expertise for small firms previously limited to short-term financing. Since that time, they have proved to be adaptable to inner city as well as rural economic development. SBIC funnels much-needed investment capital into economically depressed communities and to socially or economically disadvantaged small business entrepreneurs.

Defining an SBIC

An SBIC is a privately owned and privately operated small business investment company that has been licensed by the Small Business Administration to provide *equity* or *venture* capital and long-term loans to small firms. Often SBICs also provide management assistance to the companies they finance. These are their only functions. They cannot, for instance, sell insurance, trade in property, or become holding companies for groups of operating businesses.

New SBICs derive their initial capital from private investors and normally become eligible to obtain funds from the government or from private financial institutions through government-guaranteed loans.

An SBIC finances small firms in two general ways—by straight loans and by equity-type investments that give the SBIC actual or potential ownership of a portion of a small business' stock. In general, financings must be for at least five years, except that a borrower may elect to prepay indebtedness.

SBICs invest in practically all types of manufacturing and service industries, and in a wide variety of other types of businesses, including construction, retailing, and wholesaling. Many seek out small businesses offering new products or services because they believe these firms have unusual growth potential.

Some SBICs specialize in electronics companies, research and development firms, or other types of businesses that the SBIC's management has special knowledge of. Most companies diversify and will consider a wide variety of investments.

SBICs are intended to be profit-making entities. Their major function is to make *venture* or risk investments by supplying equity capital and extending unsecured loans and loans not fully collateralized to worthy small enterprises. Some SBICs have been organized and utilized as subsidiaries, on a profit-making basis, by national concerns. These SBICs provide equity capital and long-term loan funds to enterprises owned and managed by socially or economically disadvantaged persons. Counseling, legal aid, and management training for the benefit of the business community is coordinated on a volunteer basis. This type of SBIC, dedicated solely to assisting disadvantaged small business entrepreneurs, is eligible for SBA purchases of its 3% preferred stock and for a subsidized interest rate on its debentures during the first five years. It may also be organized on a nonprofit basis to obtain additional tax benefits for itself and its investors. Some SBICs may be incorporated bodies or limited partnerships, with corporate general partners.

Advantages to Investors

With good management, an SBIC can achieve impressive profit figures. Among the available benefits are certain tax advantages, granted by Congress as an incentive for those providing venture capital to small business through the program. Recent changes liberalizing the legislation and the regulations governing SBICs have made these companies even more attractive.

The leverage available to SBICs through government or government-guaranteed loans can be very important. An SBIC may be eligible for such a loan equal to three times its paid-in capital and paid-in surplus. These loans may be subordinated and have maturity of up to 15 years. SBICs that specialize in venture capital financing and are adequately capitalized may qualify for a fourth layer of leverage. Qualified SBICs may obtain SBA loans or SBA-guaranteed loans aggregating $35 million. There is no limit to the private capital that may be used in the formation of an SBIC.

An SBIC, as a flexible financing vehicle, can serve and has served many corporate and community purposes. It is adaptable to urban and rural economic development needs and to financing of innovative and high-technology small business concerns, and also constitutes an ideal instrument for concentrating much-needed investment capital within economically depressed communities. Especially significant is the fact that, in addition to accumulating capital for economic development, an SBIC is designed and authorized to provide one of the prime requisites for success of new business ventures—adequate management assistance.

The Need for SBICs

Small businesses generally have difficulty obtaining equity capital to finance their growth. Without up-to-date operating records and strong financial statements, small business concerns have difficulty in obtaining long-term financing.

To help close this financing gap, Congress passed the Small Business Investment Act of 1958, which authorized the SBA to license, regulate, and help finance privately organized and privately operated SBICs, which in turn would provide equity-type and long-term financing to small concerns.

Present Status of Industry

As an industry, the SBICs have total assets amounting to over $75 million dollars. They have outstanding investments in small businesses of more than $50 million dollars.

The majority of SBICs are owned by relatively small groups of local investors. However, the stock of 21 SBICs is publicly traded, and 73 are partially or wholly owned by commercial banks. A few are subsidiaries of other corporations.

Defining a Small Business

In general, the SBA considers a firm to be *small* and therefore eligible for SBIC financing if its assets do not exceed $9 million, if its net worth is not more than $4 million, and if its average net income after taxes for the preceding two years was not more than $400,000.

If a business does not qualify as small under these provisions, it may qualify under certain other criteria established by the SBA for its business loan program, or for assistance to firms that are located in areas of substantial unemployment. In determining the size of a business, the SBA also considers the size of any affiliates, including a parent company that controls the firm, and any other companies controlled by the same parent company.

Income Tax Aspects

The SBIC industry has a number of different kinds of tax advantages. One, for example, is a major tax inducement to investors contemplating commitment of funds to an SBIC. It permits an SBIC shareholder to treat gains on sales of stock as long-term capital gains, whereas such a shareholder may take an unlimited ordinary-loss deduction on losses arising from the sale, exchange, or worthlessness of the stock.

A special benefit arises from the fact that SBICs are allowed a deduction of 100% of dividends received from a taxable domestic corporation, rather than the 85% deduction allowed most corporate taxpayers.

SBICs are granted relief from the tax on excess accumulations of surplus and may qualify for relief from the tax on personal holding companies.

Specific provisions are contained in the Internal Revenue Code to allow SBICs to take full deductions against ordinary income for losses sustained on convertible debentures or on stock received through conversion of convertible debentures.

Recent legislation provides for licensing SBICs organized as partnerships, with a corporate general partner.

Advantages to Banks

A bank may, through a wholly-owned SBIC subsidiary or partial ownership of an SBIC, add a new dimension to its services to customers. A federally regulated bank may invest up to 5% of its combined capital and surplus in stock of an SBIC. Investment by state-chartered member banks is subject to the applicable provisions of state law.

How an SBIC Gets Started

What are the General Requirements?   The initial private investment may vary upward from a minimum of $150,000, depending on the area to be served. The amount must be adequate to assure a reasonable prospect of sound and profitable operation. Provisions should also be made for funds to cover organization expenses. The articles of incorporation, bylaws, partnership agreement or certificate, capitalization, and proposed policies of an SBIC are subject to SBA approval, and background information must be furnished for all officers, directors, and persons who will hold 10% or more of the SBIC ownership interest. Those proposing to form an SBIC must be prepared to have a reasonably accessible office with qualified management readily available to the public during normal business hours.

Must Paid-In Private Capital of an SBIC Be in Cash or May It Be in Mortgages or Securities? Paid-in capital must consist of cash or eligible government securities.

Is There Any Restriction on a Prospective Owner of a Proposed SBIC Borrowing Funds for His or Her Investment in the SBIC? Yes. He or she may not borrow funds for investment in the SBIC unless he or she can show a net worth equal to at least twice the amount borrowed. The SBA may require that balance sheets be submitted in this connection.

Will the Operation of an SBIC Automatically Be Exempt from Securities and Exchange Commission Regulations? No. The SEC will determine, from the circumstances in each case, whether or not the activities of the SBIC are subject to acts and regulations administered by that agency.

Can an SBIC Be Publicly Held? Yes. Although most SBICs are owned by relatively small groups of local investors, the stock of 24 SBICs is publicly traded.

What Guides Are Available on Regulatory Aspects? Every holder of a license to operate an SBIC is furnished a copy of the Small Business Administration regulations for SBICs and automatically receives all amendments to the regulations, as well as policy and procedural releases that provide additional information.

What an SBIC Does

May an SBIC Freely Perform Any and All Actions Associated with Lending or Investment? An SBIC may engage in all activities contemplated by the Small Business Investment Act, but not in any other activities.

Can an SBIC Specialize in a Particular Industry? Yes, except for real estate investments.

Can an SBIC Be Used for Real Estate Financing? A new company will not be licensed if it proposes to put more than one-third of its assets into real estate investments. However, loans secured by real estate mortgages are not counted as real estate investments if the proceeds of the loans are to be used for purposes other than real estate investments.

Are There Penalties for Failure to Observe the Regulations?   Yes. The SBA can conduct investigations and revoke or suspend licenses in the event of false statements or omissions of material facts or for willfull or repeated violations of the Act or regulations. The SBA may issue cease and desist orders, request injunctions, and act as receiver for an SBIC. Also, the SBA can suspend any director or officer of an SBIC for due cause. The Act and regulations require the filing of certain reports with the SBA. Failure to submit these on time may subject a licensee to penalty of up to $100 per day.

Can an SBIC Convert to Another Line of Business?   A licensed SBIC can engage only in the activities authorized by the Small Business Investment Act. However, a license can be surrendered if prior SBA approval is obtained. SBA approval will be conditioned on payment or acceptable settlement of any indebtedness to the SBA and elimination of any existing violations. Dissolution of the entity is not required, but its charter must be changed in accordance with its changed purposes.

Can the License of an SBIC Be Transferred?   An SBIC license cannot be transferred from one corporation or partnership to another except in connection with mergers approved by the Small Business Administration. Sometimes a license might in effect be transferred through transfer of control of the ownership interest of an SBIC. This type of transfer also requires prior approval by the SBA.

How an SBIC Grows

What Access to Long Term Funds Does an SBIC Have?   An SBIC may obtain long term funds from both government and private sources. An SBIC may request the SBA to lend, or to guarantee 100% of the loans of private financial institutions, to the SBIC in an amount equivalent to 300% of its private capital. The maximum available to an SBIC on this basis is $35 million. The debentures issued by the SBIC for these funds may be subordinated and may have a term of up to 15 years. For SBICs with private capital equal to or in excess of $500,000, funds equivalent to 400% of private capital become available if 65% of the total funds available for investment are invested or committed in venture capital investments. The maximum available to a qualified SBIC on this basis is $35 million. SBICs dedicated solely to assisting socially or economically disadvantaged small business concerns may borrow from SBA at a subsidized interest rate (usually 3% below the going cost of money to the U.S. Treasury) for the first five years of the loan. They may also sell to SBA nonvoting preferred securities on a 1:1 basis in relation to their private capital or (in some cases) portions of their private capital.

May an SBIC Borrow Money for Its Operations from Sources Other Than SBA and Without an SBA Guarantee?   Yes, and it should be noted that SBA funds, or SBA-guaranteed funds, become available only to the extent that funds are not available from private sources on reasonable terms.

Can an SBIC Merge with Another SBIC?   Yes, provided prior approval is obtained from the Small Business Administration.

Can an SBIC Merge with a nonSBIC?   Yes, when prior approval has been obtained from the Small Business Administration, and when the resulting company will qualify to hold an SBIC license.

Some Investment Rules

May an SBIC Extend Long Term Loans to, or Purchase Stock or Convertible Debenture from, a Small Concern, the Controlling Stockholders of Which Are Also Stockholders, Partners, or Members in the SBIC?   Unless an exemption is granted by the SBA, and SBIC may not purchase stock or convertible debentures of, or make a loan to, an officer, director, or owner of 10% or more of the private capital of the SBIC. The same restriction applies to any company in which the officer, director, partner or 10% owner of the SBIC is an officer or director, or owns 10% or more of the stock, or is a partner.

What Is the Maximum Rate of Interest an SBIC May Charge?   In states where state law specifies a maximum interest rate, the SBIC cannot charge a higher rate. If the state law imposes no maximum, SBA regulations specify the maximum interest rate and related charges. In any event, 15% is the maximum rate that SBICs are allowed to charge. In the calculation of the actual rate of interest and related charges to a borrower, the SBA requires that all charges, discounts, etc., be taken into account, and that the rate be computed on the basis of the outstanding balance.

Do SBA Regulations Governing SBIC Operations Cover the Negotiations Between the SBIC and the Borrower Concerning Types of Loans, Interest Rates, Discounts, and Conversion Features?   The SBIC and the small business concern negotiate the specific terms and conditions, which must conform to SBA regulations, It is not necessary for the SBIC to secure approval of every transaction; however, the SBIC should ask for approval of any negotiation or transaction that appears doubtful or borderline in relation to the regulations.

Is an SBIC Subject to Any Investment Loan Limitation?   Yes. Without prior SBA approval, the total funds loaned to or invested in equity securities of a particular small business concern held by a single SBIC may not exceed 20% of the paid-in capital and surplus of the SBIC. Two or more SBICs may participate in a single investment thereby providing a larger dollar total of financing in a single firm than any of the participating SBICs could have invested individually. Of course, the company in which the investment is made must qualify as small under SBA standards.

Various Other Rules

Is the Ownership of an SBIC Freely Transferable?   Yes, with the limitation that transfers of 10% or more of the stock, or private capital of an SBIC must be approved by the SBA.

Is There Any Restriction or Limitation on the Distribution by an SBIC While It Remains Indebted to the SBA?   Yes, where an SBIC is indebted to the SBA, distributions to shareholders or partners can be paid only out of retained earnings.

Will the Number of SBICs in Any One Area Be Limited? What Are the Restrictions About the Area of an SBIC's Operations?   Yes. A need must be shown. If there is a heavy concentration of SBICs in the area, the license applicant must show that there are types of businesses or industries that can use SBIC financing in a manner advantageous to these businesses and the SBIC.

May a Group of Residents in One State Organize the SBIC Under the Laws of a Neighboring State, and Conduct the SBIC's Investment Business in Both States?   It depends upon the laws of the particular state. Generally some of the incorporators or partners must be residents of the state in which the SBIC is incorporated or registered.

What Are SBA Requirements Concerning the Name of an SBIC?   Use of "United States," "National," "Federal," "Reserve," "Bank," "Government," or "Development" in the name of the SBIC is not acceptable. Moreover, the name should not be so similar to that of any other organization as to imply that it is associated with the other organization unless the other organization has given its approval. In addition, the name must be approved by the Corporation Commissioner of the state where incorporated, or other public body with which registered, as well as by the SBA.

May an SBIC Establish Branch Offices?   Yes, if the SBA has given its approval to do so. And, in applying for this approval, the SBIC must state the area to be served by each branch.

What Restrictions Are There Concerning the Types of Businesses to Which Loans May Be Made by an SBIC?   The regulations provide that an SBIC may not provide funds to a small business concern for relending, nor for purposes not contemplated by the Small Business Investment Act, nor for purposes contrary to the public interest, such as gambling activities or fostering a monopoly. It may not provide funds for foreign investment or for any business not conducted as a regular and continuous activity. Funds invested in real estate enterprises must not exceed one-third of an SBIC's portfolio.

First Steps

What Preliminary Steps Should Be Taken?   Visit the nearest regional office of the Small Business Administration. They are now located in Boston, New York, Philadelphia, Atlanta, Chicago, Kansas City, Dallas, Denver, San Francisco, and Seattle. You also can obtain preliminary information from any of the SBA's field offices located throughout the United States, or the headquarters office of the SBA in Washington, D.C. You are welcome to visit or write the Investment Division at 1441 L Street, N.W., Washington, DC 20416.

How Does Your Group Find Out Whether You Can Form an SBIC and Particularly Whether You Can Meet the Latest Licensing Standards?   It is suggested that you furnish SBA Headquarters (Washington, DC) with proposed plans for capitalization, management personnel, operating policies, etc.

If It Is Then Indicated That Your Group Is in a Position to Form an SBIC, What Do You Do Next?   Obtain from your nearest SBA office a copy of Form 415, a License Application form. Certain information required by this form may then be submitted to the headquarters of the SBA for informal comment. The formal application for a license may not be filed until the corporation or partnership has been formed and the capital subscribed.

What Is Some of the Preliminary Information You Will Be Required to Submit?   You will need to describe your proposed method of financing, your proposed plan of operation, your proposed articles of incorporation, and bylaws or partnership agreement. You also will need to include personal and business histories of the individuals who propose to form the SBIC. Personal interviews with Washington staff members will follow, if considered desirable by the SBA.

In Addition to the Rules and Regulations of the Small Business Administration, Are There Any Important Rules or Limitations Concerning the Number and the Affiliations of the Organizers of an SBIC?   Various states have rules and regulations of their own. The proponents must, of course, conform to the laws of the state in which they propose to organize with respect to the number and qualifications of incorporators and directors or partners or members and must conform to the laws of the state in other respects.

SBA Liquidation

The Small Business Administration believes it operates at a risk level just above that of a bank. Subsequently, it believes it should experience a higher risk rate (on an average) than a bank. And, in the aggregate, they do. However, many entrepreneurs believe that the SBA should experience an even higher risk rate and take a more aggressive lending position.

Given that the SBA has about 13,000 companies in some form of liquidation, I can't wholeheartedly recommend adopting the policy to increase the SBA's bad debt experiences. But I can advise our readers that many good "deals" exist within the SBA bad loan portfolio. In other words, one person's problem can be another person's opportunity. If you're interested, write to Tim O'Leary, Deputy Administrator, Office of Portfolio Management, SBA, 1441 L Street, NW, Washington, DC 20416.

APPENDIXES

Checklist for Starting a Successful Business

INTRODUCTION

Thinking of starting a business? You want to own and manage your own business. It's a good idea—provided you know what it takes and have what it takes.

Starting a business is risky at best. But your chances of making it go will be better if you understand the problems you'll meet and work out as many of them as you can before you start.

Here are some questions to help you think through what you need to know and do. Check each question if the answer is *yes*. Where the answer is *no,* you have some work to do.

These checklists are organized in the following manner:

1. A checklist for going into business that was field tested with a sample of several hundred potential entrepreneurs.
2. A reproduction of the free SBA booklet entitled, "Checklist for going into business. Small marketing aid #71."
3. Information questionnaire for use in the development of a business plan.

The List for Starting Your Own Small Business

Before entering a new business venture, a checklist can provide the guidance in analyzing all the elements necessary for success. The checklist guide exposes variables that may be forgotten in the rush to start a business. It's also wise to look over a checklist after you begin a new business venture. There are several excellent checklists at the end of this essay. Award yourself points up to a maximum, on varying scales, for each area—then sum up the points. The highest possible number of points on each scale should be awarded when you have an exceptionally strong plus in the area. The lowest number of points (zero) should be awarded when you are weak in an area.

ITEM #1—ARE YOU EQUIPPED FOR A BUSINESS VENTURE?

	Points
1. Have you ever been in business for yourself before?	0–5
2. Have you succeeded in business for yourself before?	0–10
3. Have you ever previously rated your abilities for managing a growing business enterprise?	0–3
4. Have you taken any courses or special training or educational seminars that will help you in your own business?	0–5
5. Have you read any books about starting your own business?	0–3
6. Have you talked to friends who have started their own businesses?	0–3
7. Has anyone in your family—your father, mother, brother, sister—been self-employed? Have you spoken to them about your venture?	0–7 Your Sum

Average score on these seven questions, on a sampling of several hundred potential entrepreneurs, was 28 out of a possible 38 points.

ITEM #2—THE IDEA STAGE

	Points
1. Is your idea an original idea? Does it have significant merit or is it a new package for an old idea?	0–7
2. Is it your idea? Will you be able to generate extensions of this idea?	0–3
3. How difficult would it be for someone else to have the same idea?	0–5
4. Have you checked to see if someone else has already had the same idea? Is your idea patentable? Have you checked the patent office?	0–10
5. Have you checked to see if other companies exist who produce the same product?	0–4
6. Have you checked the *Thomas Register* to see if this product or service is offered?	0–5
7. Have you discussed or disclosed your idea to an expert in the area in which you offer your idea?	0–3
8. Have you talked to inventors about your idea?	0–3
9. Have you analyzed the recent sales trends in this business?	0–5
10. Do you know the volume and profitability of the competitors?	0–5
11. Is there a single large successful competitor who is highly profitable?	0–10
12. Have you attempted to obtain sales orders, or commitments, or letters of intent from potential customers?	0–15
13. Do other services or products like yours exist?	0–5 Idea Sum

The average score on these 13 questions, on a sampling of several hundred potential entrepreneurs, was 65 out of a possible 75 points.

ITEM #3—HOW ABOUT MONEY?

		Points
1.	Have you saved enough money to start the business on your own?	0–15
2.	Do you know how much money you'll need to get the business started?	0–10
3.	How much of your own money can you put into the business versus how much money is needed? Do you need a partner to supply money?	0–15
4.	Do you know what sales volume is necessary to break even?	0–7
5.	Will it take less than three years before your business reaches the breakeven sales volume?	0–10
6.	Do you know how much credit your suppliers will provide? Do you know the terms of payment in your industry?	0–5
7.	What are the normal terms for selling in your industry?	0–3
8.	Are you aware of money sources that will help finance your business in the event that you exhaust your initial capital?	0–4
9.	Have you talked to a banker about your plans for a new business?	0–3
10.	Have you talked to a lawyer about your plans for a new business?	0–3
11.	Have you talked to an accountant about your plans for a new business?	0–3
12.	Have you found a good location for your business?	0–10
13.	Does the location provide expansion possibilities?	0–5
14.	Will the new location require extensive lease-hold improvement expenditures?	0–5
15.	Have you examined the trade-off of buying instead of leasing a facility?	0–5
16.	Is the location convenient for parking, buses, and for employees to get to work, and for suppliers and customers?	0–5
17.	Have you checked the lease and zoning requirements?	0–3
18.	Did you evaluate several locations before making your final selection?	0–3
19.	Have you made a scaled layout of your office or work area to study work flow or customer flow?	0–7
20.	Are you a good manager of money?	0–15
		Money Sum

The average score on the above 20 money questions, based upon a sampling of several hundred potential entrepreneurs, was 111 out of a possible 136 points.

ITEM #4—HAVE YOU MADE A REAL INVESTIGATION INTO THE POTENTIAL SUCCESS OF YOUR BUSINESS?

		Points
1.	Have you compared the standard operating ratios for your business with the industry averages and Dun & Bradstreet?	0–2

2. Have you decided firmly on a single legal form of organization? Have you researched all the alternatives? — 0–5

3. Have you written down a statement of what you want to do for your customers, suppliers, and employees, to help them understand the purpose of your business? — 0–15

4. Have you answered the difficult question, "What business am I in?" — 0–15

Success
Sum

Average score on the above four questions, based upon a sampling of several hundred entrepreneurs, was 25 out of a possible 37 points.

ITEM #5—RISK MANAGEMENT

Points

1. Have you considered the impact on your business of government regulatory agencies like OSHA, Equal Employment Opportunity Employment, etc? — 0–3

2. Have you made allowances for unpredictable expenses resulting from uninsured risks, such as bad debts, shoplifting, or fire? — 0–5

3. Do you know the kind of insurance you should purchase? Should you purchase product liability insurance? — 0–4

4. Have you determined for which hazards you should provide insurance? — 0–5

Risk
Sum

The average score on the above four questions, based upon a sampling of several hundred entrepreneurs, was 15 out of a possible 17 points.

ITEM #6—EMPLOYEE RELATION AND PURCHASING

Points

1. Have you hired your first employee? Does the employee have the requisite skills to grow on the job as well as do the job in the initial phases? — 0–10

2. Have you prepared a general wage structure and does it compare favorably with prevailing wage rates? — 0–7

3. Are your working conditions desirable? — 0–10

4. If you plan to employ your friends and relatives, are you sure the family will not get in the way of the business? — 0–10

5. Are you planning an employee incentive program? — 0–3

6. If so, is it your program or their program? — 0–7

7. Have you evaluated alternative sources of supply? — 0–7

8. Have you carefully analyzed the pros and cons of each source of supply? Each vendor? And not made friends with a single salesman or vendor and thereby chosen to buy from that vendor on a friendship basis? — 0–5

9. Have you investigated other sources of supply, not available locally, but maybe through direct mail? Cooperative purchasing? Overseas pricing? — 0–5

People
Sum

Average score—43 out of a possible 64 points.

ITEM #7—ADVERTISING AND SALES PROMOTION

		Points
1.	Do you have copies of your competitors' advertisements for the last twelve months?	0–5
2.	Do you understand how much your competitors are spending on each advertisement and percentage of sales?	0–5
3.	Have you defined your customer? Do you know how and why your customer buys?	0–15
4.	Have you determined the media, or message, which will influence your customers' buying habits?	0–7
5.	Do you know what successful and unsuccessful advertising will be for your business?	0–7
6.	Have you investigated direct mailing as an alternative?	0–5
7.	Do you have a good mailing list?	0–5
8.	Have you selected the most promising features and benefits of your business to promote?	0–10
9.	Do you know a list of media, or methods, that is most suitable for advertising your business?	0–12
10.	Do you know the cost of these media?	0–5
11.	Have you discussed marketing issues which are central to your business with a marketing expert?	0–15 Advertising Sum

Average score—65 out of a possible 89 points.

ITEM #8—PRICING

		Points
1.	Have you decided to price your product on the basis of the cost of the product or what the competitors charge for the product? Shouldn't you price it based upon what the market will bear?	0–15
2.	Have you thought through the advantages of being a price leader or a price follower?	0–10
3.	Have you considered your competitors' reactions to any of your pricing policies?	0–7
4.	Have you considered the relative importance of each market segment with different pricing policies?	0–10
5.	Have you investigated pricing issues to be sure you're not in violation of any of the codes? (Robinson-Patman, etc.)	0–3
6.	Is your pricing sufficient so that you will make a profit on each of the products you sell?	0–5
7.	Do you know what your contribution margin is on each product?	0–4
8.	Has it taken into account your breakeven volume?	0–5

9. Do you anticipate having to raise or lower your price to meet competitors in the future? 0–5

10. Do you offer special discounts for special customers? Is this a generally known policy? 0–3

11. Have you developed a chart of accounts to classify your expenses? 0–10

12. Do you know what your largest expense items are? Can you control or reduce these expenses? 0–10

13. Have you attempted to control these expenses from the very beginning? 0–10

14. Do you have a flexible expense budget to be able to handle unexpected expenses? 0–7

Pricing Sum

Average score—55 total; possible score, 89 points.

ITEM #9—MISCELLANEOUS

1. Have you been able to comply with the local town government regulations by filing the appropriate forms with the town? 0–2

2. Have you done the same for the state and the federal government? 0–2

3. Have you provided an adequate system of records in order to generate your tax payments and especially your payroll taxes? 0–3

4. Is your chart of accounts sensible? Are there items that are too large or too small? 0–2

5. Will you be able to compare your performance with existing standard operating ratios? (D&B) 0–2

6. Have you obtained a social security number or tax identification number for your business? 0–2

7. Is your business clear from sales tax exemptions? 0–2

8. Have you provided for a sense of security about these government issues to all your employees? 0–2

9. Have you complied with regulations about copyrighting, trademarks, brandnames, and trade names? 0–3

10. Have you figured out whether or not you could make more money working for someone else? 0–5

11. Are you prepared to invest boundless energy and time in this business venture? 0–8

12. Do your family and spouse go along with your desire to start a business? 0–15

13. Do you know how to discover the second product or second location or second feature of your business? 0–8

14. Have you spoken to the Small Business Administration for help? 0–10

15. Have you secured any of the SBA's pamphlets? 0–3

16. Have you gotten any help from any source? They'd recommend: Score, Ace, Small Business Institute. 0–5

Misc. Sum

Average Miscellaneous score 57
Total Miscellaneous possible points 74

Below is the breakdown of this checklist.

		Average Score	Total Possible Score
1.	Are you equipped for a business venture—7 questions	28	31
2.	How good is your idea—3 questions	65	41
3.	How about raising money—20 questions	111	136
4.	How about the potential success of your business—4 questions	25	37
5.	Risk management—4 questions	15	17
6.	Employee skills and purchasing—9 questions	43	64
7.	Advertising and sales promotion—11 questions	65	89
8.	Pricing—14 questions	55	89
9.	Miscellaneous—16 questions	57	74
		463	619

Your Sum _____   Success Sum _____   Pricing Sum _____

BEFORE YOU START

HOW ABOUT YOU?

Are you the kind of person who can get a business started and make it go? (Before you answer this question, use the worksheet on the next few pages.) _____

Think about *why* you want to own your own business. Do you want to badly enough to keep you working long hours without knowing how much money you'll end up with? _____

Have you worked in a business like the one you want to start? _____

Have you worked for someone else as a foreman or manager? _____

Have you had any business training in school? _____

Have you saved any money? _____

HOW ABOUT THE MONEY?

Do you know how much money you will need to get your business started? (Use worksheets 2 and 3 to figure this out.) _____

Have you counted up how much money of your own you can put into the business? _____

Do you know how much credit you can get from your suppliers—the people you will buy from? _____

Do you know where you can borrow the rest of the money you need to start your business? _____

Have you figured out what net income per year you expect to get from the business? Count your salary and your profit on the money you put into the business. _____

Can you live on less than this so that you can use some of it to help your business grow? _____

Have you talked to a banker about your plans? _____

HOW ABOUT A PARTNER?

If you need a partner with money or know-how that you don't have, do you know someone who will fit—someone you can get along with? _____

Do you know the good and bad points about going it alone, having a partner, and incorporating your business? _____

Have you talked to a lawyer about it? _____

HOW ABOUT YOUR CUSTOMERS?

Do most businesses in your community seem to be doing well? _____

Have you tried to find out whether stores like the one you want to open are doing well in your community and in the rest of the country? _____

Do you know what kind of people will want to buy what you plan to sell? _____

What people like that live in the area where you want to open your store? _____

Do they need a store like yours? _____

If not, have you thought about opening a different kind of store or going to another neighborhood? _____

WORKSHEET NO. 1

Under each question check the answer that says what you feel or comes closest to it. Be honest with yourself.

ARE YOU A SELF-STARTER?

I do things on my own. Nobody has to tell me to get going.

If someone gets me started, I keep going all right.

Easy does it, man. I don't put myself out until I have to.

HOW DO YOU FEEL ABOUT OTHER PEOPLE?

I like other people. I can get along with just about anybody.

I have plenty of friends—I don't need anyone else.

Most people bug me.

CAN YOU LEAD OTHERS?

I can get most people to go along when I start something.

I can give the orders if someone tells me what we should do.

I let someone else get things moving. Then I go along if I feel like it.

CAN YOU TAKE RESPONSIBILITY?

I like to take charge of things and see them through.

I'll take over if I have to, but I'd rather let someone else be responsible.

There's always some eager beaver around wanting to show how smart he is. I say let him.

HOW GOOD AN ORGANIZER ARE YOU?

I like to have a plan before I start. I'm usually the one to get things lined up when the gang wants to do something.

I do all right unless things get too goofed up. Then I cop out.

You get all set and then something comes along and blows the whole bag. So I just take things as they come.

HOW GOOD A WORKER ARE YOU?

I can keep going as long as I need to. I don't mind working hard for something I want.

I'll work hard for a while, but when I've had enough, that's it, man!

I can't see that hard work gets you anywhere.

CAN YOU MAKE DECISIONS?

I can make up my mind in a hurry if I have to. It usually turns out okay, too.

I can if I have plenty of time. If I have to make up my mind fast, I think later I should have decided the other way.

I don't like to be the one who has to decide things. I'd probably blow it.

CAN PEOPLE TRUST WHAT YOU SAY?

You bet they can. I don't say things I don't mean.

I try to be on the level most of the time, but sometimes I just say what's easiest.

What's the sweat if the other fellow doesn't know the difference?

CAN YOU STICK WITH IT?

If I make up my mind to do something, I don't let *anything* stop me.

I usually finish what I start—if it doesn't get fouled up.

If it doesn't go right away, I turn off. Why beat your brains out?

HOW GOOD IS YOUR HEALTH?

Man, I never run down!

I have enough energy for most things I want to do.

I run out of juice sooner than most of my friends seem to.

Now count the checks you made. How many checks are there beside the *first* answer to each question? How many checks are there beside the *second* answer to each question? How many checks are there beside the *third* answer to each question?

If most of your checks are beside the first answers, you probably have what it takes to run a business. If not, you're likely to have more trouble than you can handle by yourself. Better find a partner who is strong on the points you're weak on. If many checks are beside the third answer, not even a good partner will be able to shore you up.

GETTING STARTED

YOUR BUILDING

Have you found a good building for your store?   _____

Will you have enough room when your business gets bigger?   _____

Can you fix the building the way you want it without spending too much money?   _____

Can people get to it easily from parking spaces, bus stops, or their homes?   _____

Have you had a lawyer check the lease and zoning?   _____

EQUIPMENT AND SUPPLIES

Do you know just what equipment and supplies you need and how much they will cost? (Worksheet 3 on page 000 and the lists you made for it should show this.)   _____

Can you save money by buying secondhand equipment?   _____

YOUR MERCHANDISE

Have you decided what things you will sell?   _____

Do you know how much or how many of each you will buy to open your store with?   _____

Have you found suppliers who will sell you what you need at a good price?   _____

Have you compared the prices and credit terms of different suppliers?   _____

YOUR RECORDS

Have you planned a system of records that will keep track of your income and expenses, what you owe other people, and what other people owe you?   _____

Have you worked out a way to keep track of your inventory so that you will always have enough on hand for your customers but not more than you can sell?   _____

Have you figured out how to keep your payroll records and take care of tax reports and payments?   _____

Do you know what financial statements you should prepare?   _____

Do you know how to use these financial statements?   _____

Do you know an accountant who will help you with your records and financial statements?   _____

YOUR STORE AND THE LAW

Do you know what licenses and permits you need? _____

Do you know what business laws you have to obey? _____

Do you know a lawyer you can go to for advice and for help with legal papers? _____

PROTECTING YOUR STORE

Have you made plans for protecting your store against thefts of all kinds—shoplifting, robbery, burglary, employee stealing? _____

Have you talked with an insurance agent about what kinds of insurance you need?

BUYING A BUSINESS SOMEONE ELSE HAS STARTED

Have you made a list of what you like and don't like about buying a business someone else has started? _____

Are you sure you know the real reason why the owner wants to sell the business? _____

Have you compared the cost of buying the business with the cost of starting a new business? _____

Is the stock up to date and in good condition? _____

Is the building in good condition? _____

Will the owner of the building transfer the lease to you? _____

Have you talked with other businesspersons in the area to see what they think of the business? _____

Have you talked with the company's suppliers? _____

Have you talked with a lawyer about it? _____

MAKING IT GO

ADVERTISING

Have you decided how you will advertise? (Newspapers—posters—handbills—radio—by mail?) _____

Do you know where to get help with your ads? _____

Have you watched what other stores do to get people to buy? _____

THE PRICES YOU CHARGE

Do you know how to figure what you should charge for each item you sell? _____

Do you know what other stores like yours charge? _____

BUYING

Do you have a plan for finding out what your customers want? _____

Will your plan for keeping track of your inventory tell you when it is time to order more and how much to order? Do you plan to buy most of your stock from a few suppliers rather than a little from many, so that those you buy from will help you succeed? _____

SELLING

Have you decided whether you will have salesclerks or self-service? _____

Do you know how to get customers to buy? _____

Have you thought about why you like to buy from some salespersons and others turn you off? _____

YOUR EMPLOYEES

If you need to hire someone to help you, do you know where to look? _____

Do you know what kind of person you need? _____

Do you know how much to pay? _____

Do you have a plan for training your employees? _____

CREDIT FOR YOUR CUSTOMERS

Have you decided whether to let your customers buy on credit? _____

Do you know the good and bad points about joining a credit card plan? _____

Can you tell a deadbeat from a good credit customer? _____

A FEW EXTRA QUESTIONS

Have you figured out whether you could make more money working for someone else? _____

Does your family go along with your plan to start a business of your own? _____

Do you know where to find out about new ideas and new products? _____

Do you have a work plan for yourself and your employees? _____

Have you gone to the nearest Small Business Administration office for help with your plans? _____

If you have answered all these questions carefully, you've done some hard work and serious thinking. That's good. But you have probably found some things you still need to know more about or do something about.

Do all you can for yourself, but don't hesitate to ask for help from people who can tell you what you need to know. Remember, running a business takes guts! You've got to be able to decide what you need and then go after it. *Good luck!*

WORKSHEET NO. 2

ESTIMATED MONTHLY EXPENSES

Item	Your estimate of monthly expenses based on sales of $_____ per year *Column 1* $	Your estimate of how much cash you need to start your business (See column 3) *Column 2* $	What to put in column 2 (These figures are typical for one kind of business. You will have to decide how many months to allow for in your business.) *Column 3*
Salary of owner-manager			2 times column 1
All other salaries and wages			3 times column 1
Rent			3 times column 1
Advertising			3 times column 1
Delivery expense			3 times column 1
Supplies			3 times column 1
Telephone and telegraph			3 times column 1
Other utilities			3 times column 1
Insurance			Payment required by insurance company
Taxes, including Social Security			4 times column 1
Interest			3 times column 1
Maintenance			3 times column 1
Legal and other professional fees			3 times column 1
Miscellaneous			3 times column 1
STARTING COSTS YOU ONLY HAVE TO PAY ONCE			Leave column 2 blank
Fixtures and equipment			Fill in worksheet 3 on page and put the total here
Decorating and remodeling			Talk it over with a contractor
Installation of fixtures and equipment			Talk to suppliers from who you buy these
Starting inventory			Suppliers will probably help you estimate this
Deposits with public utilities			Find out from utilities companies

Item	Column 2	Notes
Legal and other professional fees		Lawyer, accountant and so on
Licenses and permits		Find out from city offices what you have to have
Advertising and promotion for opening		Estimate what you'll use
Accounts receivable		What you need to buy more stock until credit customers pay
Cash		For unexpected expenses or losses, special purchases, etc.
Other		Make a separate list and enter total
TOTAL ESTIMATED CASH YOU NEED TO START WITH		Add up all the numbers in Column 2

WORKSHEET NO. 3—LIST OF FURNITURE, FIXTURES, AND EQUIPMENT

Leave out or add items to suit your business. Use separate sheets to list exactly what you need for each of the items below.	If you plan to pay cash in full, enter the full amount below and in the last column.	If you are going to pay by installments, fill out the columns below. Enter in the last column your downpayment plus at least one installment.			Estimate of the cash you need for furniture, fixtures, and equipment
		Price	Downpayment	Amount of each installment	
Counters	$	$	$	$	$
Storage shelves, cabinets					
Display stands, shelves, tables					
Cash register					
Safe					
Window display fixtures					
Special lighting					
Delivery equipment if needed					
TOTAL FURNITURE, FIXTURES, AND EQUIPMENT (Enter this figure also in worksheet 2 under "Starting Costs You Only Have to Pay Once.")					$

Information Questionnaire

This questionnaire is to be used as background for the development of a business plan.

1. What is the present name of the company?
2. Is the company a corporation, partnership, or sole proprietorship?
3. If the company is a corporation, please set forth the date and the state of incorporation.
4. Please furnish the names of the persons who formed the company.
5. Was the company originally organized as a corporation, partnership, or sole proprietorship?
6. Please furnish the names of the initial shareholders and/or providers of funds (debt and equity) of the company. Supply dates of each sale of securities, number of shares issued, and the consideration received for the shares. If no cash consideration was received, indicate the dollar value ascribed to each consideration.
7. Please describe the nature of the company's business. Has the nature of the company's business changed or evolved since its inception? Is it intended to place future emphasis on different areas?
8. Does the company conduct business under names other than its own? If so, please set forth the names and places where they are used.
9. Does the company utilize any trademarks or tradenames? If so, submit copies.
10. What geographical area does the company serve? Are there any limitations on what markets can be reached, for example, freight, duties, service, maintenance, patent licenses, tariffs, government regulations, etc.? Does the company intend to enlarge its present areas of distribution or service?
11. Please describe the major products or services of the company.
12. In which states and/or countries other than its state of incorporation is the company licensed or qualified to do business?

13. Please furnish a listing plus a physical description of all offices, plants, laboratories, warehouses, stores, outlets, studios, or other facilities (include size of plot, square footage of enclosed space, etc.).

14. Please describe the method or methods of distribution and sales. If any contractual arrangements are involved, please describe and/or furnish copies.

15. Please list and describe, to the degree relevant, all patents, technical information, trademarks, franchises, copyrights, patent and technical information, licenses owned and/or used.

16. Please furnish a detailed five-year breakdown of sales, earnings, income, or losses of the company's major divisions, departments, and product categories. Give the percentage of total income or loss attributed to each.

17. Please furnish a detailed breakdown of major suppliers of raw materials, goods, etc. Give their names, addresses, and volume of purchases. Are other sources readily available or is the company dependent to any degree on any one supplier? What would result if the product or products of said supplier or suppliers were no longer readily procurable? Does the company have any long term contracts with its suppliers?

18. If the company utilizes the services of subcontractor and/or processors of its products or components of subassemblies, please describe the work done and the availability of other subcontractors or processors. Does the company have any long term contracts with such persons?

19. Furnish a three-year record of names, addresses, and volume of purchases of major customers or outlets for the company's products or services. The prospectus or offering circular will list names of customers who account for more than 10% of the company's business. Could this in any way be deleterious to the company?

20. Please furnish names of the company's major competitors; describe the nature and area of their competition—is it direct or indirect? What is the company's approximate rank in the industry? Are there numerous competitors? What is the degree of competition? Can new companies readily enter the field? Do the company's competitors possess greater financial resources? Are they longer established and better recognized?

21. Please furnish a complete list of all officers and/or directors plus the following data:
    a. Age
    b. Education
    c. Title and function—responsibilities
    d. Length of service with company
    e. Posts held and functions performed for company prior to present post
    f. Compensation
    g. Past business associations and posts held
    h. Special distinctions
    i. Other directorates or present business affiliations

22. Please furnish a copy of all stock option plans.

23. Please furnish a copy of or describe any bonus and profit-sharing plans.

24. Please furnish copies of or describe any other employee fringe benefits.

25. Please furnish copies of any pension plan.

26. Please state the total number of employees, full- and part-time, the major categories of employees and number within each. If the company is to any degree dependent on technology or other expertise, please give details, for example, number of Ph.D.s, M.A.s, engineers, technicians, medical personnel, etc.

27. Are your employees represented by one or more unions? Please list each union by name or number. Please furnish copies of the union contracts.

28. Please furnish a general description of labor relations, past strikes, handling of grievances, etc. Has the company experienced any difficulties in obtaining qualified personnel? Has the company had any problems with respect to personnel turnover?

29. Please describe all acquisitions of other companies, assets, personnel, etc., made by the company, or any intended acquisitions. Please furnish copies of all acquisitions agreements.

30. Please describe any major dispositions of subsidiaries, divisions, assets, equipment, plans, etc., made by the company.

31. Has any officer, director, or major shareholder ever (a) had any difficulties of any nature with the Securities and Exchange Commission, the National Association of Securities Dealers, or any state securities commission or agency, (b) been convicted of a felony, or (c) been under indictment, investigation, or threatened by the SEC, NASD, a state commission, or public agency with prosecution for violation of a state or federal statute? Has any such person ever been adjudicated a bankrupt? If the answer to any of the questions is in the affirmative, please describe the circumstances in detail.

32. Has the company made (a) any private placements of its equity or debt securities, or (b) any public sale of its equity or debt securities? If so, please furnish complete details including copies of documents used in the placement and/or sale.

33. Furnish a specimen copy of all outstanding and authorized equity and debt securities.

34. Furnish the following data regarding the distribution of the company's voting stock:
    a. classes of stock and number of shares of each outstanding;
    b. total number of shareholders plus list of shareholders;
    c. names, residence addresses, and shareholders of ten largest shareholders of each class;
    d. relationships of major shareholders to each other or to the officers and directors of the company; and
    e. details of any voting trust agreements, shareholders agreements or other arrangements to vote stock jointly.

35. Are there any options to purchase stock or other securities or warrants outstanding other than employees' stock option plans? If so, please furnish copies or describe such plan.

36. Does the company have any long-term or short-term debt, secured or unsecured, or has the company guaranteed such debt on behalf of others? Please furnish copies of the documents creating the debt or guarantee, or describe the debt or guarantee.

37. Please furnish detailed audited statements for the last five years if available.

38. Please furnish interim statements covering the period subsequent to the last audited financial statement.

39. Please furnish comparative figures of earning and net worth for five years.

40. Please furnish an explanation of any and all abnormal, nonrecurring or unusual items in earnings statements or balance sheets.

41. Please furnish a statement of cash flow if materially different from statement of net earnings.

42. Please furnish a statement as to any contingent or possible liabilities not shown on balance sheet. Please include guarantees, warranties, litigation, etc.

43. With respect to the company's inventories, please state (a) major categories, (b) method used in valuation, LIFO, FIFO, other, and (c) control systems. If your "inventories" are distinctive in any fashion, for example, film libraries, promotional displays, etc., please state how they are handled on your books.

44. What is the company's policy regarding depreciation, depletion, and amortization? Which items are capitalized and which expensed? Are there any deferred write-offs?

45. Are your company's methods of accounting similar to the rest of the industry? If not, please describe the differences and the reason for such differences.

46. Please state the status of federal and state tax examinations. When was your last examination, and are there any open questions?

47. Please describe all bank relationships and credit lines. Are factors involved?

48. Please describe any pending or threatened claims and litigation by identifying the parties, the amount involved, the names of involved, and please furnish copies of all documents with respect thereto.

49. Please describe all insurance coverages, for example, plant, equipment, properties, work interruption, key employees, other.

50. Please describe your company's projection of sales and earnings for the next three years, including explanations with respect to any increase or decrease.

51. Please furnish lists of all real estate owned by the company, including, without limitation, the following: (a) the improvements on the property, (b) the assessed valuation and amount of current real estate taxes, (c) any mortgages, including amount, rate of interest and due date, (d) any liens or encumbrances, and (e) the estimated present value.

52. Please furnish a list of all real estate leased by the company, including, without limitation, the following: (a) the amount of space, (b) the rent-fixed and contingent, (c) the term of lease, (d) the renewal options, (e) the purchase options, (f) the minimum annual gross rentals, and (g) the minimum total gross rental obligation to expiration of all leases in force.

53. Please list all equipment leased by the company if aggregate annual rentals exceed $5,000 or if the company is dependent on the equipment. If any other property is leased at a sizable aggregate annual rental, please furnish details of the lease, including, without limitation, the terms, options to renew and/or purchase, etc.

54. Please describe all depreciable property owned by the company including, without limitation, the following: (a) the original cost to company, (b) the depreciation to date, in addition to a statement as to the method employed, (c) the remaining cost, and (d) the aging of items listed (remaining depreciable life).

55. Please furnish copies of all brochures, catalogues, mailers, publicity releases, newspaper or magazine articles, literature and the like distributed by the company or concerning the company, its products, personnel, or services.

56. Please describe the company's research and development activities.

57. Please give a complete description of any unusual contracts relating to the company, its business, products, or services.

58. Please describe exactly how the net proceeds (after underwriting commission and all expenses) are to be used by the company.

59. Please describe the company's plans for expansion or growth.

60. Please set forth any information not previously disclosed in your answers that an investor would use in making a decision as to whether he or she should invest in the company.

61. Please furnish copies of the following:

    a. Certificate of Incorporation and all amendments
    b. By-laws and all amendments
    c. Employee agreements, if any

Suggested Outline of a Business Plan

Cover Sheet: Name of business, names of principals, address and phone number of business
Statement of Purpose
Table of Contents

I. The Business
   A. Description of Business
   B. Market
   C. Competition
   D. Location of Business
   E. Management
   F. Personnel
   G. Application and Expected Effect of Loan (if needed)
   H. Summary

II. Financial Data
   A. Sources and Applications of Funding
   B. Capital Equipment List
   C. Balance Sheet
   D. Breakeven Analysis
   E. Income Projections (Profit and Loss Statements)
      1. Three-year summary
      2. Detail by month for first year
      3. Detail by quarter for second and third years
      4. Notes of explanation

    F. Pro-Forma Cash Flow

        1. Detail by month for first year
        2. Detail by quarter for second and third years
        3. Notes of explanation

    G. Deviation Analysis
    H. Historical Financial Reports for Existing Business

        1. Balance sheets for past three years
        2. Income statements for past three years
        3. Tax returns

III. Supporting Documents: Personal résumés, personal financial requirements and statements, cost of living budget, credit reports, letters of reference, job descriptions, letters of intent, copies of leases, contracts, legal documents, and anything else of relevance to the plan.

appendix D

Sample Business Plans

The introductions and tables of contents of these business plans are included not as examples of either effective or ineffective business plans, but rather to acquaint the reader with several actual business plans. These were chosen more for their representation of various types of plans. They are all actual plans, disguised where needed, especially as relates to geographic location, financial information, and individual identities, which may account for some, but not all, of the inconsistencies, errors, and omissions.

BRIOX TECHNOLOGY. INC.

This is an interesting story—one with a good ending. It began when my brother, John Anthony Mancuso, acting as a salesman for a valve company in upstate New York, called on Briox Technologies. He mentioned my interest in small business to the Briox entrepreneur, David Gessner. As can be observed from the résumés in the business plan, Gessner was the holder of a technical master's degree, and as such, he elected to attend an interesting three-day workshop sponsored by the Institute of New Enterprise Development (INED) in Belmont, Massachusetts. This agency specializes in helping new entrepreneurs get started. For a small fee, Gessner attended a weekend "how to write a business plan" seminar which was held in Salt Lake City, Utah. Hence, Gessner was fairly well versed in the construction of a business plan. Moreover, as will be evident in a moment, he possessed a deep and burning desire to start, finance, and manage a small business of his own. John Mancuso suggested that he show the business plan to me.

Gessner and I met; I was impressed with him and his business, and I introduced him to a Minority Enterprise Small Business Investment Company (MESBIC). Gessner cleverly constructed the business plan to highlight the minority employment aspect of his business. The plan, as attached, was financed by several friends and relatives (angels) and by the Worcester Corporation Council, Inc. (WCCI). The business moved to Worcester, and Gessner began to operate the medical oxygen company.

This is where the story becomes interesting. It took only a few months to use up all of the original investment. During that time the company was unable to perfect the oxygenerator that was to make oxygen from water. The idea was good—even great—but the technology was only fair—maybe poor. Within six months of the private placement, the business was bust, Al Stubman* was fired, and Gessner was all alone with no money, no sales, and no product. A more sensible man would have known when to quit, and would have gone in search of a job. Instead, he sought part-time employment, did some consulting (he assisted in a small business course at WPI), and collected unemployment. The last of these actions—collecting unemployment—was the most emotional and most rewarding experience of all. Gessner collected for over one year, and these funds provided the main sustenance for his family.

With the addition of hindsight, these unemployment checks were a vital motivation to keep him going: They supplied the nourishment for the next year or so. If a person who contemplates going into a small business has never collected an unemployment check, may I recommend that he visit his unemployment office. The sign over the door will read "Employment Office" but everyone calls it the "Unemployment Office." It's a very dehumanizing process. Go see for yourself, if you haven't already.

During these never-ending months of product development, Gessner continued to improve his radical new invention, the oxygenerator. Finally, after two years of trying, he decided to shift horses.

Just as Ed Land of Polaroid was initially interested in building a business around polarized glass (supposedly for the windshields and headlights of automobiles), Dave Gessner began his business with the wrong initial product. Gessner soon improved upon the existing and proven technology pioneered by the competitors—making oxygen by filtering air. He developed a brochure, attracted new investors, acquired a new partner/investor, and began again. In the past few years, after four years, he now leads a profitable company with annual sales in the $10 million range.

I said that starting a business and succeeding at it requires perseverance and motivation—sometimes bordering on obsession. Gessner proves my points.

*See "How to Start, Finance, and Manage Your Own Small Business, revised, Joseph R. Mancuso (Englewood Cliffs, NJ: Prentice-Hall, 1984).

AMERICAN LASER, INC.

This is not an atypical story. In fact, it's recurring quite frequently. Although this story is disguised, it is true. These two fellows bought a business when their employer decided to go out of the business. And best of all, they succeeded. This may become an even more common practice in the future.

In fact, the largest employer in the entire state of Vermont, an asbestos mine, experienced a similar transaction. After years of poor financial management, the parent company announced plans to close its doors. The people were going to lose their jobs, and closing of the business was a statewide concern. The good news is what happened. The employees banded together, obtained financing from the state, and bought the company. Naturally, as with many of these stories, the elected president was the former foreman of the maintenance division. After one year under employee ownership, all the stockholders were able to have their entire initial investment returned. In subsequent years, the business demonstrated excellent profitability.

The same is true in the case of American Laser. As a division of the larger parent company, it consistently lost in excess of $1 million per year. This is devastating, given the size of the sales of the division. When these two people took over the company, they had only marginal management experience. The business plan was written in module form. This allowed the entrepreneurs to package the appropriate modules in order to maximize the appeal. The plan is a good one. However, in fact the list of customers in the plan failed to materialize in the first year. In other words, *none* of the customers listed in the report purchased products during the first year the firm was in business.

The plan failed to raise venture money. However, it did *not* fail to launch the business. Moreover, the business is extremely successful; and in the fifth year after the start of the business, the firm was sold to another business for $1 million.

After discussing the appeal of the new business with several venture sources, the founders were extremely dejected. They found the terms and conditions of any new money to be terribly limiting. Subsequently, they walked into a bank and pleaded their case with an unusual, creative, and friendly banker. Within a half an hour, the banker advanced them a personal, unsecured loan to launch their business. I was there, and I saw it happen—an unusual event if I ever saw one. Earlier in this book I said, "Pick a banker, not a bank." Later on the same page, I said, "A good banker can be a venture capitalist in disguise." This one was more than that: He became an admired friend. He received all of the loan back and kept the new growing company in town.

PERSPECTIVE, INC.

This is an excellent business plan. It is well written; the entrepreneur is successful; the idea is superior. However, the plan never raised any money: It was a failure.

It was shown to many investors, probably more than it should have been, but it was always a bridesmaid. One of the common criticisms of the plan was the inability to test the idea on a small scale. One of the investors claimed that the plan was too large an investment prior to any measurable level of success being obtainable. There was considerable negotiating about the viability of a regional publication for the senior citizens, say, in Florida, But on a regional scale, it was much less appealing financially. So the idea died.

However, as with most good ideas, it only died for this entrepreneur. Publishing, like many industries, is a special and private business, and John O'Mara had very little publishing experience. But another entrepreneur with a different business plan, totally unrelated to this venture, launched a very similar product. The data obtained by the grapevine claims that the business is now a solid financial success.

John O'Mara gained a great deal of experience in developing this business plan—so much, in fact, that he wrote another one. Soon, he left the secure arms of his large company employer in order to launch a new business called the Computer Security Institute. This venture provided newsletters, information, and seminars for larger firms interested in protecting confidential information stored in computers. I'm told that the venture is extremely successful because the initial membership fee alone, from my outside vantage point, certainly must help cover some overhead. The advantage of having customers send money in advance (membership fees) is an interesting method of financing an entrepreneurial venture.

IN-LINE TECHNOLOGY

The plan presented here is a shortened version of the actual document used to finance In-Line Technology. The actual document was about four times longer. It contained numerous photos and product descriptions. The financing was successful. The firm was able to raise the funds stated in the prospectus. The funds were supplied by friends and relatives, and the final $50,000 was provided by an extremely successful and well-known New York venture capitalist. The venture capitalist, because of his reputation, was able to negotiate an extra bonus for investing in this young but promising business. The two founders were extremely reluctant to give extra compensation to the venture sources, but they finally decided to go along.

The new money transfusion helped, and the firm began to grow. The venture source forced the additional services of a paid-for management consultant to work several days per month at In-Line Technology. This was not part of the private placement agreement, but the after-the-placement verbal persuasion was sufficient. In other words, the original private placement legal document did not specifically require In-Line to accept outside consulting advice. The legal agreement for private placements of this type and size are usually secondary to verbal agreements. In fact, the business improved based on this consulting advice.

In-Line never made money. Occasionally, it had a few months of profit but never any sustained or significant profits. It always seemed to almost make a profit in the following few years, but it never became very successful. Finally, the venture capitalist grew restless and introduced In-Line Technology to a larger firm on the West Coast—Applied Materials, Inc. The firms were merged in January of 1976, and the investors in this business plan realized a 3:1 gain. Hence, the firm raised money and performed at an unprofitable level, yet the investors and stockholders still made a profit. This is seldom the case, and without the assistance of the New York venture capitalist, the firm would still be struggling. The venture placement was determined at a breakfast meeting in New York. This was the only meeting the venture source had with the firm. He never visited the plant.

About nine months after the merger, one of the two founders was fired and the other was made a consultant. In other words, they were both eased out of the business. The partnership of Gene St. Onge and Hank Bok works well and they have just launched a new business. Based upon the funds gained from the sale of In-Line Technology, the two men have started another small business, Hydro-tech. This firm is entering the interesting area of hydroponics, which is a form of scientific farming. This business calls for year-round growing of tomatoes, cucumbers, and lettuce in greenhouses. The success of this newest business is still undetermined. It's interesting to recall some of the early comments that the likelihood of starting a new business is increased if you have previous experience in starting businesses. Many entrepreneurs will start five to six businesses in a lifetime.

B.L.T.

The reader of this business plan must be careful not to let recent events such as the energy crisis cloud proper readings of the document. This plan was written in 1969. It followed very closely on the heels of a successful public stock offering for Robo-Wash, a competitor. The plan was written by three extremely talented men who spent most of their careers on Wall Street in New York. While none of the three founders had any experience in either the gas station or car wash fields, they knew their way around Wall Street. They were experts at raising money.

The business plan is extremely simple. It is not terribly exciting to read. The strongest point is the level of management achievement of the three principals. This was enough for this start-up business to raise in excess of $1 million from a handful of venture capitalists. The money was raised over several placements, and the firm experienced continual delays and postponements in building and operating the gas station/car wash combination. The business began in fine style with a prototype gas station/car wash operating profitably in southern Connecticut. However, this was the only profitable business enterprise with B.L.T. The business as a whole never made money. The firm lost the $10 million of investment plus a good deal of bank debt. The reasons for failures were manifold. However, the business plan, as simple as it was, was sufficient just as it was to raise over $1 million.

BRIOX TECHNOLOGIES
Medical Oxygen Generator

MEDICAL OXYGEN GENERATOR

FOR HOMECARE PATIENTS

BUSINESS PLAN

SEPTEMBER, 1974

Briox Technologies, Inc.
65 Tainter Street
Worcester, Massachusetts 01610

617/757-7474

CONTENTS

159

SUMMARY

Briox Technologies, Inc. is a company in the Biomedical Equipment field which is responding to the needs of homecare service businesses and hospitals. The company was founded in September 1973 by David M. Gessner with the commitment of his personal funds. WCCI Capital Corporation of Worcester, Massachusetts, and several individuals have provided additional seed financing.

The Product

The first product is a home oxygen generating system, the OXY-GENERATOR, to replace expensive-to-deliver high pressure cylinders currently in use for the treatment of Chronic Obstructive Pulmonary Disease (COPD). The company has completed a full-scale prototype which was complete and operating on April 9, 1974.

Field Evaluation

Five demonstrator OXY-GENERATORS are being built for laboratory and field evaluation. At the recent national meeting of the American Thoracic Society in Cincinnati six board certified pulmonary specialists expressed interest in conducting field evaluations with their patients.

The Market

The total market size for home oxygen generating systems is 66,000 and is growing at an annual compounded rate of $7\frac{1}{2}$%. The company will capture at least 6% of this market by 1978 with annual sales of 5,000 units @ $2100 yielding revenues of $10.5 million with a net profit greater than 15% of sales.

Production

OXY-GENERATORS will be produced by assembly of commercial components and subcontracted subassemblies. The primary subassembly will be provided under exclusive license by TELEDYNE ISOTOPES. As the company grows the investment in manufacturing facilities will be increased in order to reduce costs and to increase capability and flexibility.

Distribution

OXY-GENERATORS will be sold to existing Respiratory Therapy Equipment Dealers who will rent them to COPD patients for use in the home. Dealer reaction to the product is positive. The company will trade exclusive distributorships within a territory for firm order commitments.

Financing Required

The company needs $100,000 to fund the development and implementation of a manufacturing plan to produce 20 units/month. Management proposes to issue an additional 25,000 shares which will bring the total issued to 85,000. Twenty thousand shares will be sold in private placement at $5.00 per share. Financial arrangements should be complete by October 31, 1974.

AMERICAN LASER CORPORATION
Employee Ownership
of High Technology Business

CONTENTS

1.0   NOTICE OF INTENTION

In making this preliminary proposal to ALI, there are many statements of the intentions of Albert D. Castro and William Lock forming a business. It should be noted:

1. This is only a preliminary document, serving as a basis of discussion only. In no way will either Mr. Castro or Mr. Lock be held to any statement, commitment, etc., without their specific signed intention to do so.

2. American Laser Corp. has full knowledge of our intention. However, there is no agreement yet between ALI with either Mr. Lock or Mr. Castro in regards to this business.

3. Estimates of completion in the glass laser field, potential sales volume, marketing plans, etc., are all only those of Mr. Lock and Mr. Castro and although they believe them to be as accurate and reliable as possible, no guarantee to their validity is implied.

2.0 SUMMARY

We, Albert D. Castro and William H. Lock are making a preliminary proposal to American Laser Corporation that it sell to us its
complete glass laser business. For this portion of what was American
Laser line of laser equipment, we are offering $85,000. We propose to
form a company within the area of Phoenix that will profit from the
substantial investment that ALI has made to develop their laser products.
Our marketing/selling plans are basically to retain two sales representatives from ALI's national organization, to concentrate our own
sales efforts in the west coast area, and to promote these products
through continued effort in applications engineering.

We plan our organization to be a small, conservative one (6 - 7
people for the first six months) but one whose sales growth should be
50% per year. A study of the market for our products and the competition indicates to us that the product line we desire is one characterized
by its high quality, its reliability, and its sales appeal. To finance this
company, we have been able to raise $25,000 between us, and our pro-
posal to ALI is that we pay them $40,000 cash and that they accept a
$45,000, three-year note from us for the rest of the payment. For this
consideration, we agree that ALI's note will be the senior debt of our
company. We will form our company with Albert D. Castro as president (and a 60% owner) and William H. Lock as vice president (and a
40% owner). Sales projections indicate a sales volume of $203,000 in
1974 and $332,000 in 1975. We expect to "break even" approximately
two years after start of business. A preliminary cash-flow analysis
indicates to us that we need at least $50,000 from some loaner.

PERSPECTIVE
Senior Citizens' Magazine

CONTENTS

SUMMARY OF BUSINESS PLAN

A MULTI-SERVICE corporation will be established dedicated to serving the needs of 30 million Americans in the 50 to 65 age group -- a group that commands the largest discretionary purchasing power in the U.S.

The initial service will be the quarterly paid-subscription magazine, PERSPECTIVE. The editorial objectives of this specialized publication will be to put the middle years in their proper context -- to show why and how they can be an exciting, challenging and independent time of life. Retirement planning will also receive a great deal of attention, with special emphasis on financial planning. In all cases the approach will be of a practical "how to" nature, attempting to establish a deep seated rapport between staff and reader.

Advertising acceptance will be promoted by offering a comprehensive readership profile package. By utilizing its computer expertise, the corporation plans to generate in-depth psychographic profiles (i.e., life style, beliefs, attitudes, etc.). The decision to offer psychographics was confirmed by the corporation's recent survey which indicated that advertising executives of consumer oriented companies were looking to supplement the demographics which they felt did not fully describe their target markets. Psychographic data will fill this void. However, standard demographic descriptions including age, sex, income and education will be included also.

The attraction of advertising is further enhanced by the absence of media directed solely to middle agers. For those advertisers selling to middle agers, there is no cost-effective magazine alternative available. The only publication addressing itself solely to middle agers is a non-profit organization -- one that does not accept advertising.

Advertising will be solicited from a variety of national firms such as health/life insurance companies, airlines, pharmaceutical firms, investment counseling services, land development organizations, travel/leisure groups, book clubs, and home study.

After eighteen months, PERSPECTIVE will switch to bi-monthly publication while retaining the $6 annual subscription price.

Circulation objectives are:

        500,000 subscribers at the end of 1st year
        700,000 subscribers at the end of 2nd year
        850,000 subscribers at the end of 3rd year
        950,000 subscribers at the end of 4th year
      1,000,000 subscribers at the end of 5th year

Another key innovation will be the guarantee to Charter subscribers that their subscription rate of $6 will NEVER be increased provided that they subscribe on a continuing basis. It is expected that this offer will have an extremely positive effect on subscription sales. Analysis has shown that this will be an economically feasible offer.

Once PERSPECTIVE has identified and cultivated a customer base, the corporation plans to expand its capabilities by offering additional services to its subscribers. Regular communications via the editorial pages will facilitate the promotion of services currently in demand by middle-aged citizens. Among these are mail order pharmaceuticals, group insurance programs, group travel, book clubs and investment counseling.

A two stage financing package is planned. The initial phase will require $60,000 to test readership acceptance. Once proven, $1,500,000 will be secured to launch operations and expansion.

The corporation plans to be profitable within two years. After five years a $1,500,000 profit (after taxes) is expected on revenues of $13,000,000.

IN-LINE TECHNOLOGIES, INC.
High Technology Investment

CONTENTS

170

I. INTRODUCTION

The electronics industry today still offers great potential to the entrepreneur for the creation of sizeable, profitable business ventures
especially in the areas of proprietary product marketing. This is true
for several reasons. First and foremost, of course, is the fact that the
dynamic state-of-the-art technology existing in the electronics industry
today affords a greater ease of market entry for the innovator. New,
unique, and different approaches to the solution of old problems are
welcomed, and are, in fact, a requirement for a successful company
engaged in the marketing of proprietary products.

For such companies the rate of growth and, of course, the rate of
profitability are limited primarily by the financial structure and support
of the organization, assuming that dynamic leadership, superior marketing capability, and exceptional technical talent are available. With a
proper financial base the growth pattern of such organization in today's
growing and expanding electronics market is highly probable.

The purpose of this business plan is to present in significant detail a
plan whereby an organization fitting the above pattern can make a substantial impact on the proprietary product market in a short period of
time with a minimum of the type of entrepreneurial risk usually found
to be an integral part of such plans. The minimization of these risks
comes about because of the following basic facts:

1. In-Line Technology, Inc. is a thriving organization that
    exists and will provide the vehicle for this plan.
2. In-Line Technology has already designed and manufactured
    90% of its fiscal year 1974 product line and is in the process
    of beginning its initial phases of marketing production tested
    and customer proved equipment.
3. In-Line Technology is supplying equipment to a rapidly
    expanding market for semiconductors that is forecasted to be
    greater than $2 billion by 1976, *almost a factor of 2 greater
    than the 1971 total .n just the United States alone.
4. In-Line Technology can accurately control and predict first
    year's bookings and shipments (with adequate financing) due to
    management's combined experience of over thirty years of
    marketing and engineering in the photo-chemical processing
    field.

---

*Market information from "Electronics' 1973 forecast of Electronics
  Markets.

In-Line Founders are in Tune with Photoprocessing Trend

A company that started as a part-time effort some 18 months ago has recently become its founders' sole business concern, and indeed, they appear in a good position to profit from semiconductor manufacturers' growing enthusiasm for automating their photoprocessing operations.

While Hendrik F. Bok and Eugene R. St. Onge worked together in the Systems division of EPEC Industries Inc., New Bedford, Mass., they saw the need for systems that could automatically handle cleaning, drying, etching, and developing. "There are a lot of different systems available," notes Bok, "but you have to buy the etcher from one company, the coater from another. To form a complete line of equipment, a plant manager needs to buy four or five makes of equipment that aren't always compatible."

The two men joined forces to make specialized turnkey photoprocessing systems, and In-Line Technology Inc. was born in Assonet, Mass. By now, In-Line has emerged from a custom-equipment phase with a number of standard items, including cleaners, coaters, dryers, developers, etchers, wet strippers, and plasma strippers, all of which are interfaced for either manual or automatic loading.

Cutting loose. During In-Line's first year, Bok and St. Onge kept their jobs at EPEC, but last October they were able to buy out EPEC'S Spray division and devote full time to In-Line, of which they are sole owners. Sales this year may reach $1 million.

Bok thinks part of their success is a result of "the imagination to come up with something new," but part of it is traceable to their backgrounds also. Bok, 47, founded his first company in 1954 in his native Netherlands. (He still speaks with a Dutch accent.) It made spray coaters, and in 1958 he brought the process with him to the U.S. where three years later he founded another company with expertise based on the same process. Joining EPEC in 1967 as a vice president, he gained experience in coating and first started to build integrated systems including sprayers, dryers, exposure equipment, and developers.

While Bok considers himself a "concept" engineer, St. Onge, 36, is a process engineer. One need they see is for better yields, and they believe their automatic production lines, which include automatic wafer handling, can help. Since wafers and plates are untouched throughout production, and the line is so timed that clean plates don't have to wait before being coated, dirt caused pinholes and other faults are cut down.

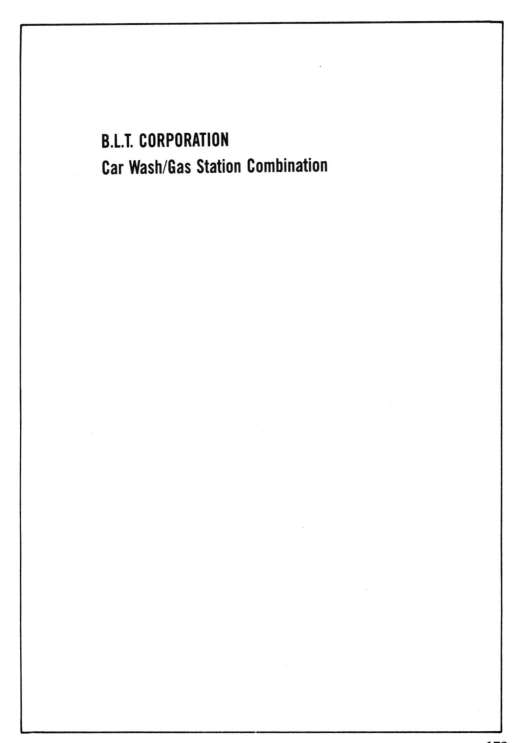

B.L.T. CORPORATION
Car Wash/Gas Station Combination

THE B. L. T. COMPANY

PARTICIPATION IN A TECHNOLOGICAL AND
MERCHANDISING REVOLUTION

THE AUTOMOBILE SERVICE INDUSTRY IS IN THE EARLY STAGE OF A TECHNOLOGICAL AND MERCHANDISING REVOLUTION. THE COMBINATION OF TWO ESSENTIAL AUTOMOTIVE NEEDS--CAR WASHING AND GASOLINE--HAS PRODUCED A HIGHLY PROMOTABLE AND EXTREMELY PROFITABLE SERVICE.

TECHNOLOGICAL REVOLUTION

The technological revolution is the result of the development and perfection of a new generation of car wash equipment. This equipment is highly automated and inexpensive to operate and maintain.

MERCHANDISING REVOLUTION

The merchandising revolution is the result of combining the purchase of gasoline with the car washing function. This combination has created a new and highly promotable service which offers the consumer distinct economic and convenience benefits previously unavailable.

PROFITABILITY

The profitability of the modern gas pumping-car wash unit is based upon the following fundamental business principles: Low labor, high gross margins, and minimal inventory and accounts receivable.

THE B. L. T. COMPANY CONCEPT

The B. L. T. Company was organized to capitalize on the technological and merchandising revolution and the fundamental business advantages outlined above. The B. L. T. Company intends to multiply the profitability of an individual car wash and gas pumping-car wash unit through the establishment of a national chain of wholly owned and franchised installations.

Each wholly owned car wash unit is expected to generate between $25,000 and $40,000 pre tax annual earnings on an investment of approximately $50,000. Each franchised unit is expected to generate initial income from the sale of equipment of between $5,000 and $10,000, plus continuing income of between $3,000 - $6,000 annually.

Each wholly owned gas pumping-car wash unit is expected to generate between $50,000 and $70,000 pre tax annual earnings on an initial investment of about $65,000. Each franchised gas pumping-car wash unit is expected to generate initial income from the sale of equipment of between $7,000 and $12,000, plus continuing income of between $5,000 - $7,000 annually.

Sample Partnership Agreement and Corporate Checklist

A note on the sample Partnership Agreement and Corporate Checklist. These forms have been made available by General Business Services, Inc. of Rockville, MD. GBS is a nationwide company providing tax and business counseling services to small businesses. We have modified the forms slightly. To obtain originals, ask your GBS representative for GBS form 8418: Partnership Agreement, or GBS form 8438: Corporate Checklist.

SAMPLE PARTNERSHIP AGREEMENT

Agreement made _____ , 19___ , between _____ of _____ , City

of _____ , County of _____ , State of _____ , and

_____ of _____ (address), City of _____ ,

County of _____ , State of _____ , hereinafter referred to as partners.

ITEM ONE

NAME, PURPOSE, AND DOMICILE

The name of the partnership shall be _____ . The partnership shall be conducted for the purposes

of _____ . The principal place of business shall be at

_____ unless relocated by majority consent of the partners.

ITEM TWO

DURATION OF AGREEMENT

The term of this agreement shall be for _____ years, commencing on _____ , 19___ , and

terminating on _____ , 19___ , unless sooner terminated by mutual consent of the parties or by operation
of the provisions of this agreement.

ITEM THREE

CONTRIBUTION

Each partner shall contribute _____ Dollars ($_____) on or before _____ ,
19____ to be used by the partnership to establish its capital position. Any additional contribution required of partners shall only
be determined and established in accordance with Item Seventeen.

ITEM FOUR

BOOKS AND RECORDS

Books of accounts shall be maintained by the partners, and proper entries made therein of all sales, purchases, receipts, payments, transactions, and property of the partnership, and the books of accounts and all records of the partnership shall be
retained at the principal place of business as specified in Item One herein. Each partner shall have free access at all times to
all books and records maintained relative to the partnership business.

ITEM FIVE   DIVISION OF PROFITS AND LOSSES

Each partner shall be entitled to _____ percent (_____ %) of the net profits of the business and all losses occurring
in the course of the business shall be borne in the same proportion, unless the losses are occasioned by the wilful neglect or
default, and not mere mistake or error, of any of the partners, in which case the loss so incurred shall be made good by the

partner through whose neglect or default the losses shall arise. Distribution of profits shall be made on the _____ day

of _____ each year.

ITEM SIX

PERFORMANCE

Each partner shall apply all of his experience, training, and ability in discharging his assigned functions in the partnership and
in the performance of all work that may be necessary or advantageous to further business interests of the partnership.

177

ITEM SEVEN

BUSINESS EXPENSES

The rent of the buildings where the partnership business shall be carried on, and the cost of repairs and alterations, all rates, taxes, payments for insurance, and other expenses in respect to the buildings used by the partnership, and the wages for all persons employed by the partnership are all to become payable on the account of the partnership. All losses incurred shall be paid out of the capital of the partnership or the profits arising from the partnership business, or, if both shall be deficient, by the partners on a pro rata basis, in proportion to their original contributions.

ITEM EIGHT

ACCOUNTING

The fiscal year of the partnership shall be from_____ to_____ of each year. On the

_____ day of_____ , commencing in 19__, and on the_____ day

of_____ in each succeeding year, a general accounting shall be made and taken by the partners of all sales, purchases, receipts, payments, and transactions of the partnership during the preceding fiscal year, and of all the capital property and current liabilities of the partnership. The general accounting shall be written in the partnership account books and signed in each book by each partner immediately after it is completed. After the signature of each partner is entered, each partner shall keep one of the books and shall be bound by every account, except that if any manifest error is

found therein by any partner and shown to the other partners within_____ months after the error shall have been noted by all of them, the error shall be rectified.

ITEM NINE

SEPARATE DEBTS

No partner shall enter into any bond or become surety, security, bail or co-signer for any person, partnership or corporation, or knowingly condone anything whereby the partnership property may be attached or be taken in execution, without the written consent of the other partners.

Each partner shall punctually pay his separate debts and indemnify the other partners and the capital and property of the partnership against his separate debts and all expenses relating thereto.

ITEM TEN

AUTHORITY

No partner shall buy any goods or articles into any contract exceeding the value of_____ Dollars ($_____) without the prior consent in writing of the other partners; or the other partners shall have the option to take the goods or accept the contract on account of the partnership or let the goods remain the sole property of the partner who shall have obligated himself.

ITEM ELEVEN

EMPLOYEE MANAGEMENT

No partner shall hire or dismiss any person in the employment of the partnership without the consent of the other partners, except in cases of gross misconduct by the employee.

ITEM TWELVE

SALARY

No partner shall receive any salary from the partnership, and the only compensation to be paid shall be as provided in Items Five and Fourteen herein.

178

ITEM THIRTEEN

DEATH OF PARTNER

In the event of the death of one partner, the legal representative of the deceased partner shall remain as a partner in the firm, except that the exercising of the right on the part of the representative of the deceased partner shall not continue for a period

in excess of _____ months, even though under the terms hereof a greater period of time is provided before the termination of this agreement. The original rights of the partners herein shall accrue to their heirs, executors, or assigns.

ITEM FOURTEEN

ADVANCE DRAWS

Each partner shall be at liberty to draw out of the business in anticipation of the expected profits any sums that may be mutually agreed on, and the sums are to be drawn only after there has been entered in the books of the partnership the terms of agreement, giving the date, the amount to be drawn by the respective partners, the time at which the sums shall be drawn, and any other conditions or matters mutually agreed on. The signatures of each partner shall be affixed thereon. The total sum of the advance draw for each partner shall be deducted from the sum that partner is entitled to under the distribution of profits as provided for in Item Five of this agreement.

ITEM FIFTEEN

RETIREMENT

In the event any partner shall desire to retire from the partnership, he shall give _____ months' notice in writing to

the other partners and the continuing partners shall pay to the retiring partner at the termination of the _____ months' notice the value of the interest of the retiring partner in the partnership. The value shall be determined by a closing of the books and a rendition of the appropriate profit and loss, trial balance, and balance sheet statements. All disputes arising therefrom shall be determined as provided in Item Eighteen.

ITEM SIXTEEN

RIGHTS OF CONTINUING PARTNERS

On the retirement of any partner, the continuing partners shall be at liberty, if they so desire, to retain all trade names designating the firm name used, and each of the partners shall sign and execute assignments, instruments, or papers that shall be reasonably required for effectuating an amicable retirement.

ITEM SEVENTEEN

ADDITIONAL CONTRIBUTIONS

The partners shall not have to contribute any additional capital to the partnership to that required under Item Three herein, except as follows: (1) each partner shall be required to contribute a proportionate share in additional contributions if the fiscal year closes with an insufficiency in the capital account of profits of the partnership to meet current expenses, or (2) the

capital account falls below _____ Dollars ($_____) for a period of

_____ months.

ITEM EIGHTEEN

ARBITRATION

If any differences shall arise between or among partners as to their rights or liabilities under this agreement, or under any instrument made in furtherance of the partnership business, the difference shall be determined and the instrument shall be

settled by _____ , acting as arbitrator, and his decision shall be final as to the contents and interpretations of the instrument and as to the proper mode of carrying the provision into effect.

ITEM NINETEEN

RELEASE OF DEBTS

No partner shall compound, release, or discharge any debt that shall be due or owing to the partnership, without receiving the full amount thereof, unless that partner obtains the prior written consent of the other partners to the discharge of the indebtedness.

ITEM TWENTY

ADDITIONS, ALTERATIONS, OR MODIFICATIONS

Where it shall appear to the partners that this agreement, or any terms and conditions contained herein, are in any way ineffective or deficient, or not expressed as originally intended, and any alteration or addition shall be deemed necessary, the partners will enter into, execute, and perform all further deeds and instruments as their counsel shall advise. Any addition, alteration, or modification shall be in writing, and no oral agreement shall be effective.

In witness whereof, the parties have executed this agreement on _____ the day and year first above written.

Courtesy of General Business Service, Inc.

A. The formation of a corporation constitutes the formation of a separate legal entity under state law. It is essential that the services of a competent local attorney be obtained to help the client file the Articles of Incorporation and meet the terms of the state law.

B. Below is a sample election for the corporation to be treated as a Section 1244 small business corporation. This is included so that the client may have it available to discuss with his attorney.

C. Following is a list of steps that will be necessary for a new corporation. It should not be deemed to be all inclusive. It is not intended to be used as substitution to the client of a competent attorney.

1. Incorporators -- Have a meeting of the incorporators and determine the following:

   a. The corporate name
   b. The classes and number of shares to authorize
   c. Business purpose for which the corporation is formed
   d. Initial capital needed
   e. Determine the directors
   f. Location of business
   g. Determine corporate officers and salaries
   h. Check on thin incorporation

2. Determine Start-Up Date -- If the corporation is to take over a going business, a start-up date should be set at some time in the future, so that all steps can be taken without unnecessary haste.

3. Corporate Name -- Check at once with the Secretary of State to see if the corporate name is available.

4. Notify the following:
   a. Insurance Company -- have policies changed. May also be necessary to increase coverage.
   b. Creditors -- inform all creditors of former business.
   c. Customers -- inform all customers of former business.
   d. State and local authorities -- such as state unemployment and disability department and county assessor.

5. Transfer of Assets and Liabilities -- If the corporation is to take over a going business, determine what assets and liabilities are to be turned over to the corporation, and shares or notes to be issued in exchange. Does it qualify as a tax-free exchange under IRC Sec. 3.

6. Banks -- Select bank or banks and furnish resolution authorizing who is to sign checks and negotiate loans.

7. Identification Number -- File application for an Identification No., Federal Form SS-4.

8. Workmen's Compensation -- File for coverage.

9. Unemployment Insurance -- File for coverage.

10. Special Licenses -- Check on transfer of new license such as food, drug, cigarette, liquor, etc.

11. Final Returns -- If the new corporation is taking over a going business,

file Sales Tax, FICA Tax, Unemployment Tax and Workmen's Compensation final returns for the old business after the corporation takes over the operation of the new business.

12. Federal Unemployment -- Determine if final Form 940, Employer's Annual Federal Unemployment Tax return is to be filed on old business.

13. Sales Tax -- Obtain a new sales tax vendor's license on the first day of business. Do not use any tax stamps purchased by the former business or do not use the plate from the former business.

14. Tax Elections:

a. Election under Subchapter S -- Determine if the corporation is going to elect to be taxed as a partnership under Subchapter S. If so, prepare and file Form 2553, Election by Small Business Corporation, within thirty days after the first day of fiscal year or date new corporation commences to "do business."

b. Section 1244 Stock -- If corporation is eligible, issue stock in accordance with a written plan included in the minutes.

c. Year Ending -- Determine the date the corporation's year will end.

d. Accounting -- Determine the method of accounting the corporation will use.

SAMPLE PLAN FOR SEC. 1244 STOCK OFFER   (for inclusion in minutes)

This Corporation is a small business corporation as defined in Sec. 1244(c)(2) of the Internal Revenue Code of 1954.

The Board of Directors wishes to offer for sale and issue shares of its common stock authorized by its Certificate of Incorporation; and

That the offer, sale and issue of such shares be carried out in such a manner that, in the hands of qualified shareholders, such shares will receive the benefits of Sec. 1244 of the Internal Revenue Code of 1954; and

Whereas, there is not now outstanding any offering, or portion thereof, of this Corporation to sell or issue any of its stock; and

*Now, therefore, be it resolved, that the President of this Corporation and such other officers as he may designate be, and hereby are, authorized and directed to offer for sale and to sell and to issue up to   shares of the common stock in the total amount of $ * at $ per share payable in cash or other property** during the period from the date hereof to   ** or to the date when this Corporation shall make a subsequent offering of any stock, whichever shall first occur.*

*   Total amount subject to limitations.

** Stock issued for stock or securities may not qualify.

***This period must not be more than two years from the date of the plan.

Courtesy of General Business Service, Inc.

Blank Forms for Projection of Financial Statements

PROJECTION OF FINANCIAL STATEMENTS

SUBMITTED BY _____

		ACTUAL	PROJECTIONS →									
SPREAD IN HUNDREDS ☐	DATE											
SPREAD IN THOUSANDS ☐	PERIOD											

PROFIT and LOSS

1	NET SALES											1
2												2
3												3
4	Less: Materials Used											4
5	COST OF GOODS SOLD											5
6	GROSS PROFIT											6
7	Less: Sales Expense											7
8	General & Administrative Expense											8
9	Depreciation											9
10												10
11	OPERATING PROFIT											11
12	Less: Other Expense											12
13	Add: Other Income											13
14	PRE-TAX PROFIT											14
15	Income Tax Provision											15
16	NET PROFIT											16

CASH PROJECTION

17	CASH BALANCE (Opening)											17
18	Add: Receipts: Cash Sales & Other Income											18
19	Cash Sales Plus Receivable Collections											19
20												20
21												21
22	Bank Loan Proceeds											22
23	Other Loan Proceeds											23
24	TOTAL CASH AND RECEIPTS											24
25	Less: Disbursements: Trade Payables											25
26	Direct Labor											26
27	OPERATING & OTHER EXPENSES											27
28												28
29	Capital Expenditures											29
30	Income Taxes											30
31	Dividends or Withdrawals											31
32	Bank Loan Repayment											32
33	Other Loan Repayment											33
34	TOTAL CASH DISBURSEMENTS											34
35	CASH BALANCE (Closing)											35

BALANCE SHEET

36	ASSETS: Cash and Equivalents											36
37	Receivables											37
38	Inventory (Net)											38
39												39
40	CURRENT ASSETS											40
41	Fixed Assets (Net)											41
42												42
43												43
44												44
45	TOTAL ASSETS											45
46	LIABILITIES: Notes Payable-Banks											46
47	Notes Payable-Others											47
48	Trade Payables											48
49	Income Tax Payable											49
50	Current Portion L.T.D.											50
51												51
52	CURRENT LIABILITIES											52
53	Long-Term Liabilities:											53
54												54
55												55
56	TOTAL LIABILITIES											56
57	NET WORTH: Capital Stock											57
58	Retained Earnings											58
59												59
60	TOTAL LIABILITIES AND NET WORTH											60

RMA's Projection of Financial Statements, Form C-117, may be completed by the banker, the customer, or both working together. It is designed to be flexible and may be used as a:

1) <u>Projection</u> tool to provide a picture of the customer's present and future financial condition. Actual and estimated financial data form the basis of the calculations.

2) <u>Tool for analysis</u> of the customer's borrowing needs and debt repayment ability.

3) <u>Budget</u> to aid in planning for the customer's financial requirements and repaying the banker's credit accommodation.

INSTRUCTIONS: In the first column, enter the actual PROFIT AND LOSS STATEMENT and BALANCE SHEET of the date immediately prior to projection period. Then, in each subsequent column, covering a projection period (e.g., month, quarter, annual):

- Enter on the "date" line, the ending date of each projection period (e.g., 1/31, 3/31, 19____)
- Enter on the "period" line the length of each projection period (e.g., 1 mo., 3 mos., 12 mos.)
- Then, follow the line-by-line instructions below:

Line No.	Title	Instructions

PROFIT AND LOSS STATEMENT

Line No.	Title	Instructions
1	NET SALES	Enter actual or beginning net sales figure in the first vertical column. We suggest you project future net sales based upon a % sales increase or decrease. Estimate acceptable % figure and record here _____%. (This % is generally calculated based on historical changes in net sales. However, consideration must also be given to factors, such as general business conditions, new products and services, and competition.)
2 through 5	COST OF GOODS SOLD	Enter all relevant components of customer's cost of goods sold calculation. Project future cost of goods sold based upon % increase or decrease. Estimate acceptable percentage figure and insert here _____%. (This figure is generally estimated as a percentage of sales based on prior years.)
6	GROSS PROFIT	Line 1 minus line 5.
7 through 10	Sales Expense; General and Administrative Expenses; Other	Enter all items. Project future expenses based on an increase or decrease. Estimate acceptable percentage figure and insert here _____%. (This figure is generally estimated as a percentage of sales based on prior years. Anticipated increases in major expenses, such as lease, officers' salaries, etc., should also be considered.)
11	OPERATING PROFIT	Line 6 minus the sum of lines 7 through 10.
12 through 13	Various adjustments to Operating Profit	Enter all items and estimate future adjustments.
14	PRE-TAX PROFIT	Line 11 minus the sum of lines 12 through 13.
15	Income Tax Provision	Common methods used for calculating Income Tax Provision include the most current year's tax as a % of the Pre-Tax Profit.
16	NET PROFIT	Line 11 minus the sum of lines 12 through 15.

CASH PROJECTION CALCULATION

Line No.	Title	Instructions
17	CASH BALANCE	Enter opening cash balance. For subsequent periods, enter the closing cash balance (Line 35) from previous period. Or enter an adjusted amount to reflect a desired cash balance.
18 through 21	Receipts	Enter total cash sales & other income plus receivables collected. Receivable collections must be calculated separately. This requires an analysis of the customer's sales and collection patterns:

(1) Estimate the portion of each month's sales collected in that month and subsequent months.

(2) From the sale's figure last month and the previous month(s), calculate how much of the existing receivable figure will be collected in the current month.

(3) Deduct the collected receivables balance calculated in (2) above from the month-end balance of accounts receivables.

(4) Add this month's sales figure to the remainder of receivables calculated in (3) above. This figure is the new accounts receivable figure for the end of the current month.

EXAMPLE Assumptions:

Projection calculation - monthly

Monthly Net Sales:	9/30 - $250M
	10/31 - $300M
	11/30 - $150M

| Accounts Receivable balance: | 9/30 - $250M |
| | 10/31 - $367M |

The average collection period is 45 days. This means that 66.7% (30 days ÷ 45 days) of each month's sales will be collected the following month and the remaining 33.3% in the second month.

To determine receivable collections for November --

Accounts Receivable balance, 10/31		$367M
Deduct: 66% of 10/31 sales	200M	
33% of 9/30 sales	83M	283M
		84M
Add: 11/30 sales		150M
Accounts Receivable Balance, 11/30		$234M

Line No.	Title	Instructions
22 through 23	Bank Loan Proceeds/ Other	Enter actual or projected bank loan proceeds on line 22. Enter any other receipts on line 23.
24	TOTAL CASH AND RECEIPTS	Enter sum of lines 17 through 23.
25 through 33	Disbursements	Enter actual or estimated cash disbursements on these lines.
34	TOTAL DISBURSEMENTS	Enter sum of lines 25 through 33.
35	CASH BALANCE (Closing)	Line 24 minus line 34. Note: The closing cash balance on line 35 may be entered on line 17 in the next column. However, if the closing cash balance is negative, or below the desired opening cash balance, then bank loans (line 22) may be needed to raise the closing cash balance to zero, or to the desired opening cash balance. The bank loan necessitates planning for repayment (line 31 and 32) in subsequent columns.

185

BALANCE SHEET

(36 through 44)	**ASSETS**	
36	Cash and Equivalents	Enter cash and readily marketable securities--current year only. For subsequent years use the closing cash balance (line 35).
37	Receivables	Enter actual receivables in the first column. To project, use previous receivables figure plus projected net sales (line 1), minus projected cash sales and receivables collections (line 19).
38	Inventory	Enter actual inventory in the first column. To project, add purchases to beginning inventory. Then, subtract materials used to calculate the ending inventory amount (lines 2 through 4). If the inventory purchase figure is not available, balances can be calculated based on historic turnover ratios.
40	Current Assets	Enter sum of lines 36 through 39.
41	Fixed Assets (Net)	Enter fixed assets. To project, add previous year's fixed assets and any fixed asset additions. Then, deduct estimated accumulated depreciation.
42 through 44		Enter other non-current assets (stockholder's receivables, intangibles, etc.).
45	TOTAL ASSETS	Add lines 40 through 44.
(46 through 56)	**LIABILITIES**	
46	Notes Payable-Banks	Prior period balance plus loan proceeds (line 22), less repayments (line 32).
47	Notes Payable-Others	Prior period balance plus note proceeds (line 23), less repayments (line 32).
48	Trade Payables	Prior period balance plus purchases less payments (line 25). If the inventory purchase figure is not available, balances can be projected based on historic payables turnover.
49	Income Tax Payable	Add prior period balance to income tax provision (line 14) and deduct income taxes paid (line 30).
50	Current Portion Long-Term Debt	Estimate current maturities by entering the sum of prior period debt's maturities and additional bank loan proceeds scheduled repayments.
51		Enter the sum of any other current liabilities.
52	CURRENT LIABILITIES	Enter the sum of lines 46 through 51.
53 through 55	Long-Term Liabilities	Enter long-term liabilities here. Calculate long-term debt by adding previous period long-term debt (line 53) to loan proceeds (line 22 & 23), and subtracting current maturities (line 50).
56	TOTAL LIABILITIES	Enter sum of lines 52 through 55.
(57 through 59)	**NET WORTH**	
57	Capital Stock	Enter current capital stock figure. An increase will occur if capital stock is sold; a decrease will occur if existing stock is repurchased or retired.
58	Retained Earnings	Add prior period retained earnings to projected net profit (line 16), and deduct dividends or withdrawals (line 31).
59		Enter other equity items.
60	TOTAL LIABILITIES AND NET WORTH	Enter sum of lines 56 through 59.

Actual Business Plans

1. Storage Technology Inc.
2. *Venture* Magazine, Inc.
3. Shopsmith, Inc.

These three business plans are copies of the *original* documents used to launch three of America's premier multimillion dollar businesses. They are taken from the Archive of Business Plans, housed at the Center for Entrepreneurial Management Inc., 83 Spring Street, New York, N.Y. 10012 (212–925–7304). This nonprofit worldwide membership association of small company presidents released the following press releases to describe its archive. The three plans are offered only as examples of what was actually used to launch major U.S. businesses, not as examples of good or bad business plans.

**THE CENTER FOR
ENTREPRENEURIAL
MANAGEMENT**
83 Spring Street
New York. N.Y. 10012
(212) 925-7304

Joseph R. Mancuso, President

FOR IMMEDIATE RELEASE

BUSINESS PLAN ARCHIVES

Entrepreneurs are the cowboys of today's business world. Instead of being launched out of a pen on the back of a Brahma bull, they are being let loose on the backs of fledgling businesses - which can be an equally bumpy, and short-lived, proposition. In Silicon Valley, about 50 miles south of San Francisco, a B.Y.O.B. on a party invitation has nothing to do with a bottle - it means Bring Your Own Business Plan! the ticket of admission to this growing fraternity of mavericks.

If you've ever wondered what turns good ideas into money, you need wonder no more. No, it's not some modern form of alchemy, though to the uninitiated it might seem just as elusive. The catalyst is the business plan, the blueprint of the business world. And Joseph Mancuso, president of The Center for Entrepreneurial Management and author of How to Prepare & Present a Business Plan, has an ongoing fascination with the business plans that were used to launch America's top businesses. Says Mancuso, "I'm collecting these old plans in the same way that someone else might collect old cars: they aren't exactly for driving any more, but they still have the charm of a Model T."

The purpose of this unique archive, according to Mancuso, is to preserve the original documents for future reference. "It would be a shame if we lost the plans that launched businesses like Hewlett-Packard, or McDonald's, or Polaroid. They should probably be kept in the Library of Congress, but since no one there seems to be making the effort, we decided to do it."

The Center for Entrepreneurial Management is a non-profit, membership association of small business owners and entrepreneurs, located at 83 Spring Street, New York, NY 10012; (212-925-7304). The business plan archive is available for public inspection Monday through Friday from 10:00 a.m. to 4:00 p.m.

"Several of these plans are truly fascinating and well worth a trip to New York City just to see them," says Mancuso. "I especially like Jesse Aweida's plan that started

Storage Technology in 1969, because it's so simple and straightforward. And, of course, it's a joy to see how Nolan Bushnell (founder of Atari) used his knowledge and experience to develop the plan that launched his current success, Pizza Time Theatre. We also have one of the early versions of Freddy Smith's Federal Express."

In addition to the plans for famous businesses, Mancuso has acquired plans for solid performers like Steven Anderson's Medical Graphics, as well as several plans for current start-ups which he feels have a shot at becoming famous. "It's a real education in entrepreneurship to study these old plans," says Mancuso, "because they are actually a window onto the entrepreneurial personality. The business plan is the tangible personification of the entrepreneur's dream."

Thus far, CEM has solicited business plans primarily from the Inc. and Venture "100" lists of the country's fastest growing businesses. However, entrepreneurs in general are encouraged to send along a copy of their business plans for inclusion in CEM's growing archive. The plans will not be reproduced, and will be available for on-sight inspection only.

2270 South 88th Street
Louisville, Colorado 80027
(303) 673-5000

Jesse I. Aweida
Chairman and
Chief Executive Officer

 Storage Technology Corporation

August 10, 1983

Mr. Joseph Mancuso
The Center for
Entrepreneurial Management
83 Spring Street
New York, New York 10012

Dear Mr. Mancuso:

In accordance with your request of July 15, enclosed
is the first business plan of the company dated
June 1969. Our date of incorporation is August 11,
1969.

I wish to thank you for the subscription to your
newsletter ENTREPRENEURIAL MANAGER also. I look
forward to receiving it.

Very truly yours,

Jesse I. Aweida

/v

190

NEW BUSINESS PLAN: DATA STORAGE DEVICES*

Rough draft. Contents of this document are CONFIDENTIAL and should not be disclosed. This plan was prepared by Jesse I. Aweida, June, 1969.

Summary

This proposal summarizes all the pertinent information related to the establishment of a new business in the fastest expanding segment on the computer industry, namely, the I/O area. At no time has the market been as ready and accepting of such a venture as the present. Some of the highlights of this proposal are briefly summarized below:

- The talent and experience of the founding group in the type of business to be pursued is superior to any in the industry.
- The product is the fastest expanding segment in the computer industry.
- The market in this type of equipment for OEM manufacturers is upwards of $80 million annually. Sales are expected to multiply rapidly, and we expect to become leaders in the high-performance tape drive business within five years.
- With the advanced and highly reliable design that the founders will produce, it is a conservative estimate that this company will capture a minimum of 30% of this market within five years, which is $24 million.
- Profitability is assured by the market requirements of this product, proven productivity and experiences of the founding group, and the low-cost manufacturing means that will be employed.

Data Storage Devices

Statement of Objectives: The company is being formed for the purpose of engaging in the development, production, and marketing of computer peripheral products with early and profitable operation as the prime goal.

*This name was later changed to Storage Technology.

1. Product Line

   i) Initial Product: IBM 2420 plug-to-plug compatible drives, equal in operation to the IBM hardware but superior in reliability.

   ii) Short Term: Add a lower speed model to the initial product line. Offer a controller that interfaces between the drives and the processor.

   iii) Long Term: Low-cost tape drive line. Initial product in this line will be a low-speed device that uses a cassette.

      Also, at all times, the company will pursue new technologies for introduction into new devices, thus broadening the base and accelerating the growth.

2. The company aims to become the leader in the tape drive and other related businesses. The capabilities, experience, and background of its founding group supports this aim.

3. Our product will be superior to any in the market. The IBM 2420 line will be used as a base to which improvements will be added. Only the knowledge and experience of the founding group can accomplish such an objective in the time allowed.

4. Timely introduction of the product will be accomplished through a relatively short development cycle for this type of equipment, which is 18 months from start of operations to first customer shipment.

5. Service to our customers will be emphasized throughout our operations. High degree of reliability and availability coupled with quick service will be implemented to gain early and continuing customer acceptance and satisfaction.

6. Early growth and profit will result in a healthy return on our stockholders' investment.

Industry

The Product to be offered falls in the fastest expanding segment of the computer industry, namely, the input–output area. Computer hardware generally consists of three distinct segments: central processor, memory, and input–output. Under the input–output products fall low-speed devices, such as punched cards and printers, as well as high-speed high-performance devices, such as disk drives and tape drives. The disk drives are used for direct access applications as extensions of the main memory, while tape drives are used for large capacity storage where the information is processed serially for applications, such as payroll, inventory control, and other commercial and scientific types of jobs. The low cost of the tape media and the large capacity storage available makes tape drives economically attractive with continued projected growth.

Tape drives and disk drives often compete for the same application. The random access capability of disk drives makes them attractive, but the economics of having a complete library on line is not feasible. The low-cost storage of magnetic tape and the great many jobs that adapt themselves to serial processing coupled with the huge libraries and program developed for tape applications are keeping the tape drive market growing at a healthy rate. 1968 Auerbach Corporation's report on magnetic tape recording compares magnetic tape and disk packs. Among other things, it shows that the cost per million bytes stored on tape is $1.03, while disk storage for the same capacity is $22.30.

Product Line

Initial Product. The Company plans to pursue vigorously and at an accelerated pace the development, production, and marketing of two models of tape drives that are plug-to-plug compatible with the IBM 2420 line. These products will be superior to any other products on the market. Reliability will be built in the hardware by a simplified design, substituting electrical circuitry and pneumatics for mechanical mechanisms whenever possible, reducing the number of adjustments, using the reliable phase encoding method of recording, and by offering automatic threading as a standard feature. Cartridge loading and NRZI capabilities will be offered on an optional basis.

Characteristics of these two models that will be developed concurrently are shown in Figure 1.

Figure 1

	PRODUCT LINE	
	DSD 2425	*DSD 2427*
Tape speed (ips)	100	200
Start time (ms)	3	2
Rewind time (sec)	72 (linear)	60 (linear)
Loading Method	Auto	Auto
Driving Method	Single capstan	Single capstan
Density (bpi)	1600	1600
Recording Method	Phase encoding	Phase encoding
Data rate (kb)	160	320
IBG (inches)	.6	.6
Tracks	9	9
Using Systems	360/30 and up	360/50 and up
	OEM	OEM
Features:		
Recording	NRZI	NRZI
Cartridge loading	Yes	Yes

Short Term Product. In the second year of business and after the initial product is developed, the company will pursue the development of a lower speed drive and a controller.

LOW-SPEED DRIVE: This drive will move tape at 50 ips and will have all the reliability and set-up time improvements of the initial product. Design emphasis will be given to reducing cost without affecting reliability. This device will be aimed at small system users, i.e., 360/20 and 360/30, most of whom do not take advantage of the IBM 2420 line due to either unavailability of a low enough data rate or cost.

CONTROLLER: The controller will be designed to handle the company's drives and their IBM equivalent. It will be offered concurrently with the low-speed drive and will have the capability to control it. The addition of a controller to the product line will give the company flexibility in satisfying market demands. It will give us the ability to offer improvements in reliability and performance without having to hold them back due to the unavailability of a competitive controller that can handle them. For example, we will not be able to offer the lower speed drive on the schedule shown due to the unavailability of a competitive controller at that time.

Long Term Products. For the long term, the company plans to extend its basic line both in speed and density of recording.

Also, a low-speed, low-cost line will be introduced. This line will consist of devices that generate ½-inch compatible tapes as well as noncompatible devices that use cassettes.

Schedule. Development, production entry, and first customer shipment schedule for the initial and short-term products are shown in Figure 2.

Figure 2. Product Introduction Schedule.

Competition

Computer manufacturers generally offer input–output devices with their systems. Most companies manufacture their own I/O equipment, including tape drives; others purchase them from OEM manufacturers. The most advanced tape drive subsystem offered to date is the IBM 2420, which reestablished IBM as the leader in this field. Other computer manufacturers, such as Burroughs and Univac, usually buy their tape drives from OEM manufacturers. Honeywell and CDC, on the other hand, have been developing their own. None of the computer manufacturers have come up with a significant high-performance tape drive announcement recently, making it possible that they may purchase their future high-performance tape drive requirements from OEM sources.

In the OEM area, the key competitors are Potter, Telex, and Ampex. The first two have announced their intention to produce IBM 2420 compatible devices, and Potter has recently demonstrated an engineering model of a 200 ips drive.

The basic competitive strategy to be used by the company will consist of offering a superior product at a lower cost with a small price differential between the different models. The superiority of the initial product will be in the area of reliability and serviceability. Performance, on the other hand, will match that of the IBM 2420 to allow for plug-to-plug compatibility.

Our competitive position will be further enhanced by offering an IBM plug-to-plug compatible controller that will give us flexibility and freedom in offering performance and operational improvements. None of the OEM competitors offer controllers; therefore, they cannot offer improvements that are not consistent with what the computer manufacturers' controllers can handle.

To further gain early customer acceptance and satisfaction, a strong service organization will be established early and expanded as required.

A brief summary of the key OEM competitors is given below.

Potter.   Potter Instrument was incorporated in 1942 as a manufacturer of counters and timers. The company now has a line of computer peripherals and a numerical control system for machine tools. The computer peripherals include printers, a random access tape loop device, and a range of tape drives for the military and OEM market. Their SC1080 tape drive is a single capstan IBM-compatible unit designed as a replacement for the IBM 729 and 2401 drives.

Potter's main facilities are situated in Plainview, Long Island and consist of four plants with approximately 170,000 square feet of floor space. In addition they have 12,000 square feet of space in Puerto Rico. Yearly sales are over $30 million, with tape transports accounting for over 60% of their business.

Potter markets to OEM and through MAI. They market the end user. The agreement with MAI retains the Washington, DC area for direct marketing to end users by Potter. The tie-in with MAI has had the effect of almost doubling Potter's tape drive sales during the past year.

Potter has announced and delivered 150 ips at 1600 bpi phase encoded drives to Burroughs early this year. They have also made known their intentions of building a 200 ips drive with automatic threading.

Technical support to system manufacturers is provided, but field service is the responsibility of the system manufacturer or the marketing organization. This is also the case with MAI, which leases and sells Potter drives to the end user.

Potter's main marketing stragety consists of lower prices, which generally run ⅓ less than IBM.

Telex.   The tape drive subsidiary of Telex Corporation is Midwestern Instruments. Their other two subsidiaries are Telex Communications and Home Entertainment (Viking). Midwestern offers a drive that is compatible with the IBM 729 and 2401, along with other tape recording and reproducing equipment.

They sell tape drives in two markets: OEM and end user. Selective marketing is done, in that the marketing effort is directed toward blue-chip accounts in large metropolitan areas. This contains the problem of service to selected geographical areas and permits orderly build-up of trained service people. (In April 1969, Telex reached an agreement with ISS, a new disk drive manufacturer whereby Telex will also market ISS's disk drives in the U.S. and Mexico.)

Net sales of Telex are around $50 million annually, and Midwestern products in total account for approximately 20% of Telex's business.

Midwestern's marketing strategy consists of offering compatible drives at purchase prices up to 55% below IBM's. The big question is one of hardware performance and field service. Their plug-to-plug compatible drive uses a pneumatic drive system with questionable reliability.

A year ago Telex announced a 200 ips and 1600 bpi phase encoded drive. This drive has not been shown and its state of development is not known. If their plan is to speed up the present pneumatic capstan design to 200 ips, they'll have many technical problems and will still end up with an unreliable drive. That is possibly the reason for their silence regarding this new product. If, on the other hand, they have decided to build a new drive mechanism, it will take them at least two years to develop a product competitive with the IBM 2420.

Ampex.   The primary product line of the Ampex Corporation includes all phases of magnetic recording. This includes the design and manufacture of digital and analog tape drives, magnetic components, and magnetic tape.

They have been successful in analog instrumentation recorders and video. Their product line now includes a single capstan tape drive that is directly interchangeable with IBM's 729 and 2401 NRZI drives.

The digital tape unit division has about 400 employees and approximately 60,000 square feet devoted to magnetic tape handlers.

Ampex has been selling their digital tape drives to system manufacturers. In 1968 they announced and demonstrated their TM 16 single capstan drive, which is fully compatible with IBM's 729 and 2401. They also announced that this new tape drive will be serviced by Ampex Corporation's nationwide service organization.

During the past few years, Ampex has been slowly losing its position as a leader in the tape drive business and has raised basic questions as to their ability to compete in this market. Many of their key tape drive people have left, which in turn resulted in a weak tape drive operation. This weakness was recently demonstrated by their loss of a substantial contract with DPF&G, which consisted of supplying the leasing company with IBM plug-to-plug compatible tape drives valued at over $10 million.

Ampex has not supplied 1600 bpi phase encoding type of recording on any of their devices to date, which further supports their weakness in this field.

Based on the above, Ampex's ability to deliver high-performance drives competitive with the IBM 2420 line within the next two to three years is highly questionable.

Business and Computer Devices.   This new company was formed during the last part of 1968 by ex-Potter people for the purpose of developing low-cost, low-performance tape drives. In April 1969, they made known their intent to develop and produce IBM 2420 compatible drives for DPF&G under a $10 million contract.

The expertise in high-performance drive development does not exist in this new company, and their efforts to hire the required talent have not been successful to date.

Characteristics of the major competitive tape drives are shown in Figure 3. The DSD 2425 and DSD 2427 are the two new models to be offered by our company.

Product Development

The engineering team will consist of capable and talented tape drive subsystem engineers who have broad experience and proven accomplishments in tape drive design. Their aim will be to develop a product that matches the performance characteristics of the IBM 2420 line (to allow for plug-to-plug compatibility) but with improvements in reliability and service for a relatively low manufacturing cost.

Figure 3: Characteristics of Competitive Drives

	AMPEX TM16	MAI 2406	TELEX 4840	IBM 2420–5	IBM 2420–7	DSD 2425	DSD 2427
IBM 2420 Compatibility	No	No	Not Proven	—	—	Yes	Yes
Rent/Month ($)	—	550	—	580	1050	440	625
Purchase (K$)	18	23.9	—	30.16	54.6	17	22
Speed ("/sec)	112.5	112.5	200	100	200	100	200
Start/Stop (ms)	3/3	4/4	2/2	3	2	3	2
Rewind (sec)	90	100	—	72	60	72	60
Load method	Manual	Manual	—	Auto	Auto	Auto	Auto
Drive (capstan)	Single	Single	—	Single	Single	Single	Single
Recording	NRZI	PE	PE	PE	PE	PE	PE
Density (Bpi)	800	1600	1600	1600	1600	1600	1600
Data rate (kb)	90	180	320	160	320	160	320
Cartridge	No	No	—	Yes	Yes	Yes	Yes
Announce date	Avail	Avail	5/68*	12/68	1/68	8/70	8/70
Delivery date	Avail	Avail	—	11/69	11/68	1/71	1/71

*Not shown yet

One basic design will be established for all the tape drive models. Differences will be restricted to speed and read–write circuit changes, which account for less than 10% of the hardware.

Modularity of design will be stressed throughout. All major subassemblies will be designed in easily replaceable packages, which are adaptable to efficient manufacturability and serviceability.

Reliability will be further enhanced by using the latest known technology in tape motion and controls, by using the reliable phase encoding method of recording, and by developing a simple design that eliminates or minimizes the need for most adjustments, one that replaces the inherently unreliable mechanical mechanisms by electronic circuitry and pneumatics wherever possible. Gentle handling of tapes and reduction in set-up time will be also stressed. Cartridge loading and NRZI capabilities will be offered on an optional basis.

The engineering effort will not terminate with the product release to manufacturing. The completion of the prototypes will signal the start of the second engineering phase, which will be a product stabilization phase. This effort will consist of stress testing, field trials, and the establishment of a Field Product Engineering group. The aim of this effort is to shake down the product prior to First Customer Shipment. Testing will be performed across the range of environmental and operational conditions, using varied customer programs and evaluating the effects of parts' tolerances and quality.

The Product Field Engineering group will be active during this stage and after customer shipments, with the sole aim of insuring good product operation and customer satisfaction.

The above program will result in early stabilization of the manufacturing process, thus allowing for an efficient manufacturing plan with the feasibility of early hard tooling.

The modularity of design will have the added advantage of maximizing the product up-time. The customer engineer only has to isolate the problem to a major subassembly; the quick replacement of such assembly will get the product on the air again. Malfunctioning subassemblies will be repaired and used again. This method has the added advantage of eliminating the need for highly trained service personnel to service our equipment.

Marketing

At no time has the market been as ready and accepting of independent tape drive manufacturers as the present. Attaching competitive input–output devices on IBM and other manufacturers' systems is getting end users' acceptance and has been multiplying at a rapid rate. Over 1500 competitive high performance drives were installed during the last half of this period, a trend that is expected to continue.

The high-performance tape drive market has been expanding at over 30% annually. This rate of growth is faster than that of the basic computers. The reason for it is the continued upgrading of users from small to larger and more powerful systems, which require high-performance devices to improve the throughput; also, emphasis on higher reliability and higher performance makes a great many of today's drives obsolete and creates the need to replace them by newer, better devices. It is estimated that by 1974, approximately 75,000 2420 or equivalent types of drives will be installed. On this total, approximately 65% will be installed on IBM systems.

The company aims to capture 6.5% of the total high-performance tape drive market by our fifth year of business. Since we plan to concentrate our marketing activity on users of IBM systems, this portion of the business adds up to approximately 10% of the tape drives installed on IBM hardware that year.

The company's marketing activity will start immediately after start of operations and will consist of concentrating on computer manufacturers, leasing companies, and large users, with the aim of obtaining a sizable contract. During this period, the company plans to pursue the possibility of reaching an agreement with a large user or an independent corporation that has the resources, organization, and know-how to handle both marketing and service of our products.

Public announcement of the initial products will take place one year after start of operations and will be heavily publicized in trade journals, brochures, and shows. The drives will be exhibited at IFIPS, Computer Machinery, and other conferences. By this time, the company would have either worked out an agreement with another concern for marketing and service or decided to market its own products. If the latter is decided, regional offices will be established in New York, Chicago, and Los Angeles, and selling will be concentrated on end users in these highly industrialized areas. After drives have been built and successfully accepted, more sales officers will be established with the possibility of adding an International Division. It is estimated that by 1974 peripherals on internationally installed systems will be equal to half those installed domestically.

Manufacturing

The manufacturing operation will start concurrently with the development cycle when manufacturing and quality engineers are assigned to work hand-in-hand with the development people. This early entry program will result in a value engineering design. It is also expected that processes, vendors, and tooling will be established by the time the product is released to manufacturing. This in turn will result in compressing the manufacturing entry cycle and reducing product cost.

Initially, specialty vendors will be used whenever possible and tooling expenses will be kept to a minimum. As the production volume increases and the cash flow position justifies it, more of the work will be brought in-house. In-house work will result in broadening our direct labor base, minimizing our dependence on outside vendors, and above all, increasing our profitability.

It is estimated that 200 direct manufacturing hours and $6500 material cost will be spent on each unit.

Great emphasis will be given to the quality assurance and materials management functions. The product will go through extensive testing prior to shipment to insure a high level of reliability. Also, the materials management function will be planned to insure the company's ability to deliver the required quantities on schedule and to have the ability to respond quickly to added requirements.

Financial Plans

Initial financial support will be required for the development and manufacturing entry cycles, which will take 18 months from start of operations.

Budgetary and control systems will be incorporated to insure sound financial operation. Expenditures will be carefully monitored and related to the financial plans. These plans are shown on the following pages.

ASSUMPTIONS:

1. Product development and administration costs are figured as 10% of sales each.
2. Marketing expenses are figured as 8% of sales.
3. Tax provision includes one-third, to be paid with tax return.

Sales Forecast

	8/1/69 1ST YEAR	8/1/70 2ND YEAR	8/1/71 3RD YEAR	8/1/72 4TH YEAR	8/1/73 5TH YEAR
Units					
200 ips					
100 ips	—	56	308	520	850
Controller	—	—	20	70	150
50 ips	—	—	40	140	300
New Products[1]	—	—	—	Yes	Yes
Revenue					
($000)					
200 ips					
100 ips	—	1070	5850	9880	16150
Controller	—	—	400	1400	3000
50 ips	—	—	520	1820	3900
New Products	—	—	—	1750	2800
Total Revenue	—	1070	6770	14850	25850
Sale prices					
200 ips	$22,000				
100 ips	$17,000				
Average	$19,000				
Controller	$20,000				
50 ips	$13,000				

[1]New Products developed and produced during this period, such as cassette drives, low-speed drives, higher density drives, and controllers.

Cost of Product Shipped ($000)

	1ST YEAR	2ND YEAR	3RD YEAR	4TH YEAR	5TH YEAR
Product Cost					
200 ips					
100 ips	—	990	2850	4160	6800
Controller	—	—	380	820	1500
50 ips	—	—	450	1200	2100
New Products	—	—	—	760	1300
Total Product Cost	—	990	3680	6940	11700

4. Accounts receivable are figured as 70% of sales.

5. Accounts payable are figured as 20% of other expenses and other expenditures not including taxes.

6. Accrued expense increase is figured as 5% of labor.

7. Miscellaneous expenses include interest and personnel costs.

8. Direct material purchase is figured as 30% of sales for 3rd year and 27% of sales for 4th and 5th years.

Income Statement Forecast ($000)

	1ST YEAR	2ND YEAR	3RD YEAR	4TH YEAR	5TH YEAR
Net Sales					
200 ips					
100 ips	—	1070	5850	9880	16150
Controller	—	—	400	1480	3000
50 ips	—	—	520	1820	3900
New Products	—	—	—	1750	2800
Total Sales	—	1070	6770	14850	25850
Cost of Goods Sold	—	990	3640	6940	11700
Gross Profit	—	80	3130	7910	14150
Other Expenses					
Product Engineering		120	120	105	105
New Product Dev.	519	483	677	1485	2585
Marketing	20	161	540	1190	2070
Administrative	69	131	508	1485	2585
Total	608	895	1845	4265	7345
Pretax net income					
(loss)	(608)	(815)	1285	3645	6805
Tax	—	—	—	1750	3400
Net Income	(608)	(815)	1285	1895	3405
Cumulative Net Income	(608)	(1423)	(138)	1757	5162

9. Manufacturing direct labor is figured as $1600 per box for 3rd year and $1800 per box for 4th and 5th years.
10. Expense labor is figured as 30% of sales for 3rd, 4th, and 5th years.
11. Other expenses are figured as 50% of expense labor for 3rd, 4th, and 5th years.

Management

Experience and occupational history of the management team is technical and in the specific field to be served by the company. Charts for the first two generations of the company's organization, as well as résumés of the principals, follow.

Legal counsel for the company is the law firm of Holland and Hart.

Cash Forecast

	1ST YEAR	2ND YEAR	3RD YEAR	4TH YEAR	5TH YEAR
Direct Mfg Labor	—	115	589	1314	2340
Expense Labor					
Administrative	53	71			
Marketing	19.6	134			
Engineering	242	314			
Manufacturing	35.1	302			
	349.7	821	2020	4450	7730
Other Expenses					
Development Materials	90	80			
Rent & Occupancy	18	30			
Supplies & Tooling	20	100			
Equipment Rental	15	15			
Professional Fees	10	20			
Insurance	5	10			
Travel	15	20			
Miscellaneous[1]	50	127			
	223	402	1010	2225	3865
Other Expenditures					
Income Tax Provisions	—	—	—	1750	3400
Direct Materials					
Purchase	—	810	2020	4000	6950
Capital Asset Purchase	35	60	100	200	250
	35	870	2120	5950	10600
Total Cash Required	608	2208	5739	13939	24535
Cash Provided					
Accounts Receivable	—	750	5060	12430	20620
Accounts Payable					
Inclusive	51	204	426	856	1464
Accrued Expenses	17.5	47	130	210	390
Taxes	—	—	—	525	1000
Additional Equity or Loan[2]	600	1200	200	1500	—
Total Cash Provided	668.5	2201	5296	15021	23474
Cash Balance	60.5	52.5	123.5	1583	522

[1]Includes interest payments and personnel costs.
[2]Public stock issued during 2nd or 4th year.

Organization Chart—First Year.

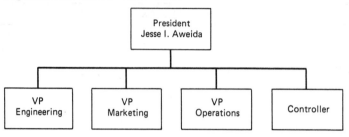

Jessie I. Aweida

Jessie I. Aweida, age 38, has been associated with IBM Corporation from 1956 until now. He holds a BS degree (1956) in Mechanical Engineering from Swarthmore College and an MS degree (1960) from Syracuse University, which he earned as a result of participating in a company sponsored work-study program.

Organization Chart—Third Year.

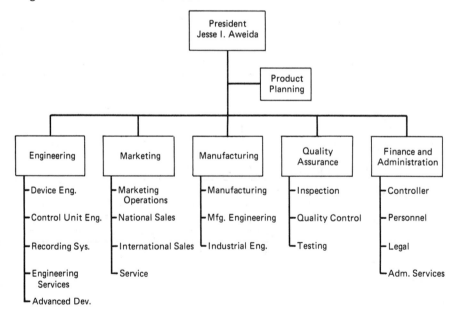

At IBM he is a Senior Engineer and head of the Advanced Tape Drive Department. His main responsibility during the past four and one-half years has been that of Program Manager and Chief Designer of the IBM 2420 Tape Drive Subsystem, which he managed from inception in 1965 to the present. This assignment consisted of complete program responsibility: He established program objectives, technologies, and design direction for both the drive and the control unit. He also managed and solved the major technical problems, met cost objectives, and directed the product engineering and customer acceptance efforts. He was personally responsible for the design of the tape path and the automatic threading systems, which along with other features account for the excellence and success of the IBM 2420. The 2420 is the most advanced tape drive in the market today and is enjoying excellent customer acceptance.

Prior assignments at IBM included that of Development and Design Manager of an on-line library device during 1963–1965 and Project Engineer with responsibility for the tape motion area of the IBM 7340 Hypertape Drive during 1960–1963. His efforts on the 7340 program were instrumental in the successful development of the single capstan drive system, which has become an industry standard. During his first four years at IBM (1956–1960) he performed analysis work on input–output equipment, the majority of which was on tape drives and controls.

During the past nine years, and especially the last four and one-half years, Mr. Aweida worked very closely with marketing, product planning, manufacturing, quality control, and customer engineering, an experience that gives him the required qualifications to produce a product line from conception to successful acceptance by the customer.

Mr. Aweida was awarded the Master Design Award by Product Engineering in 1962; he holds four patents and was awarded IBM's First Invention Award in 1967.

First Year Financial Requirements

The first year financial requirements as shown in Table 1 are based on:

- Schedule and manpower costs as shown in Tables 2 and 3
- Establishing a small model shop
- Developing and building prototypes of the 100 and 200 ips drives nine months after the start of operations
- Limited study and design efforts on the controller during this period

Table 1. 1st Year Budget Requirements

	1	2	3	MONTH 4	5	6	3Q	4Q	FIRST YEAR TOTAL
Manpower									
Administration	4.1	4.1	4.1	4.1	4.1	4.1	12.3	15.9	52.8
Engineering	14.3	16.9	16.9	19.8	19.8	19.8	54.4	54.4	216.3
Marketing	2.2	2.2	2.8	2.8	2.8	2.8	12.9	12.9	41.4
Manufacturing	—	1.2	1.2	1.2	3.4	3.4	13.0	15.7	39.1
Total Manpower	20.6	24.4	25.0	27.9	30.1	30.1	92.6	98.9	349.6
Other Expenses									
Materials	2.0	4.0	5.0	5.0	15.0	15.0	28.0	16.0	90.0
Rent & Occup.	1.5	1.5	1.5	1.5	1.5	1.5	4.5	4.5	18.0
Supplies & Tool	1.0	2.0	2.0	2.0	2.0	2.0	4.5	4.5	20.0
Prof. Fees	—	1.5	1.5	1.0	1.0	1.0	2.0	2.0	12.0
Insurance	1.0	—	—	1.0	—	—	1.5	1.5	5.0
Travel	1.0	1.0	1.0	2.0	1.0	1.0	4.0	4.0	15.0
Personnel Cost	2.0	2.0	2.0	2.0	2.0	2.0	6.0	7.0	25.0
Misc.	4.0	2.0	2.0	2.0	2.0	2.0	6.0	6.0	26.0
Capital Equip. & Rental	—	12.0	12.0	10.0	3.0	3.0	5.0	4.0	49.0
Total Other Expenses	12.5	26.0	27.0	26.5	27.5	27.5	61.5	49.5	258.0
Total	33.1	50.4	52.0	54.4	57.6	57.6	154.1	148.4	607.6

Table 2. First-Year Schedule.

	Month 1	2	3	4	5	6	7	8	9	10	11	12
200 ips												
100 ips												
Design	XXXXXXXXXXXXXXX——————————————											
Critical Parts Procurement	XXXXXXXXXXX											
Prototypes												
Procurement		XXXXXXXXXXXXXXXXXXX										
Build			XXXXXXXXXX									
Debug						XXXXX						
Test								XXXXXXXXXXX				
Design Improvements												
Completed BM (Drawings)											XX	
Controller												
Study and Architecture		XXXXXXXXXXXXXXXXXXXX										
Design								XXXXXXXXXXX				

206

Table 3. Headcount and Manpower Cost ($000)

| | MONTH | | | | | | | |
	1	2	3	4	5	6	3Q	4Q
Administration								
President	2.2	2.2	2.2	2.2	2.2	2.2	6.6	6.6
Secretary	.6	.6	.6	.6	.6	.6	1.8	1.8
Financial	.3	.3	.3	.3	.3	.3	.9	4.5
Accountant	1.0	1.0	1.0	1.0	1.0	1.0	3.0	3.0
Total	4.1	4.1	4.1	4.1	4.1	4.1	12.3	15.9
Engineering								
VP Engineering	2.2	2.2	2.2	2.2	2.2	2.2	6.6	6.6
Proj. Engineers	5.0	5.0	5.0	5.0	5.0	5.0	15.0	15.1
Eng. & Designers	4.4	7.0	7.0	7.0	7.0	7.0	20.3	20.3
Technicians	1.0	1.0	1.0	2.0	2.0	2.0	6.0	6.0
Draftsman	.7	.7	.7	2.1	2.1	2.1	6.3	6.3
Model Maker	1.0	1.0	1.0	1.0	1.0	1.0	3.0	3.0
Sec/Clerk	—	—	—	.5	.5	.5	1.5	1.5
Total	14.3	16.9	16.9	19.8	19.8	19.8	54.4	54.4
Marketing								
VP Marketing	2.2	2.2	2.2	2.2	2.2	2.2	6.6	6.6
Mgr of Service	—	—	—	—	—	—	4.5	4.5
Secretary	—	—	.6	.6	.6	.6	1.8	1.8
Total	2.2	2.2	2.8	2.8	2.8	2.8	12.9	12.9
Manufacturing								
VP Manufacturing	—	—	—	—	2.2	2.2	6.6	6.6
Engineers	—	1.2	1.2	1.2	1.2	1.2	6.4	6.2
Purchasing	—	—	—	—	—	—	—	2.9
Total	3—	1.2	1.2	1.2	3.4	3.4	13.0	15.7

Initial headcount—14
Year end headcount—17

SHOPSMITH, INC.: GENERAL REVIEW

This plan was submitted by:

Shopsmith, Inc.
Mr. John R. Folkerth
112 East Dixon Ave.
Dayton, Ohio 45419
Phone: 513–298–3190

Introduction

Shopsmith, Inc., an Ohio corporation, is being formed for the purpose of producing and selling the indoor line of woodworking machinery formerly manufactured by the Magna American Corporation, namely the Shopsmith Mark V, the Sawsmith, and related accessories and equipment. Magna American Corporation has given Shopsmith, Inc. a one-year option to purchase all their assets pertaining to this product line, which includes all engineering drawings, tooling, special machinery, in-process and finished inventory, advertising and promotional material, patents, copyrights, and trademarks.

For clarity, this presentation has been arranged in the following categories:

Product History	Purpose of the Corporation
Sales History	Management
Terms of Sale from	Financing
Magna American Corporation	Conclusion

History

The Shopsmith line of woodworking equipment was originally developed and sold by Magna Engineering Corporation. This company was sold to Yuba Consolidated Industries in 1957 and subsequently sold to Magna American Corporation, a corporation specifically formed for this acquisition, in 1961.

Through 1964, Magna's chief product in the indoor line was the Shopsmith Mark V, a very successful machine selling over 125,000 units during the ten years it was in production. In 1964, the Mark VII was introduced to replace the Mark V. This unit wasn't as successful although approximately 10,000 units were sold up to the time all production was terminated in 1967. Of these two models, it is our intention to sell only the Shopsmith Mark V.

The Shopsmith is a woodworking machine that combines five basic tools in one: a 34-inch lathe, a 9-inch circular saw, a disc sander, a horizontal drill, and a vertical drill press. It is unique in the woodworking field and, as such, has no direct competition.

The other major indoor product was the Sawsmith. This radial arm saw was introduced in 1960 and had total sales of approximately 26,000 units against strong competition.

A major asset for both products is that they are engineered to accept a number of accessories, thus expanding their potential usage. These major accessories include a jointer, a bandsaw, a jigsaw, a belt sander, and a compressor/sprayer. In addition, the product line includes all the minor accessories and supplies normally sold with this type of equipment.

In 1967 Magna American Corporation moved their operations from Cincinnati, Ohio, to Raymond, Mississippi. This decision was made in order to take advantage of lower labor rates and tax concessions so that their main product, garden tillers, might be produced competitively. In contemplation of this move, Shopsmiths, Sawsmiths, and a large number of spare parts were produced ahead.

Production of the garden tiller line was started but found to be very difficult because of the shortage of skilled labor. This has been a continuing problem and, because of the significantly higher skills needed to produce the Shopsmith line of equipment, it has not been feasible to initiate production of Shopsmiths and Sawsmiths. However, sales of minor accessories and spare parts have continued to date, mainly from the inventory produced in 1967.

Sales History

The following sales figures have been provided by Magna American Corporation. As their operations included a number of other products, they are not able to provide net profit figures specifically for the indoor line. Also, since 1967, all sales have been made from inventory except for minor additions of the faster selling small accessories and spare parts.

	SALES	GROSS PROFIT	% PROFIT
Year Ended			
6/30/1962	$ 2,090,523	$ 647,006	30.9
6/30/1963	2,585,494	852,717	33.0
6/30/1964	2,609,477	890,485	34.1
6/30/1965	1,749,334	561,753	32.1
6/30/1966	1,618,340	531,062	32.8
For 11 months ending			
5/31/1967	690,052	192,672	27.9
5/31/1968	485,125	151,058	31.1
5/31/1969	212,483	63,541	29.9
5/31/1970	149,760	79,563	53.1
For the 8 months ending			
1/31/1971	73,553	45,755	62.2

It should be remembered that for the last several years there has been no sales effort and a continually diminishing product selection. All sales have been on a completely unsolicited basis.

Terms of the Sale from Magna American Corporation

Magna American Corporation has agreed to sell to Shopsmith, Inc. all their assets pertaining to the production and sale of their indoor line of woodworking equipment, consisting of Shopsmith, Sawsmith, and related accessories. The terms of this sale are as follows:

1. Shopsmith, Inc. will pay cash at the time of the purchase for all of their inventory on the basis of:

100%   on all finished goods inventory

70%   for the in-process inventory pertaining to the Shopsmith Mark V and the Sawsmith

40%   for all other in-process inventory

Since sales from this inventory will continue until the time of the purchase, the cost of this inventory to Shopsmith, Inc. cannot be exactly determined, but it should be approximately $130,000.

2. Shopsmith, Inc. will pay $150,000 for the balance of the assets: $20,000 at the time of the purchase ($5,000 of which was paid at the time the option was granted) and the balance at 6% interest to be paid in ten yearly payments, the first payment due 18 months from the time of the purchase. (After the third year, Magna American Corporation has the option to convert any remaining debt into common stock at any time at a price of seven times the earnings per outstanding share during the third year, minimum price of $1.00 [one dollar] per share.) These assets include:

1. All the special machinery necessary to produce this product line. This machinery had an original cost of over $300,000, and the replacement cost would be much higher.
2. All the jigs, fixtures, tooling, stamping dies, die casting dies, etc. necessary for high-speed production of this equipment—original cost in excess of $500,000.
3. All the engineering studies and drawings pertaining to the original design and production of this equipment.
4. All the sales promotional material developed to sell this equipment. This includes brochures, operational manuals, books specially commissioned to explain the equipment, a series of six films for training courses, a TV program, TV commercials, and many other items.
5. All trademarks, patents, etc. pertaining to this equipment: 24 patents, 3 U.S. design patents, 3 U.S. trademarks, and 9 foreign patents.

Purpose of the Corporation

The primary purpose of Shopsmith, Inc. is the production and sale of Shopsmith Mark V's Sawsmiths and their related accessories.

As the purchase from Magna American Corporation includes all the tooling and special machinery to produce this equipment, we expect to be in production within six months from the time our option is exercised. This time will be necessary to get the machinery moved to Dayton, Ohio, and reconditioned; subcontractors established; the assembly line set up; and personnel trained. Through agreement with Magna American Corporation, we will have the services of Mr. Ed Gronefeld to supervise the reconditioning of the machinery and to help us get production initiated. We are fortunate in having Mr. Gronefeld working with us as he was responsible for building much of the special machinery and for the actual production of the Shopsmith line of equipment for Magna American Corporation.

As part of the move to Dayton, the transfer of the minor accessories and spare parts inventory will be as immediate as possible so that sales of these items can be resumed with little interruption. As can be seen in the "Sales History," these sales amount to more than $100,000 per year and are extremely profitable as a large portion of them are made at retail prices.

When production was terminated in 1967, Magna American Corporation had over 800 dealers selling Shopsmiths and Sawsmiths. Since then, many of them have continued as dealers selling accessories and parts. Several have actually developed significant businesses in purchasing used Shopsmiths and Sawsmiths, reconditioning, and then selling them. As there has been a considerable demand built up over these years, our entire production during the balance of the first year and well into the second year will go into reestablishing those dealers' inventories.

As Magna American Corporation had an extensive sales organization to sell this equipment, we have been able to locate a number of these men and have talked to several of them regarding our plans and the possibility of their working with us. We are confident we will be able to hire a sales manager already familiar with many of the former dealers and thoroughly knowledgeable in the product line. This will be important in working with our new dealers and expanding our sales efforts as will be required in our second year.

As a strong dealer organization will be the basis of our future success, our initial efforts will be concentrated in this area. However, we do have a number of plans concerning alternate methods of distribution and expansion of the product line to assure our continued growth in years to come.

Management

At this time there are only two employees working for the company. They are Mr. Harold E. Folkerth, Chairman of the Board and Secretary, and Mr. John R. Folkerth, President and Treasurer. At this time they receive no remuneration and will not until such time as the financing has been completed and the purchase made.

Mr. Harold E. Folkerth is currently President of Continental Technical Service, Inc. and Vice President of Continental Consultants, Inc. He has spent more than thirty years in the field of production and design engineering and manufacturing. As Chairman of the Board, he will not be working full-time for the company. However, he does intend to spend as much time as necessary to assure the success of Shopsmith, Inc. His compensation has been set at a token $100 per month.

Mr. John R. Folkerth attended Vanderbilt University for three years, studying business administration, and he completed his degree at the University of Dayton in Industrial Engineering. He then worked for Continental Technical Service, Inc. for eight years, starting in the machine shop and the design room. When he resigned in 1961, he was Vice President and General Manager. He then joined Merrill Lynch, Pierce, Fenner and Smith, Inc. as an Account Executive and was employed there until he resigned on July 2, 1971 to work full-time toward getting Shopsmith, Inc. started.

His salary has been initially set at $18,000 per year plus stock options and will not be raised until the company becomes profitable. From that time, his compensation will be determined by the Board of Directors in line with the profitability of the company. He will devote full time to the company.

As we anticipate that it will take approximately six months to get set up and into production, we do not anticipate hiring any additional executive personnel for some time. As mentioned elsewhere, Mr. Gronefeld will be working with us for at least six months reconditioning the machinery, setting up the production line, and training production personnel. As our initial production is committed, it will be six to eight months before it will be necessary to develop our sales organization beyond the efforts of the President.

Financing

At present, Shopsmith, Inc. has no tangible assets other than the option agreement with Magna American Corporation. We estimate that it will take approximately $350,000 to $400,000 to make the actual purchase and provide operating capital until we are producing and selling the product line. These requirements are as follows:

Inventory purchase	$130,000–$140,000
Down payment on equpiment	15,000
Costs of moving the equipment, reconditioning it, and setting up production	190,000
Safety factor	40,000–50,000

We have given considerable study to the costs of getting this product into production. As close as can be estimated, we will have a maximum deficit cash flow of $192,000, peaking in the eighth month after the purchase is consummated. However, since it is impossible to foresee all possible contingencies, we feel that success is much more assured with some capital set aside as a safety factor.

We are presently exploring several avenues of acquiring this financing. The method we eventually choose will be the one which allows Shopsmith, Inc. the strongest possible capital structure. These methods are:

1. Private placement of all capital requirements
2. Private placement of a portion of capital requirements with either private loans, bank loans, or SBA-guaranteed bank loans to furnish the balance
3. Private placement for a portion of the financing needed and a public stock offering to raise the balance
4. A public stock offering of such a size to provide all the required capital

Conclusion

At the present time, we have completed all the initial steps preparatory to starting into business. Plans have been made to assure a smooth transfer of assets; a plant layout is being completed; available manufacturing space has been inspected and tentatively determined; personnel requirements have been reviewed and some key men have been conditionally approached; our product line is being costed and retail prices determined; a number of dealers have been interviewed and their requirements provided for in our planning; and, finally, our marketing plans have been formulated and include what we feel are the means to almost unlimited future growth. The details of our plans are available in a separate study along with our projected costs, manufacturing and sales estimates, profit and loss schedule, and cash flow projections.

We are continuing to review all these areas for possible improvement, but our primary concern at this time is to arrange the required financing. Once this has been completed, we are prepared to exercise our option with Magna American Corporation immediately and do what is necessary to get into production.

One final item is that, although all our plans have been forumulated on the assumption that we will be located in Dayton, Ohio, we can and are willing to locate elsewhere if such a move would assure the best opportunity for financing.

Basic Products

The primary product of Shopsmith, Inc. will be the Shopsmith Mark V. This is an all-purpose woodworking tool that combines five basic tools in one: a nine-inch circular saw, a thirty-four inch lathe, a twelve-inch disc sander, a horizontal drill press, and a vertical drill. Accessories that can be utilized on this equipment are a jointer, a bandsaw, a jigsaw, a belt sander, and a compressor/sprayer. Thus, with one variable power source, a buyer has at his disposal all the tools normally found in the most complete workshop. It has been thoroughly engineered and can almost be considered a perfect machine. Over 120,000 of these units have been produced and sold, compiling an outstanding record of dependability and ruggedness. We have included a brochure at the end of this section.

The Shopsmith Mark V is unique in its field. It is the only single piece of equipment that can fulfill any power woodworking operation with either the basic unit or with its available accessories. It is compact and easily stored, an important feature with the space limitations of contemporary housing. It is well designed for appearance and, including accessories, is thoroughly protected with over 15 current patents.

The other major product that will be produced later is the Sawsmith, a ten-inch radial arm saw. It is a superior product, but there is considerable competition in the field, mainly from Black & Decker, Rockwell-Delta, and Sears, Roebuck & Co. Their products are good, but we feel that they are not comparable to the Sawsmith either in styling or in quality. However, they do have outstanding national distribution, which is something we have to reestablish. Also, Sawsmith does have some unique characteristics. A variable speed control assures the proper blade speed for different operations and allows the use of most of the accessories that are available for the Shopsmith. As with Shopsmith, this allows the owner to have available with one tool almost all the normal power operations.

Other products to be marketed immediately are the major and minor accessories for the Shopsmith and Sawsmith. The major accessories have been designed so that they can be attached quickly to and use the power source of the Shopsmith/Sawsmith, or they can be used individually on a power stand that we will produce. The minor accessories include all the auxiliary items that are used with this type of equipment, such as sandpaper discs, belts, and drums; saw and dado blades; drills; grinding wheels; etc. These are profitable items and, as they must be periodically replaced, provide continuing sales.

A Sawsmith brochure is included at the end of this section along with a general accessory catalog.

History of Product

The original Shopsmith was conceived and developed by Dr. Hans Goldschmidt right after World War II to answer the problem of the home woodworking craftsman who either could not afford and/or didn't have the space available to store the number of power tools normally required to do even the simplest craft project. Once the working model had been produced, he, in partnership with Mr. Frank Chambers and Mr. Robert Chambers, formed Magna Engineering Corporation to produce and sell Shopsmiths.

At that point, they were fortunate in being able to form an association with Montgomery Ward & Co., who gave them their first order for 200 units and then purchased their full production for the next two years. This association lasted for a number of years and, one time, Magna Engineering Corporation was producing a number of individual power woodworking tools exclusively for Montgomery Ward under their "Power-Craft" label. Shopsmiths were always sold by Montgomery Ward under the Shopsmith name.

After the second year, Magna Engineering was able to satisify the requirements of Montgomery Ward so that they were able to start establishing their own independent dealer system, which eventualy spanned the country with over 800 dealers.

During those early post-war years, Magna Engineering Corporation was one of the glamour stories of the era. From the original concept, their "Shopsmith" became the standard of the home woodworking field, a feeling that many still hold. In effect, they recognized the demand for a quality product by the home craftsman and did much to establish this field into what it is today, a major consumer industry.

The first Shopsmith unit had a six-inch saw blade capacity and was designated the 1OE. Magna Engineering then modified and improved the unit, enlarging the size so that it had a seven-inch blade. This unit, the 1OER, was in production until 1954, during which time over 125,000 were made and sold. In 1954, they introduced a completely new unit, the Mark V, which is the model we plan to produce. The Mark V was a major improvement over the earlier models. A more powerful motor, which was completely enclosed, was provided. This was not only safer; it gave them the means to provide a variable speed control, an important item for operational efficiencies. The Mark V also provided the mounting and power drive for the attachment of accessories. These major accessories became extremely profitable for the company and they allowed the owner to utilize the Mark V for all possible woodworking operations, thus making it literally an "all-purpose machine." This was a very successful model selling over 120,000 units until production was terminated in 1964.

In the meantime, Magna Engineering Corporation was sold to Yuba Consolidated Industries of San Francisco in 1956. This company was an early conglomerate. Their original field was mining and, through a number of acquisitions, they became an extremely large corporation with interests in many areas. The primary reason for the sale to Yuba was because the principals of Magna Engineering recognized the necessity of producing the unit in a more central location, because of the prohibitive costs of shipping from California, and they didn't want to leave the area. Also, they felt that Yuba Consolidated had the financial resources to make the move properly and to expand the independent dealer organization into areas that couldn't be covered efficiently from their California location.

Yuba Consolidated Industries moved the production facilities to the Cincinnati, Ohio, area and merged it with another of their acquisitions, Weber Engineered Products of Cincinnati. Weber was a large company producing garden tillers (over 100,000 per year) and lawnmowers, which they later dropped. In addition to being a major supplier of garden tillers to Sears, Roebuck & Co., they also had an independent dealer system, selling the product line under the name of "Choremaster." They also had a seasonal selling pattern complementing that of the Shopsmith line, so it was felt this merger would strengthen both companies. This new division was called the Yuba Powered Products Division of Yuba Consolidated Industries, Inc. Mr. John Snowball, formerly of Weber Engineered Products, was made President of the division. Within the organization, the Shopsmith line was called the "indoor line," and the tiller and lawnmower operations the "outdoor line."

Yuba Consolidated Industries continued to expand in the early 1950s and did very well until there was a minor recession in the heavy equipment industry starting about 1957. By 1960, Yuba was in financial trouble and began selling off their profitable divisions in order to raise cash. Mr. Snowball, along with two other officers, was able to get outside financing from both local investors and Boston Capital Corporation to purchase this division in 1961. The corporation they formed to make this purchase is called Magna American Corporation. Quickly after the sale, Yuba Consolidated Industries filed for protection from their creditors under Chapter 11 of the bankruptcy act.

In 1960 the Sawsmith, a ten-inch radial arm saw, was introduced to meet the competition from DeWalt and to round out their product line. It is an excellent unit and did well against strong competition. Its peak sales year was 1961, with sales of almost 6,000 units. Altogether, sales of the Sawsmith were approximately 26,000 units through 1969.

In 1964, Magna American Corporation introduced the Shopsmith Mark VII. This is a deluxe version of the Mark V incorporating some new features, and it completely replaced the Mark V in 1965. This model had some early mechanical problems and, although corrected, caused considerable dealer resistance to the unit. This is why we will not be producing it and intend to make and sell the Mark V.

At this time it was decided to move the company to Raymond, Mississippi, which was accomplished in 1967. In addition to getting new financing from Mississippi Steel Corporation, who eventually purchased 100% of the stock, Magna was provided a new plant, tax concessions, and significantly lower labor rates. This was extremely important because of the price pressure they were under from Sears on their garden tiller line.

Because of the yearly model changes on the tiller line, compared to the fixed design of the Shopsmith line, they decided to set up the new model tiller production first in the new plant. Therefore, in contemplation of this production gap, they produced ahead a large number of Shopsmiths, Sawsmiths, and major and minor accessories. It was anticipated that it would take approximately nine months to get their production under control on the new tiller line, and they would then be able to set up the production lines for Shopsmith and Sawsmith.

However, Magna immediately ran into production difficulties, primarily because of the lack of skilled labor in the area. To this date, their reject and efficiency rates are still a major problem. As they have been concentrating their full management and production efforts on solving these problems, they have not been able to initiate production on the Shopsmith line of equipment. In addition, they have realized that the lack of skilled personnel in the area makes it improbable that they would ever be able to produce this equipment efficiently with the quality that is required. Therefore, although sales have continued through the present and there is still a considerable inventory of spare parts, there has been no actual production of this equipment since 1967.

Sales History

We are listing below the dollar volume and gross profits from the sale of the equipment since 1962. As all of their sales were originally made through their dealer organization, the high profit margins of the last two years are primarily because many of these sales have been made directly to the consumer at full retail prices.

The summary sheet that follows gives the breakdown of product sales in addition to showing the unit sales from 1949.

	SALES	COST OF SALES	GROSS PROFIT	% PROFIT
Year				
6/30/1962	2,090,523	1,443,517	647,006	30.9
6/30/1963	2,585,494	1,732,777	852,717	33.0
6/30/1964	2,609,477	1,718,992	890,485	34.1
6/30/1965	1,749,334	1,187,581	561,062	32.1
6/30/1966	1,618,340	1,087,278	531,062	32.8
For 11 months ending				
5/31/1967	690,052	497,380	192,672	27.9
5/31/1968	485,125	334,067	151,058	31.1
5/31/1969	212,483	148,942	63,541	29.9
5/31/1970	149,760	70,197	79,563	53.1
For the 8 months ending				
1/31/1971	73,553	27,798	45,755	62.2

Reason for Sale

As was discussed under "History of Product," this equipment has not been produced since 1967. Also, because of the skilled labor situation, they do not feel that it is practical to resume production. As they could no longer supply units, their salesmen were either shifted to tiller sales or dropped, and their dealer organization has pretty well evaporated.

When they were approached by us, their situation was that they had a good product with no visible way of exploiting the potential. Therefore, they were open to our proposition of buying the Shopsmith/Sawsmith portion of their operations for cash plus convertible debt.

Sales Approach

In determining the most efficient manner of selling the Shopsmith line of equipment, we find that there are some basic differences in what we must do in order to get started and the way we eventually want to distribute the product line. These sales approaches are not completely incompatible, but care must be taken that overemphasis on near-term requirements does not jeopardize our future potential for growth. Our short- and long-range sales plans are as follows:

SHORT TERM

1. Sell almost all our production through independent dealers.
2. Develop direct mail sales for areas without dealer coverage.

Sales History

FISCAL YEAR	10 ER UNIT SALES	MARK V UNIT SALES	MARK V DOLLAR SALES	MARK VII UNIT SALES	MARK VII DOLLAR SALES	SAW-SMITH UNIT SALES	SAW-SMITH DOLLAR SALES	MAJOR ACCESS. UNIT SALE	MAJOR ACCESS. DOLLAR SALES	MINOR ACCESS. DOLLAR SALES	SPARE PARTS DOLLAR SALES	TOTAL SALES
1949–1950	25,737											
1950–1951	28,087											
1951–1952	24,116											
1952–1953	26,157											
1953–1954	13,100	11,865										
1954–1955		26,948										
1955–1956		24,108										
1956–1957		21,874										
1957–1958		16,988										
1958–1959		9,778	2,004,490					15,327	554,162	843,215	40,763	3,442,630
1959–1960		9,185	1,882,925			5,541	1,125,499	16,520	596,789	694,967	28,945	4,329,122
1960–1961		6,043	1,238,815			5,970	1,105,422	10,920	394,496	663,861	64,648	3,467,242
1961–1962		3,833	784,483			2,746	526,090	6,986	220,216	413,151	55,202	1,999,142
1962–1963		4,129	912,268			3,197	647,605	8,842	311,922	440,273	60,037	2,372,105
1963–1964		2,058	432,180	3,076	762,205	3,200	585,870	6,040	212,750	494,110	65,374	2,107,790
1964–1965		347	63,674	2,818	689,401	1,889	341,533	3,565	175,041	419,368	70,089	1,759,160
1965–1966				2,714	635,804	2,003	420,555	4,404	211,392	365,070	62,830	1,695,651
1966–1967				1,356	381,924	460	90,000	1,212	58,176	141,257	42,400	713,857
1967–1968				517	139,590	328	60,352	1,212	58,176	188,007	39,000	485,125
1968–1969				190	51,803	72	14,062	303	14,000	136,300	41,006	257,171

LONG TERM

1. Continue selling our product line through the larger independent dealers.
2. Establish a system of retail outlets stocking a full line of woodworking equipment and accessories and featuring Shopsmith products. These will be called "Shopsmith Craft Centers."
3. Develop a direct mail catalog sales program.

Over the short term, our efforts will necessarily be concentrated on selling all the units that can be efficiently produced. To accomplish this, we must rely almost entirely on the dealers formerly associated with Magna American Corporation. However, there are certain disadvantages in working with independent dealers, which are:

1. We must maintain a strong sales organization so that we can keep in continual contact.
2. As most of these dealers are strictly retail establishments, we must either provide or arrange for service facilities that are convenient, prompt, and efficient.
3. Invariably, there is intense competition for floor space to display the products.
4. As this equipment should be demonstrated for successful selling, it is up to our salesmen to familiarize and train the dealer's salesmen as to how it is used and the most effective methods of selling it.
5. Since a dealer's own money is involved, it is up to our salesmen to work continually with him to assure that the full product line is on display and that he maintains sufficient inventories.
6. Dealers must be convinced of the value of after-hours promotional work, such as "Sawdust Parties" and woodworking instruction courses.
7. Cooperative efforts must be solicited from dealers in advertising, running TV shows, and participation in such things as homeowner's shows and state and county fairs.
8. Because of space limitations, new products are difficult to introduce.

Regardless of the above, the independent dealer organization will be very important to us as it provides a ready source of significant sales. Also, it must be remembered that those dealers who became the most successful in the past were those most cooperative in these areas. This will be a factor in determining those with whom we will be establishing relations.

Of the total of 866 dealers who worked with Magna American Corporation, about 65 sold over 150 units per year, and approximately 150 of them sold over 50 units per year. We hope to recruit 100 to 125 of these large dealers over the first two years. If this group of dealers can average 75 units per year, our sales projections for these years will prove very conservative. Our criteria on which dealers to solicit actively are:

1. Proven sales volume in the past
2. Location in relation to other large dealers in order to facilitate our salesmen working with them, cooperative area advertising, sales promotions, etc.

3. Ability to handle the service required themselves or the proximity of good independent service facilities

4. Their willingness to work with us in keeping full inventories, the training of sales personnel, and other promotional activities

It is important to consider that in areas where we do establish independent dealers, we will not be able to set up Shopsmith Craft Centers. Therefore, we are going to try to confine these areas as much as possible. However, once a dealer is established, it will be both efficient and to our advantage to work with other dealers, regardless of their size, to assure proper coverage of the area. In addition, there are a number of smaller dealers who have carried the Shopsmith line of equipment for years and who are extremely loyal. It will be necessary to include them in our independent dealer organization.

Our present plans are to send a form letter to selected former dealers as soon as we have a firm indication of our production schedules. We hope that this letter will accomplish two things. The first is to let them know that we are bringing the product back into production. We will also request that they provide the following information:

1. If they are interested in being dealers,
2. At the prices which will be quoted, how many units do they estimate they can sell per year, and
3. Any suggestions that they may have on product improvement or dealer relations.

All the replies we receive will be answered as quickly as possible, either by mail or by phone as appropriate. Although our production for the first couple of months is tentatively committed, the answers to this letter will determine the priorities of our sales activities. The dealers who indicate that they want to represent us will be kept informed of our progress at periodic intervals.

As we get back into production, we will do a moderate amount of national advertising. This will be done principally to inform present Shopsmith owners that parts and accessories are available and where to request information. From the indications we have had, we will be able to count on considerable sales in this area. Also, although this equipment normally needs to be seen and demonstrated to be sold, there are a number of men across the country who are already sold but haven't been able to buy a Shopsmith or a Sawsmith. Although these sales would be limited, they would be very profitable as there will be no sales effort and we would receive the full retail price. Any inquiries from an area where we have an established dealer would be referred to that dealer.

As we work with the large dealers to increase their market penetration, we will begin pilot stores to develop our own distribution system in the form of Shopsmith Craft Centers. These small retail stores will cater to the woodworking enthusiast. In addition to carrying the complete Shopsmith line, they will handle as complete a selection as possible to stationary and portable power tools, hand tools, hardware, and stains and varnishes, along with craft plans and patterns, premium hardwoods, veneer sheets and trim, etc. They will also provide saw sharpening and equipment repair. It is our intention to provide all the merchandise and service necessary to the individual interested in woodworking either seriously or on a casual basis.

If successful, the benefits to Shopsmith, Inc. will be incalculable. In addition to the stores themselves returning a good profit, their concentration of sales efforts on the Shopsmith product line will be tremendously beneficial to our market penetration and profits. It will also give us an excellent means of testing new sales promotions and experimental advertising, as well as test marketing and instant national exposure of any new products. Most important, this plan answers almost all of those problems previously listed concerning working with independent dealers.

This system of Centers, either company owned or franchised, will be expanded across the country as quickly as possible once the concept has been proven. With our administrative controls, we can establish these Centers in areas where developing and servicing an independent dealer system could only be marginally profitable. Liaison with the Craft Centers can be handled very efficiently through a system of district supervisors.

Another program we will be pursuing concurrent to the development of the Craft Centers is the mass distribution of a catalog featuring Shopsmith, along with the other woodworking equipment and materials we sell through the Centers. We are sure this will become an important source of business and can be fully developed with a minimum of expense as both the mailing list and the merchandise selection will be generated from our other activities.

The initial mailing list will come from the warranty cards that have been returned by buyers of Shopsmiths, Sawsmiths, and major accessories. As over 400,000 of these items have been sold, this group will give us a sizable mailing list even after it has been cleaned up. We also expect good response from our ads telling owners we are back in business and that parts and accessories are available.

The mailing list will be expanded by adding new Shopsmith/Sawsmith owners and from our advertising. Primarily, we will be advertising our regular product line but, as new items are included in the catalog, they will also be advertised individually. If we find it necessary, mailing lists can be purchased.

At first, our catalog will be a simple brochure on the Shopsmith product line. As merchandise is selected for the Craft Centers, it will automatically be included in the catalog. In this manner our catalog will offer a good selection of items within a short time.

Other than the sales and profits directly attributable to catalog sales, we anticipate benefiting in other ways from this program. Initially, it will provide some major unit sales, and it will give present owners a way of purchasing major and minor accessories until we have an independent dealer or Craft

Center in their area. In some areas of the country, the catalog will always be the owner's most convenient source of accessories and supplies.

As we expand our Craft Center system, we expect the catalog to complement it in many ways. As with Sear's catalog stores, customers will be able to phone in orders and pick up merchandise at the Craft Centers. Giving them a substantial portion of their normal mark-up along with the impulse buying that will be generated when the customer comes into the store should assure their cooperation. Also, we think the Centers will find that most customers will prefer to buy where they can take home their purchases immediately, and the catalog will support their sales by showing the merchandise available. Since the catalog will eventually carry a much greater selection than the stores can handle, a simple code will show that although an item isn't carried in the store, a phone call to the Center will get it ordered from the factory immediately.

We will encourage our independent dealers to participate in catalog sales on the same basis as the Craft Centers. They can also carry in stock any item they wish from our catalog, and all our promotional programs will be designed to include them.

Although we are confident that our Shopsmith Craft Centers will be extremely successful, we have alternatives available if necessary. First of all, we will have a solid core of independent dealers. Although it would take longer and be much more difficult, this dealer system could be expanded indefinitely until it covers the major population centers across the country. This was done very successfully before and it can be done again.

Another substantial source of business would be getting our product carried by either Sears Roebuck, Montgomery Ward, or J.C. Penney. Montgomery Ward did sell Shopsmiths until about 1966. Actually, they put the original Magna Engineering Corporation in business with their first order, and in their peak years, they sold approximately 14,000 Shopsmiths a year. Through the years it was a very rewarding relationship. However, we feel that there is a much greater long-term potential for sales through a system of Craft Centers, and we do not feel that we can do both. However, if the Shopsmith Craft Center program should be terminated, we would do everything possible to get either Montgomery Ward, Sears, or J.C. Penney to carry our product line.

Even if we don't have the support of the Craft Centers, we will be continuing our program of developing direct mail sales through a catalog as we will have already determined our basic merchandise selection and lined up suppliers. At this point, the profits generated by these sales will support its continued expansion.

We feel that the Shopsmith line of equipment is unique and of such quality that all it needs to be sold is the proper exposure. We are confident that the sales approaches we have outlined here will give us sufficient distribution to assure substantial growth for years to come.

Shopsmith Craft Centers

In our market surveys referencing sale of the Shopsmith line of equipment, we have come to the following conclusions:

1. The Shopsmith product line must be properly promoted and displayed to assure customer interest.
2. It is almost necessary to have sales personnel available specifically trained to demonstrate and sell this equipment.
3. With this size investment, the customer must be assured of efficient and fast service.
4. Keeping a complete stock of major and minor accessories available stimulates sales considerably.
5. Special sales efforts are required, such as TV programs, "Sawdust Parties," and trade shows (i.e., homeowner's shows and state and county fairs).
6. Follow-up programs, such as woodworking courses, assure proper product use, which in turn generates very important referral sales.

In working through an independent dealer organization, we have the advantage of wide exposure, but the factors that produce good dealer results are beyond our control. The successful Shopsmith dealer will work with us in the above areas because he has seen his efforts return handsome profits. However, many dealers are not willing to expend the efforts required and, in effect, are riding on the promotional efforts of other participating dealers. In addition, even poor dealers require continued sales coverage and factory backing, a very expensive situation.

We feel that the answer to this problem lies in the establishment of a franchised chain of Shopsmith Craft Centers. These Centers will be strategically placed small retail stores that specialize in woodworking equipment and materials. The main items for sale will be Shopsmiths and Sawsmiths, major and minor accessories, and spare parts. In addition, there will be a full line of power tools and hand tools. It will not be a hardware store, but it will carry all those items normally found in one that relates to woodworking.

The Centers will also carry wood finishing materials, such as stains, varnishes, and paints; an extensive line of cabinet and furniture hardware; and a full line of general woodworking hardware. Several items we plan to sell—not normally available—are wood veneer, a full selection of woodworking project plans, and a good selection of premium hardwoods.

The Centers will offer two services sometimes difficult to find: saw sharpening and power tool repair. Depending on the Center owners, there are other services that may be offered.

It is our intention that a Shopsmith Craft Center be a place where the home craftsman can go to get expert and friendly advice, service, and any tools or materials that he needs for his woodworking projects.

All the different subjects included under supplementary information, particularly the basic franchise agreement, the financial risk to the franchise buyer, and the liability of the Craft Centers to Shopsmith, Inc. are very tentative, and we have approximately one year before we must have definite agreements finalized. In the meantime, it will be necessary for us to work with one of the several available consulting firms specializing in franchising programs. In addition to the help they can give us with the basic agreements and recruiting methods, they can be very valuable to us in areas of bookkeeping systems, inventory control, advertising programs, etc.

Because of the length of this section, we are providing the following table of contents:

Sales Approach
Supplementary Information
Required Support from Shopsmith, Inc.
Basic Franchise Agreement
Financial Risk to the Franchise Buyer
Liability of Centers to Shopsmith, Inc.
Advantages to the Franchise Buyer
Merchandise to be Offered
Services to be Offered

Sales Approach

These Centers will be franchised to individuals and will be established in all areas of the country except those where we have large independent dealers. (In anticipation of this policy we plan to initially approach only those dealers who have proven successful in the past because we do not feel that we can establish a Center where it can in any way be considered competition for a dealer who has worked with us in good faith.)

The advantages of selling the Shopsmith product line through this type of system are numerous. The Centers will provide adequate space to display properly the full product line and personnel knowledgeable in its use and how to sell it. Also, it is a definite sales advantage for the buyer to know that any time he wants to add accessories or needs supplies, service, or advice, they are immediately available.

With these Centers available, we can expand our product line to cover the full range of woodworking power and hand tools (see section "New Products"). Under the system of independent dealers, any new product not directly related to Shopsmith/Sawsmith would have to be sold to dealers and would probably have to replace another brand that they are already carrying. This is always a difficult task, and few new products would justify the sales efforts required. The Centers would provide major new product exposure immediately.

The Centers would be located in middle to upper-middle class neighborhoods. Any building properly located could be used, but it is likely our initial efforts will be concentrated in small shopping centers where space is somewhat standardized and parking is available.

The interior appointments and fixtures will be no problem. All these items can be standardized with enough flexibility to take care of almost any space variations and can either be built by Shopsmith, Inc. or to our specifications at minimum cost.

All of the inventory would be supplied from Dayton. Each store would have perpetual inventory control with quick replacement of sold stock. Subsidiary warehousing will be established wherever necessary as the Centers spread across the country.

Our present idea is that, in the metropolitan areas, the Centers should be open from about 4:30 in the afternoon to 9:00 in the evening; in rural areas, from about 11:30 in the morning to 5:30 in the afternoon. They would be open normal hours on Saturdays. We feel that any sales lost because of short hours would be negligible. Also, in metropolitan areas, these working hours will allow the use of high school or college students as inexpensive part-time help.

The profit potential of the Centers cannot be determined at this time. From the studies we have made, we are sure that they can be operated at a profit, and we have indications that they will be very profitable. However, because of the reasons outlined below, we feel that if we can assure the individuals buying the franchise that the Center will be even moderately profitable, our entire franchising program will be extremely successful.

The individuals we recruit to buy these franchises are the key to the success of the program. First of all, they must have the inclination and the ability to demonstrate and sell this type of equipment. In addition, they must be able to service the product and have the knowledge necessary to work with customers on their woodworking requirements. Initially, we intend to sell franchises only to financially responsible individuals at or near retirement age. This is because we feel that there is a large pool of talented men in this group, many of them very concerned with continuing responsible employment. Thus, this program can attract good men without having to assure them of large, quick profits.

Another thing that we will encourage is to have Centers owned by two or more partners, another inducement to men of this age. Under this arrangement, they would be able to arrange convenient working schedules and vacations. In other words, it will give the owners a responsible position where they can meet the public, in an area that they are already interested in, and where we have relieved them of much of the administrative burden normally associated with owning your own business. Coupled with reasonable hours and the limited-risk franchise agreement we have worked out, the response of the men we have discussed this program with has been most encouraging.

Our schedule for establishing Shopsmith Craft Centers is as follows. As soon as our Shopsmith sales are progressing at a satisfactory rate, hopefully in about nine months, we will hire or assign two men to this division. One will be the man we intend to have supervise the whole program; the other will be the one who will run the first store. This store will be owned by Shopsmith, Inc. Their initial duties will to be to determine the product selection, line up suppliers, rent space, design the store layout, purchase the necessary display cases and racks, develop accounting and control systems, etc. Once this has been done, probably in three to four months, the first store will be opened. We hope that we will have pretty well settled what products we will offer and that we will have worked out any problems in the accounting and control procedures with six to nine months of actual experience. At that time, we will franchise two additional stores in the Dayton area. They will be independently owned but closely supervised by our Director. Even with this supervision, we estimate that they will have to be in operation six months to one year before we are sure enough of all our product selection, systems, and controls to aggressively expand the franchise system.

As can be seen, we are planning to approach this program rather cautiously until we are sure of its success. In this way we will be able to terminate the program quickly with minimum cost if it proves unsuccessful. However, we are confident that it will be successful and will eventually prove to be a tremendous asset to Shopsmith, Inc.

Supplementary Information

The establishment of an extensive franchise system is a major undertaking. There are a number of industries that have utilized this method of distribution, and the problems are unique in each area. However, there are franchised hardware store systems and also company owned hardware chain stores whose systems can be studied, copied, or adapted to our operations as appropriate. In recent years there have been major administrative advances in remote management control, inventory control, stock ordering, computerized central purchasing, computerized warehousing, and numerous other areas that need to be incorporated into our planning as we grow.

In the meantime, there are a number of different areas that must be considered in our planning, and, for clarity, we have broken them down and reviewed them separately. They obviously must be studied further, and it is our intention to modify our present thinking as our experience dictates. As previously mentioned, our first store will be experimental to establish our systems and to test our merchandise selection. The next two stores will be set up and run under our direction to prove out the whole concept.

The balance of this section reviews our basic thinking on the different areas of this program under consideration.

Required Support From Shopsmith, Inc.
for Shopsmith Craft Centers

As our sales programs and dealer system become established, we will either hire or assign a man to develop our Shopsmith Craft Centers. He and the man we hire to eventually run the first store will find suitable space and, working with our own support personnel and outside consultants as necessary, determine the merchandise selection and establish all the control systems.

The next two stores can be established by our Director working with the men we franchise the stores to. Again, some support will be required from other Shopsmith, Inc. personnel, but it will be nominal at this point.

Once these three stores have proved our concept, procedures, and systems, we will begin franchising new Centers as quickly as possible. As we expand, the support necessary will be as follows:

1. A man who will advertise in the local area for potential franchise buyers or contact men who have made previous inquiries. He will be responsible for interviewing, testing, reviewing our agreement and store requirements, and, finally, selecting those men who will purchase the franchises. He will sign the agreement and set up their training schedules in Dayton. The number of franchises assigned to a given area will depend on the population, marketing area covered, and the average incomes in the area.

Once the agreements are signed and training schedules arranged, his responsibilities will be over; he will then move on to the next area to be covered.

2. Once the agreements have been signed, a man will be assigned to the area to oversee all the details in establishing the individual Centers. He will work with local real estate agents to secure locations. The space layout will be submitted to Dayton for interior design (and exterior alterations if necessary). It will be his responsibility to contract the work locally. Dayton will provide all the necessary fixtures and the initial stock of merchandise at the proper time.

3. As the franchise owners complete their training and the new Centers are opened, a man will be assigned to the area temporarily to help them get started. The District Supervisor will also be available.

This man will probably be from our training school in Dayton. He will already know the franchise owners, and this assignment can be handled between training sessions as they will be of limited duration. The District Supervisor will then be responsible for any further assistance required.

4. In Dayton, we will have a man who will be responsible for working with the new franchise owners. With support personnel as required, he will familiarize them with our established procedures in the following areas:

A. General operating and selling philosophies of Snopsmith, Inc.
B. Store layout and display maintenance
C. General selling techniques

D. Training on the operation of the Shopsmith equipment and how to demonstrate and sell it

E. Inventory control and stock ordering

F. Accounting procedures

G. Store and merchandise protection

H. Operating the equipment for the services offered (for example, saw sharpening)

I. Basic equipment repair

All new franchise holders will complete their stay in Dayton by working for some period in the Dayton Craft Center.

5. At first, all replacement stock will be warehoused in Dayton. In the future, we may have to establish satellite warehouses in diffrent parts of the country, but they will be controlled from Dayton.

6. All purchasing, testing of new lines, establishing suppliers, etc. will be handled by our purchasing department.

7. Design of new stores, remodeling stores, design or determining specifications of display fixtures, etc. will be handled through our engineering department.

8. The local advertising for each area, promotional sales, etc. will be handled through our regular advertising agency working through our sales department with the individual franchise owner.

9. The Director of the Craft Centers group will be directly responsible for liaison between Shopsmith, Inc. and the individual Centers, eventually working through District Supervisors. It will be up to him to make sure that we maintain a close relationship with all the individual Centers.

Basic Franchise Agreement

The actual franchise agreement will have to be written by our attorneys, but it will include the following provisions, subject to revision as we gain experience in this area.

1. The franchise agreement will be for an indefinite period but will be subject to termination by either the franchise owner or Shopsmith, Inc. on each yearly anniversary of the agreement signing.

2. Shopsmith, Inc. will be responsible for getting the individual Center ready to start operation. We will also provide advice, forms, and systems to assure efficient and profitable operation of the Centers.

3. Shopsmith, Inc. will provide the original selling inventory and will replenish the stock as necessary. All inventory not manufactured by Shopsmith, Inc. will be supplied to the Center at actual cost plus transportation charges.

4. The franchise owner will agree to keep his Center fully stocked, and all merchandise is to be sold at prices set by Shopsmith, Inc. unless otherwise agreed. He will also agree to participate in sales promotions and other programs initiated by Shopsmith, Inc.

5. Any change in ownership must be agreed to by Shopsmith, Inc.

6. Shopsmith, Inc. has the right to purchase any Center at the rate of three times annual earnings. This will be the same basis on which partners can be bought out by other partners. The calculation of earnings will include the salaries and profit distributions of the owners.

7. Shopsmith, Inc. will own 20% of each Center and will receive 7% of total sales, payable monthly. Shopsmith, Inc. will not participate in any earnings nor will it hold any equity interest in the earned surplus in any Center in case of dissolution.

8. The franchised Center will not stock any new items nor offer any new services without the explicit approval of Shopsmith, Inc.

9. At any time that a franchise agreement is terminated, Shopsmith, Inc. will have the right to require that all merchandise be returned, FOB Dayton, Ohio.

Financial Risk to the Franchise Owner

We have tried to make the terms of the franchise agreement very tight in areas necessary for us to control the quality, type, and pricing of the merchandise and services offered. However, we are offering the potential franchise buyer terms so that his potential liability can be calculated at any time.

At the time the franchise agreement is signed, we will require a deposit of $10,000. This will be utilized as follows:

1. $2,000 will be paid as a franchise fee.

2. There will be no charge for the store location, set up and interior design, and training services provided by Shopsmith, Inc. However, the franchise owner is responsible for the cost of leasehold improvements, fixtures, and equipment. Three of the original $10,000 has been allocated toward these costs, and the balance will be paid at $100 per month. It is anticipated that $4,000 will cover the major portion of these costs. The life of this equipment will be figured at four years, and if the franchise is terminated, the prorated balance will be refunded to the franchise owner.

3. $3,000 will be allocated toward the purchase of inventory. There will be interest charged at the rate of 5% on the balance due on the inventory, and it is to be paid off at the rate of $150 per month. As an alternative to paying off the cost of inventory, Shopsmith, Inc. will keep title and will add 2% to the 7% override on monthly sales. The $3,000 initial payment will be considered a security deposit. All replacement orders must be paid for immediately on a bimonthly billing basis.

4. The remaining $2,000 is to cover advertising. The amount of the advertising will be determined largely by the franchise owner, with help from our advertising department. The cost of advertising will be split on a 75%–25% basis, Shopsmith, Inc. paying the 25%. When the first $2,000 has been used, the franchise owner will continue to determine his own advertising and will charge our 25% portion toward the 7% (or 9%) monthly payment. All advertising must be approved in advance by Shopsmith, Inc.

   5. The franchise owner is responsible for all rent and utility charges.

As we have already mentioned, the franchise holder can compute his potential liability at any time. For example, if he decides to terminate the agreement at the end of the first year, his liability will be approximately as follows:

1. $2,000 franchise fee
2. Approximately $1,000 for the leasehold improvements, fixtures, and equipment
3. No cost for inventory, as that would be returned to Shopsmith, Inc.
4. About $2,000 for advertising
5. About $1,000 for miscellaneous costs
6. About $4,000 for rent and utilities. Any time left on the lease is the liability of Shopsmith, Inc.

The total cost of the above will be approximately $10,000, excluding the time of the franchise owners. Against this maximum potential loss is any profit made during the year. Therefore, with the owners working the stores themselves, it is hard to visualize them having much actual cash risk.

Potential Liability of Each Shopsmith Craft Center to Shopsmith, Inc.

With the limitations of liability we have provided to the franchise owners, we have somewhat expanded our own possible costs in case of termination.

   There are several reasons a franchise might be terminated other than unprofitable operation. Areas like the death of an owner or the incompatibility of partners will be covered in the franchise agreement and will not involve Shopsmith, Inc. (other than the right of approval of a change in owners).

   In the event the franchise holder(s) decides to terminate operations before the expiration of four years, we will have the option of either liquidating the operation or continuing it, either ourselves or with new franchise owners. In any case, we will pay the franchise holders immediately for the following:

1. The inventory, either left in place or returned to Dayton, Ohio, at the option of Shopsmith, Inc.
2. Any remaining value on the calculated life of the fixtures and equipment
3. Any remaining value on the calculated life of the leasehold improvements

As no original lease will be written for more than four years, our maximum liability would be for three years of lease payments. Whether this is written off or not will depend on whether we continue operating the Center. In the event that operations are discontinued, the lease payments and the remaining value of the leasehold improvements would be a complete loss. However, it is extremely unlikely a Center would need to be abandoned.

The $2,000 we receive as a franchise fee approximates our costs in getting a Center started, so none of this amount would be available.

Since all the stores will carry approximately the same merchandise, disposal of the inventory will be no problem. As the fixtures and equipment will be standardized and of good quality, they can be refurbished and used in another location.

If the franchise agreement is terminated after the fourth year, Shopsmith, Inc. would have no liability other than payment to the franchise owner for the returned inventory.

Advantages to the Franchise Owner

Our primary objective in establishing a franchised system of Craft Centers is to assure us a highly efficient sales outlet for our present and future products. In addition, we have every intention of realizing a good profit on the Centers themselves. Therefore, it is definitely in our best interest to do eveything possible to attract highly qualified men to purchase franchises and to do anything necessary to assure their success.

We do feel our franchise program is extremely attractive and has a number of unique features designed to interest those men we most want to work with. One is that, unlike most retail establishments, the working hours are not excessive. Another attractive feature is that it will not be expensive initially and that the potential liability is limited. This is of considerable interest to older men whose future earning capacity is somewhat fixed. Finally, the most important thing is that the Centers will feature a well-known line of superior equipment, and the work itself should be very interesting in addition to being highly profitable.

We have set the percentage of monthly sales charge at a figure that should net us approximately 2% after all our costs. This will work out to be very profitable to us and low enough that the franchise holder cannot operate less expensively on his own. These services include computerized inventory and bookkeeping, mass purchasing, quick replacement of sold stock, legal and tax advice, preticketed merchandise, free national advertising, and professional help and cost participation on local advertising. It should be kept in mind that even the voluntary buying associations have a mark-up of 8% to 10%.

Another advantage will be that all our Centers will be basically the same. Therefore, the problems encountered will have probably been solved in some other store, and any sales ideas and operational suggestions will be of general benefit. We plan to have a regular newsletter and will have contests and suggestion awards to foster a fellowship among the franchise holders.

We feel that the basic sales approach in the Craft Centers should be competent presentation of quality equipment with no high-pressure selling. The owners should be concerned with establishing and holding a good reputation in their community, which will give them personal satisfaction, as well as substantial monetary rewards.

Merchandise to Be Offered

In reviewing the following list, it must be kept in mind that it is very much subject to change. That is the main reason we intend to have our first Center open six to nine months before the next two stores are opened. We estimate that these three stores will have to be in operation another six months to one year before we will be ready to start an aggressive program of franchising additional Craft Centers. Our merchandising ideas at present are:

Shopsmith, Sawsmith, and all major and minor accessories

Act as a dealer for a complete line of major woodworking machinery until we produce our own (under a private brand label)

Complete line of screws, nails, and fasteners

Complete line of woodworking hand tools

Complete line of portable power tools under private label

Complete line of power tool accessories

Paint, finishes, stains, thinners, etc.

As complete a line as possible of cabinet and furniture hardware

Complete selection of woodworking books

A large selection of woodworking patterns

High quality, pre-cut furniture kits

Complete line of glue, gluing clamps, etc.

A good inventory of premium hardwoods

Complete line of general and carved mouldings and wood fiber carvings

Wood veneer sheets, trim, and special tools

Some hobby lines, possibly large car and ship models, large clocks, musical instrument kits, hi-fi cabinet kits, etc.

Possibly carrying some of the large kits now available, such as boats, truck campers, etc.

Services to Be Offered

There are only two specific services that we have definitely decided to offer at this time.

1. Saw sharpening—This is a service that is very difficult to find in some areas, and a successful sharpening operation can net up to $400 per week. Competition comes mainly from small shops or men working from their homes and shouldn't be difficult to overcome. Also, it is a natural service to be offered in this type of store.

2. Power tool and equipment repair—This is also a service that is often difficult to find. All Center owners must be able to repair the Shopsmith line of equipment, and repair service on other equipment will be offered. This other repair work can be subcontracted if necessary. In either case, it again is a natural function of this type of store and will serve to gain the confidence of the customer in addition to being very profitable.

There are a number of other possible services that can be offered, but we must give them extensive trial before they are considered definite.

1. Key making—This service can be worthwhile, particularly for the amount of space required. However, there is competition from many types of retail establishments as well as regular locksmiths.
2. Custom planning and moulding—This service is not likely to be very profitable but may be valuable to serve our customer's needs.
3. Picture framing—This can be done either by the store owner or subcontracted.

It should be kept in mind that franchise owners will differ in skills and amounts of time available. Therefore, one might do the tool repair for a number of area Centers and another may do picture framing for those who did not wish to do it themselves.

We are sure that other services can be performed profitably by the Centers and will present themselves as we gain more experience.

Management and Personnel

At this time, there are only two employees officially working for the Company. However, a management team that will be able to start immediately has been selected, with key supporting personnel also selected and available as required.

Mr. Harold E. Folkerth, Chairman of the Board, will not be devoting full time to the Company unless it proves necessary. However, he is willing to spend as much time as is required to assure the success of the Company. He is currently Vice President of Continental Consultants, Inc. and has spent close to forty years in the field of production and design engineering and manufacturing. His counsel and advice will prove invaluable in areas of engineering and production.

Mr. John R. Folkerth, President, attended Vanderbilt University for three years, majoring in economics and business administration. He then completed his education at the University of Dayton in Industrial Engineering. Next, he worked for Continental Technical Service, Inc. for eight years, starting in the machine shop and moving to the design room. When he resigned in 1961, he was Vice President responsible for finance and administration. He then joined Merrill Lynch, Pierce, Fenner, and Smith, Inc. as an Account Executive for ten years until his resignation on July 2, 1971. In addition to supervising the day-to-day operations of the Company, he will be responsible for the duties that will eventually be assumed by the Vice President, Administration, in the areas of finance and general administration.

The man who will be our Vice President, Sales, is currently employed as the National Sales Manager of a small paper company in the Dayton area. Before joining this company, he spent over ten years in sales with one of the country's largest paper companies. He is making an equity investment and has been working with us in the beginning stages of forming Shopsmith, Inc. He will join the company as quickly as it is formed. His starting duties will be to work with the President in coordinating all the required details in organizing the company, and he initially will be active in all areas except purchasing and production. As our marketing organization develops, he will be primarily concerned in this area.

Mr. Robert Ginn is scheduled to join us in the fifth month. He is presently working as the manager of a retail store and will continue working there until we need him. He was formerly Sales Manager of the West Coast area for Magna Engineering Corporation, after working in direct sales for several years. He is well known by a number of the dealers and has a proven record of performance.

Mr. Norville Wehrheim will join the company in the seventh month and will be responsible for working with dealers in sales training and demonstration techniques, and he will make public demonstrations. He is extremely talented in these areas after spending more than eight years as National Training Manager for Magna Engineering Corporation and Yuba Consolidated Industries, Inc. He is personally known by almost the entire former dealer organization.

These three men will be able to handle effectively our requirements until some time during the second year. At that time, we anticipate continuing the policy of hiring salesmen experienced in selling Shopsmiths whose effectiveness and ability is a matter of record.

An important area related to sales is advertising and promotion. This will be the responsibility of *Mr. Mel Hucke,* presently a partner of HH Art Studios of Dayton, Ohio. Although his firm will be doing the work on a fee basis, Mr. Hucke is making a significant equity investment and will be on the executive committee. Therefore, we will benefit not only from his talent in the advertising and promotional fields, but also from his extensive experience in running a very successful business for over 30 years.

To handle the production, *Mr. Ed Gronefeld* will be working for us for the first six months as a result of our agreement with Magna American Corporation, and he is available to work directly for us after that time. His initial duties will be in the reconditioning of the machinery and in helping to train the production personnel. Once we are set up, he will become our Promotion Foreman. We are fortunate in having Mr. Gronefeld available to work with us as he was responsible for building much of the special machinery and for the actual production of the Shopsmith line of equipment for Magna American Corporation.

Because of the quantity and the critical nature of the purchased parts in this product, we are also fortunate in having *Mr. Carse Weglein* available as our Purchasing Agent. He was responsible for all the purchasing, inventory control, and traffic control for Magna American Corporation. He is thoroughly knowledgeable in the product requirements and has built strong personal relationships with the suppliers we will be utilizing. He is presently working but is willing to join Shopsmith, Inc. as quickly as we can use him.

At this time, the position of Vice President, Production, has not been filled. We have been in contact with Mr. Frank Field, formerly Vice President, Operations, of Magna American Corporation. In this position, he was responsible for all engineering and manufacturing operations. He is not presently working, and we have not worked out anything definite with him at this time. Furthermore, there are several other men in the area that we have talked to who would be extremely capable in this position. Also, if we form this corporation as a joint venture with an established manufacturer, their contribution would be primarily in the production area, so their man would fill this position. Therefore, we will not be making any firm commitments for this requirement until everything else has been finalized.

Another important area is Service and Quality Control. We have already been working with Mr. Jim Kiernan, who proved very capable in this position for Magna American Corporation while they were still in Cincinnati. Mr. Kiernan has not actually committed himself to working full-time for the company but has promised to act as a consultant whenever necessary. We feel that he will be available when we can offer him something definite.

As the success of any organization depends on the quality of its personnel, we are fortunate in being able to assemble a team capable and, to a great extent, already thoroughly familiar with the product. Also, because of the respect they hold for the product and their knowledge of its potential, we have available to us on a consulting basis many of the executive personnel formerly associated with Magna Engineering Corporation. This gives us a tremendous advantage in getting the Company started properly as these men are familiar in all aspects of this very successful operation. Many of their suggestions have already been incorporated in our planning. They are:

Dr. Hans Goldschmidt. Dr. Goldschmidt is the inventor of the original Shopsmith and was one of the three principals of Magna Engineering Corporation. He has a Ph.D. in Mechanical Engineering and is still very active as an independent inventor.

Dr. Goldschmidt has expressed a very personal interest in seeing Shopsmith produced again. In addition to being eligible for royalty payments, he feels that Shopsmith's potential is better now than ever and wants to be involved as a consultant in the areas of product improvement and new product development. In addition, he has already given us invaluable assistance by introducing us to men formerly associated with Magna Engineering Corporation and by giving us suggestions on who would best fill our personnel requirements.

Mr. Frank G. Chambers.   Mr. Chambers, a graduate of the Harvard School of Business, was one of the three originators of Magna Engineering Corporation. At present he is President of Continental Capital Corporation, a very successful small business investment corporation located in San Francisco.

Mr. Chambers is helping us with our financing requirements and has expressed his willingness to help us in the future in financial and administrative areas.

Mr. Roy Maddox.   Mr. Maddox first joined Magna Engineering Corporation in sales in the Southern California territory. He proved to be one of their most successful salesmen and finally became the General Sales Manager for the Shopsmith line. He is presently Executive Vice President of Operations of Mobility Unlimited, Inc., a subsidiary of Magna American Corporation. With their permission, he has offered to act as a consultant at any time he can be of help.

Mr. George Goodrich.   Mr. Goodrich started with the Yuba Power Products Division in sales of Shopsmith and was finally responsible for the East Coast marketing area before he was promoted to Sales Manager and then National Marketing Manager. He resigned when Magna American Corporation moved to Mississippi.

Mr. Goodrich has already been of significant aid to us in discussing our marketing plans and personnel requirements. He has volunteered his services to us as a consultant at any time we may need him.

Mr. Goodrich has his Master's Degree in Marketing and is presently with Cincinnati Melacron Company in their Special Products Division.

Mr. John W. Edgemond.   After their first several years in business, Magna Engineering Corporation submitted the Shopsmith to Stanford Research Institute for a thorough engineering analysis. Mr. Edgemond was assigned by Stanford to head the project and, in submitting his final report, recommended a number of changes and improvements. Magna was so impressed that they hired Mr. Edgemond to design a completely new Shopsmith incorporating these suggested changes, which became the Shopsmith Mark V.

Mr. Edgemond has already been able to help us considerably in areas of possible design changes and product improvement. He is also very knowledgeable in production techniques and has offered to help us on a consulting basis. He is presently Staff Engineer at Maxwell Laboratories, Inc.

Mr. Charlie Reed. Mr. Reed was formerly the Manager of Material and Method Engineering for Magna Engineering Corporation and is presently Director of Materials of Envirotech Systems, Inc.

Since Mr. Reed was responsible for all purchasing for the Shopsmith Mark V, he has already been able to give us considerable insight into the requirements and particular problems involved. He will be available to give us the benefit of his experience at any time we can utilize him.

Mr. Morgan Baldridge. Mr. Baldridge is the owner of Hobby Models, Inc. of Peoria, Illinois. They were a very successful dealer for Shopsmith, and at one time expressed an interest in purchasing the Shopsmith product line.

Mr. Baldridge is very loyal to Shopsmith and has offered his services on a full-time basis. We feel that he could prove very effective in dealer relations and in working with the dealers in improving their sales.

Mr. R. J. DeCristoforo. Mr. DeCristoforo is a well-known author on general woodworking and wrote the books on both the Shopsmith and the Sawsmith.

He feels that there is still a tremendous potential for the product line and is willing to work with us in developing his ideas on product improvement, new product development, and general promotional activities.

Magna Engineering Corporation was very successful due both to a superior product and a very strong management and sales organization. We have been extremely gratified by the response of these men, and their willingness to help us indicates a measure of their faith in this product and its future.

As can be understood, we are not in a position to offer anything definite to potential employees. However, we have had positive indications that we will be able to assemble a management team that has a thorough knowledge of the product line and that has proven ability in its production and sales.

Sales Projection: First Year

In projecting the sales for the first year, we are in an unusual position for a new company. In this case, our sales will be limited only by what we can produce while maintaining the highest possible quality. This situation has been made possible by the fact that, when Magna American Corporation sold out the units they produced in anticipation of the move to Mississippi, they had an organization of approximately 800 dealers. Many of these are most anxious to resume their dealerships and the number of units necessary to replenish their inventories will require all of our production well into the second year.

We estimate that it will take approximately six months to initiate production. It will require this amount of time to recondition the machinery, check out the dies and tooling, set up the production line, and train personnel.

When we actually start production, we are scheduling a much slower rate than the maximum possible in order to assure the quality of the product. We are starting at a rate of ten units per day for the first month, twenty units per day for the second and third months, and thirty units per day for the next three months. This will take us through our first year of business.

The monthly production schedule and the production personnel requirements for the first year as follows:

MONTH	PRODUCTION (PER DAY)	PRODUCTION (PER MONTH)	PRODUCTION PERSONNEL	MACHINISTS
4th	-0-	-0-	-0-	1
5th	-0-	-0-	3	2
6th	-0-	-0-	5	2
7th	10	184	7	3
8th	20	368	15	5
9th	20	368	20	5
10th	30	528	20	5
11th	30	528	20	5
12th	30	528	20	5

The total number of major units produced during the first year at the above rate is 2,504, plus major and minor accessories.

In order to arrive at the total dollar sales for the first year, we have broken down sales into three different areas.

The first and largest area is the sale of major units. As outlined above, we have projected sales of 2,504 major units during the first year. To give these sales a dollar value, we have utilized a figure of $400 per unit. In arriving at this dollar amount, we analyzed the sales records of Magna American Corporation and found that for every dollar of sales of major units, sales of major and minor accessories and spare parts averaged 56.8 cents. We then multiplied this factor by our net average sale price of the Shopsmith and Sawsmith to arrive at an approximate $400 of total sales for each major unit sold.

The second area is sale of spare parts. These sales are currently running approximately $10,000 per month. Because of the transfer of inventory during the first month, we have not scheduled any sales during this month but have increased the second month's sales to $14,000 and $10,000 per month thereafter. We have projected these part sales separately from what we include in the sale of spare parts generated by the sale of major units because of the large number of units presently in use.

The third area is sale of major accessories. Because these accessories have not been available for some time, we are projecting $55,000 in sales from this area, independent of the accessory sales generated from the sale of major units.

As can be seen on the following chart, our total sales for the first year are projected at $1,170,600.

MONTH	SPARE PART SALES	MAJOR ACCESSORY SALES	MAJOR UNIT SALES	TOTAL (MONTH)	TOTAL (YEAR)
1st	-0-	-0-	-0-	-0-	-0-
2nd	14,000	-0-	-0-	14,000	14,000
3rd	10,000	2,000	-0-	12,000	26,000
4th	10,000	3,000	-0-	13,000	39,000
5th	10,000	4,000	-0-	14,000	53,000
6th	10,000	5,000	-0-	15,000	68,000
7th	10,000	6,000	73,600	89,600	157,600
8th	10,000	7,000	147,200	164,200	321,800
9th	10,000	7,000	147,200	164,200	486,000
10th	10,000	7,000	211,200	228,200	714,200
11th	10,000	7,000	211,200	228,200	942,400
12th	10,000	7,000	211,200	228,200	1,170,600

Cost Projections: First Year

In this section we are including a summary sheet detailing our projected general and administrative expenses and sales expenses. Another sheet shows those expenses normally included in the "Cost of Goods Sold." We are doing this because we will be incurring these expenses before we actually start production. As can be seen, all but one of these expense items terminate after the sixth month, since we will then be in production and these costs will be included before figuring the gross profit on sales.

Following each of the summary sheets, we are including detailed explanations of how we arrived at each individual cost item.

We have endeavored to cover all the costs that will be incurred in establishing this company. Although it is impossible to cover all contingencies, we feel that these estimates are as accurate as possible.

Supplementary Information: Cost of Goods Sold

This section explains the individual cost items on the following sheet.

ITEM 1. Salary—Production Manager

ITEM 2. Expenses—Production Manager: In order to help us get started, Magna American Corporation has agreed to loan us the service of Mr. Ed

Cost Projections: First Year

	(DURING FIRST SIX MONTHS)						
Salary—Prod. Manager	-0-	-0-	-0-	1,150	1,150	1,150	-0-
Prod. Mgr.—Expenses	-0-	400	650	650	650	650	3,450
Laborers at Magna	1,067	333	-0-	-0-	-0-	-0-	-0-
Boxing—Shipping Mat.	633	67	-0-	-0-	-0-	-0-	-0-
Shipping Costs	1,283	1,167	-0-	-0-	-0-	-0-	-0-
Machinery Rebuilders	-0-	844	1,386	1,386	1,386	1,386	-0-
Mach. Rebuilder Helper	-0-	347	563	563	563	563	-0-
Stock Clerk	292	542	542	542	542	542	-0-
Mechanic—Handyman	187	607	607	607	607	607	-0-
Misc. Tools & Equip.	-0-	733	167	-0-	-0-	-0-	-0-
Air System Suppliers	-0-	1,167	333	-0-	-0-	-0-	-0-
Mach. & Tool Repair Mat.	-0-	1,067	2,333	2,600	2,000	2,000	-0-
Fork Lift Truck Rental	-0-	8	110	110	110	110	-0-
Pick Up Truck Rental	-0-	10	125	125	125	125	-0-
Industrial Engineer	667	867	867	867	867	867	-0-
Payroll Taxes (12%)	266	420	475	614	614	614	-0-
Depreciation	1,140	1,140	1,140	1,140	1,140	1,140	-0-
Amortization—Plant Imp.	29	29	29	29	29	29	-0-
Plant Rental	1,275	1,275	1,275	1,275	1,275	1,275	-0-
Utilities	400	400	400	400	400	400	-0-
Janitor Wages	346	346	346	346	346	346	-0-
Janitor Supplies	243	19	19	19	19	19	-0-
Machinist	-0-	-0-	-0-	650	650	650	-0-
Machinist (#2)	-0-	-0-	-0-	-0-	650	650	-0-
Mechanical Technician	-0-	-0-	-0-	-0-	563	563	-0-
Assembly Girls	-0-	-0-	-0-	-0-	390	780	-0-
Total	7,828	11,768	11,367	13,083	14,076	14,466	3,450

Gronefeld, free for three months and at $1,150 per month for another three months. If Mr. Gronefeld is subsequently hired by Shopsmith, Inc., we have agreed to pay them for his first three months, which is the $3,450 item in the seventh month in the expense line (Item 2). This appears because we definitely feel that we will want to employ him. Mr. Gronefeld was responsible for the production of Shopsmiths and Sawsmiths for Magna American Corporation and for helping develop much of the special machinery, so he will be of invaluable help. The expenses shown are for travel and living costs during the initial six-month period.

ITEM 3. Laborers at Magna American Corporation: Mr. Gronefeld will be responsible for the shipping of the equipment from Raymond, Mississippi. This expense item is for men to help box and load the machinery, tooling, and inventory. We are estimating that it will require three men for five weeks at $2.50 per hour.

ITEM 4. Boxing and Shipping Materials: We have estimated these costs at $700. This will include materials for skids for the machinery, and boxing for many of the tools and for the inventory.

ITEM 5. Shipping Costs: Magna American Corporation is going to allow us the use of their truck to ship all the material to Dayton at their actual cost of $.37 per mile. This truck has a capacity of 20 tons, and we estimate it will take seven trips at an average cost of $350 per trip, for a total of $2,450.

ITEM 6. Machinery Rebuilders—At $4.00 per hour

ITEM 7. Machinery Rebuilder Helper—At $3.35 per hour: Working with Mr. Gronefeld, we estimate that it will take two good machinery rebuilders with a good helper to get all the equipment and machinery in proper working order. They will start as soon as everything arrives in Dayton (about six weeks from the date of purchase), and we will probably require their services through the sixth month.

ITEM 8. Stock Clerk: We will need to hire this man to start right away. The inventory will be the first thing to be shipped, so shelving will have to be prepared and procedures worked out. He will be responsible for filling and shipping parts orders, so we need him to get things organized as quickly as possible. His rate will be $3.00 per hour.

ITEM 9. Mechanic–Handyman: This man's responsibilities will be such things as installing the permanent storage and shop partitions, putting in shelving, stringing lights, installing the air supply system, setting up the assembly lines, running errands, etc. His rate will be $3.50 per hour.

ITEM 10. Miscellaneous Tools and Equipment: This expense item includes things such as hand tools, inspection equipment, pullers, grinders, etc. that will be required for general use and to recondition the machinery. We estimate that they will cost approximately $900.

ITEM 11. Air System Supplies: We estimate that it will take about $1,500 for the piping, hoses, nozzles, etc. to get the compressed air to the machinery and other areas where it will be needed.

ITEM 12. Machinery and Tool Repair Material: We have budgeted $10,000 to cover the material costs of reconditioning the machinery and tooling. Although there is no way of being sure, we feel that this amount will be more than adequate.

ITEM 13. Fork Lift Rental—At $110 per month

ITEM 14. Pick-up Truck Rental—At $125 per month

We will need both of these items by the eighth week, which is the reason for the small figure in the second month. Our initial rental will be for one year, after which we may find that we don't need either one of them or that it would be cheaper to purchase them.

ITEM 15. Industrial Engineer: His first duty will be to provide a detailed plant layout to enable us to place the machinery efficiently when it has been checked out. We also will be able to erect partitions, install lighting, and run the required electricity and compressed air. When this is completed, we will want him to lay out the subassembly and assembly lines, then work out an inventory control and production control system. His rate will be $200 per week and we will need him for six to eight months.

ITEM 16. Payroll Taxes: We have estimated that the taxes directly attributable to payroll cost will run approximately 12%.

ITEM 17. Depreciation

ITEM 18. Amortization—Plant Improvements

As per the latest depreciation guidelines, we are depreciating all the machinery and improvements over a 12-year life. Other than the original machinery purchase from Magna American Corporation, all the purchases going into the depreciation and amortization accounts are detailed in the section "Cash Flow—First Year."

ITEM 19. Plant Rental—Total cost at $1,500 per month

ITEM 20. Utilities—Total cost at $500 per month

For both of these expense items, we are allocating 85% of the total cost toward "Cost of Goods Sold" and the other 15% is included in the "General and Administrative Costs" expenses.

ITEM 21. Janitor Wages—Total cost at $433 per month

ITEM 22. Janitor Supplies—Total cost at $25 per month

For these expense items, we are allocating 80% to "Cost of Goods Sold" and 20% to "G. & A. Costs." To get started, we are budgeting $304 for supplies for the first month.

ITEM 23. Machinist

ITEM 24. Machinist (No. 2)

Since we will want to start actual assembly in the seventh month, we will need to have the machining operations for the first run completed before then. In addition, the machinists will need training on the machinery, sample parts will have to be inspected, and we will need parts for the accessories as early as the fifth month. Therefore, we are scheduling the first machinist to be hired at the beginning of the fourth month and the second at the beginning of the fifth month. Their rate will be $3.75 per hour.

ITEM 25. Mechanical Technician—$3.25 per hour

ITEM 26. Assembly Girls—$2.25 per hour

We will hire a mechanical technician at the beginning of the fifth month so Mr. Gronefeld and the Industrial Engineer can work with him on setting up the subassembly and assembly lines correctly. As he will supervise this operation, he will also be responsible for training the assembly girls. Two will be hired in the middle of the fifth month and two more at the beginning of the sixth month. There will be some subassembly operations and some accessory assembly that they will be able to start on immediately.

Supplementary Information: General and Administrative Costs and Sales Costs

This section explains the individual cost items on the following summary sheet.

ITEM 1. Chairman of the Board: As previously mentioned, his salary will be $100 per month unless at some time in the future it becomes necessary for him to devote full time to the company.

ITEM 2. President: The President's salary will be fixed at $18,000 per year plus stock options until the company becomes profitable. From that time, his compensation will be determined by the Board of Directors in line with the profitability of the Company.

ITEM 3. Secretary–Bookkeeper: This secretary will be hired soon after we start operating. She will be working with our accountant to set up the books in addition to handling our initial clerical requirements. As our activity picks up, her duties will eventually be limited to keeping the books and payroll. Her salary will be $520 per month.

ITEM 4. Secretary—General and Billing: This secretary will be hired at the beginning of the third month to handle the billing and other secretarial duties that the bookkeeper had been handling. Her salary will be $430 per month.

ITEM 5. Secretary—General

ITEM 6. Secretary—General

As can be seen on the summary sheet, these women are scheduled to be hired in the fifth and eighth months, when our increased activity will require their services. Their salaries will be $430 per month.

ITEM 7. Administrative Travel: This is to cover the travel expenses necessary to get the company started, such as trips to Mississippi, checking suppliers, calling on dealers, etc. After that, considerable travel will be necessary in working with the dealers, trade shows, etc.

ITEM 8. Payroll Taxes: We have estimated that the taxes directly attributable to payroll costs will run approximately 12%.

ITEM 9. Consulting and Professional Fees: This item covers a number of necessary services we will require, such as legal fees, a certified public accountant, promotional services, credit reports, and other general advisory services.

ITEM 10. Franchise Taxes: These are the fees necessary to become qualified to do business in each of the individual states.

ITEM 11. Office Supplies: There are some basic supplies that we will need immediately and others that we will need as we go along. The printing of all the forms we will need causes this expense item to be quite high during the first three months, after which it drops off considerably.

ITEM 12. Miscellaneous General and Administrative Expenses: This expense item is to cover hard-to-account-for items that are needed in any business.

ITEM 13. Insurance—General and Liability: This item is intended to cover all our insurance requirements, such as fire, theft, valuable papers, liability, product liability, etc.

ITEM 14. Classified Advertising: It will be necessary to advertise for some of the personnel we will require, particularly the machinists and production personnel.

ITEM 15. Telephone: The $350 figure for the first month is to cover installation charges. As can be seen, the costs for this service will increase gradually over the year as our activity picks up.

ITEM 16. Utilities—Total cost of $500 per month

ITEM 17. Plant Rental—Total cost at $1,500 per month

For both of these expense items, we are allocating 15% of the total cost to "G. & A. Costs" and 85% to "Cost of Goods Sold."

ITEM 18. Depreciation—Office Equipment

General and Administrative Costs and Sales Costs

	J	F	M	A	M	J	J	A	S	O	N	D
General and Administrative												
Chairman of the Board	100	100	100	100	100	100	100	100	100	100	100	100
President	1,500	1,500	1,500	1,500	1,500	1,500	1,500	1,500	1,500	1,500	1,500	1,500
Secretary—Bookkeeper	280	520	520	520	520	520	520	520	520	520	520	520
Secretary—Gen'l & Billing	-0-	-0-	430	430	430	430	430	430	430	430	430	430
Secretary—General	-0-	-0-	-0-	-0-	-0-	-0-	-0-	430	430	430	430	430
Secretary—General	-0-	-0-	-0-	-0-	-0-	-0-	400	400	400	400	400	400
Administrative Travel	550	333	200	200	300	300	390	622	622	742	742	742
Payroll Taxes	236	264	339	339	390	390	100	100	100	100	100	100
Consult. & Professional	133	200	300	200	100	100	100	-0-	-0-	-0-	-0-	-0-
Franchise Taxes	-0-	25	50	50	50	50	100	100	100	100	100	100
Office Supplies	200	500	1,000	100	100	100	50	50	50	50	50	50
Misc. G. & A. Expenses	100	100	100	100	50	50	100	100	100	100	100	100
Insurance—Gen. & Liability	100	100	100	100	100	100	50	-0-	-0-	-0-	-0-	-0-
Classified Advertising	50	50	50	-0-	-0-	50	200	200	200	200	300	300
Telephone	350	100	100	100	100	200	100	100	100	100	100	100
Utilities	100	100	100	100	100	100	225	225	225	225	225	225
Plant Rental	225	225	225	225	225	225						

Depreciation—Off. Equip.	22	22	22	22	22	22	22	22	22	22	22	22
Amortization—Lease Imp.	6	6	6	6	6	8	8	8	8	8	8	8
Auto Depreciation	120	120	120	120	120	120	120	120	120	120	120	120
Amortization—Preoperating & Organization Expense	200	200	200	200	200	200	200	200	200	200	200	200
Janitor Wages	87	87	87	87	87	87	87	87	87	87	87	87
Janitor Supplies	61	6	6	6	6	6	6	6	6	6	6	6
Total G. & A.	4,422	4,560	5,557	4,507	4,938	5,088	5,238	5,750	5,750	5,870	5,970	5,970
Sales Costs												
Sales Manager	-0-	-0-	-0-	-0-	-0-	-0-	1,500	1,500	1,500	1,500	1,500	1,500
Expenses—Sales Mgr.	-0-	-0-	-0-	-0-	-0-	-0-	1,000	1,000	1,000	1,000	1,000	1,000
Salesman	-0-	-0-	-0-	-0-	-0-	-0-	-0-	-0-	-0-	1,000	1,000	1,000
Car Rental—Sales	-0-	-0-	-0-	-0-	-0-	-0-	-0-	-0-	-0-	130	130	130
Expenses—Salesmen	-0-	-0-	-0-	-0-	-0-	-0-	-0-	-0-	-0-	900	900	900
Sales Promotion Nat.	-0-	-0-	200	200	200	200	200	200	200	200	200	200
Advertising	-0-	2,000	2,000	-0-	-0-	1,000	1,000	1,000	2,000	2,000	2,000	2,000
Direct Mail	-0-	-0-	-0-	-0-	-0-	-0-	200	200	200	200	200	200
Total Sales	-0-	2,000	2,000	2,000	200	1,200	1,400	3,900	4,900	6,930	6,930	6,930
TOTAL	4,422	7,560	7,557	6,507	4,932	6,288	6,638	9,650	10,650	12,800	12,900	12,900

ITEM 19. Amortization—Leasehold Improvements

The cost of the equipment and alterations included in these two expense items are detailed in the section "Cash Flow—First Year."

ITEM 20. Automobile Depreciation: It will be necessary to have a car for administrative travel. At this time we don't know if it will be best to purchase or rent. However, the expense to the company will be approximately the same in either case.

ITEM 21. Amortization—Preoperating and Organization Expense: This expense will total approximately $12,000, which we are amortizing over a five-year period.

ITEM 22. Janitor Wages—Total cost at $433 per month

ITEM 23. Janitor supplies—Total cost at $25 per month

For these expense items, we are allocating 20% to "G. & A. Costs" and 80% to "Cost of Goods Sold." To get started, we are budgeting $? for supplies for the first month.

ITEM 24. Sales Manager—Salary at $15,000 to $? per year

ITEM 25. Expenses—Sales Manager

We will be hiring our sales manager at the beginning of the eighth month. As our initial production will already be sold, his initial duties will be in customer relations work for the expansion of the business in the second year. As these activities will require a considerable amount of traveling, we have budgeted his expenses at $1,000 per month.

ITEM 26. Salesman

ITEM 27. Car Rental—Sales

ITEM 28. Expenses—Salesman

This man will be hired at the beginning of the tenth month, primarily to work with the individual dealers. He will be traveling constantly, so the company will be providing a car and travel expenses. Additional salesmen will not be required until the second year.

ITEM 29. Sales Promotional Material: There are a number of items required for the promotion of these products, and it will be necessary to have a large supply on hand when we start selling the units. These items include the following:

Dealer display cabinet

Sales literature on the main products

Sales literature on the major accessories

Operational manuals of all the major units and accessories

Other manuals and promotional material

ITEM 30. Advertising: During the first year, advertising will be limited to that required to support individual dealers. It will not be until the second year that we will require a national advertising campaign.

ITEM 31. Direct Mail: As can be seen from the amount budgeted, our direct mail activities during the first year will be largely experimental in order to see if our products can be sold in this manner. If successful, we will be doing considerably more of it during the second year.

Profit and Loss Projections: First Year

The following summary sheet gives the monthly profit and loss projections, utilizing the figures developed in other sections of this study. As can be seen, the company should start operating profitably in the seventh month and show an after-tax profit for the year of $72,015.

Cash Flow: First Year

The following summary sheet gives a detailed analysis of our projected cash flow during the first year. As can be seen, we end the year with a deficit cash flow even though we anticipate having a profitable year. This is not unusual in starting a new business. We are fortunate to be able to utilize the inventory we are purchasing from Magna American Corporation for immediate sales and in our production, for this holds down the deficit cash flow considerably.

These cash flow figures do not take into consideration the payments that will be made to Magna American Corporation for the purchase of the business, of which approximately $150,000 will be due at the time the purchase is consummated. Following the summary sheet, we are including detailed explanations of how we arrived at most of the income and expense items.

Our peak negative cash flow comes in the eighth month at approximately $156,000 and declines thereafter. During the early months of the second year, our cumulative cash flow will turn positive, and we cannot visualize circumstances where it would ever be negative again—other than sporadically for unusual reasons.

There are three items that could alter our cash flow considerably. One assumption we have made is that we will be paid by our customers in 30 days. This may be optimistic, and if so, we have arranged bank financing on our receivables. On the positive side, we have shown that our product costs will be paid immediately, which will not be completely necessary. The other factor that could considerably alter this cash flow is the use of the inventory. The inventory we are purchasing from Magna American Corporation has a book value of approximately $160,000, of which we are scheduling the use of only $65,000 in spare part sales and in our production during the first year. Our use of this inventory could be as much as $30,000 to $50,000 higher than this during the first year.

Supplementary Information

This section explains the individual items on the following summary sheet.

ITEMS   1–12. All these items are self-explanatory. They are expense items that, because of their nature, must be either depreciated or amortized. In the

Profit and Loss Projections: First Year

12-MONTH PERIOD

	1	2	3	4	5	6	7	8	9	10	11	12
Monthly Sales												
Spare Parts	-0-	14,000	10,000	10,000	10,000	10,000	10,000	10,000	10,000	10,000	10,000	10,000
Major Accessories	-0-	-0-	-0-	-0-	-0-	2,000	2,000	2,000	2,000	2,000	2,000	2,000
Major Units (at 400)	-0-	-0-	-0-	-0-	-0-	55,000	73,600	147,200	147,200	211,200	211,200	211,200
Gross Profits on above												
Spare Parts	-0-	7,700	5,500	5,500	5,500	5,500	5,500	5,500	5,500	5,500	5,500	5,500
Major Accessories	-0-	-0-	-0-	-0-	400	800	800	800	800	800	800	800
Major Units (% Profit)						at 10%	at 15%	at 20%	at 20%	at 25%	at 25%	at 30%
Major Units—Profit	-0-	-0-	-0-	-0-	-0-	5,500	11,040	29,440	29,440	52,800	52,800	63,360
Total Gross Profit	-0-	7,700	5,500	5,500	5,900	12,000	17,340	35,740	35,740	59,100	59,100	69,660
Costs												
General & Admin.	4,422	4,560	5,557	4,507	4,930	5,088	5,238	5,750	5,750	5,870	5,970	5,970
Sales	-0-	2,000	2,000	2,000	2,000	1,200	1,400	3,900	4,900	6,930	6,930	6,930
Cost of Goods Sold	7,828	11,768	11,367	13,083	14,070	6,280	3,450	-0-	-0-	-0-	-0-	-0-
Total Costs	12,250	18,328	18,924	19,590	21,014	20,754	10,088	9,650	10,650	12,800	12,900	12,900
Profits (loss) for month	(12,250)	(10,628)	(13,424)	(14,090)	(15,414)	(14,454)	7,252	26,090	25,090	46,300	46,200	56,760
Profit (loss) for year	(12,250)	(22,878)	(36,302)	(50,392)	(65,806)	(80,260)	(73,008)	(46,918)	(21,828)	24,472	70,672	127,432

Net profit for year: 127,432

Income Taxes
- 25% first $25,000: 6,250
- 48% balance: 49,167
- Total Taxes: 55,417

Profit (after taxes): $72,015

Projected Cash Flow: First Year

	12 MONTHS											
Cash Outflow												
Air Compressor	2,000											
Fencing—crib & storage		600										
Office Equipment	500		1,000									
Office Machinery	500		500									
Leasehold Improvements (off.)	100	200		300								
Leasehold Imp. (in plant)												
Electrical Work	700	1,300										
Air Supply System	1,167	433										
Equipment												
Standard Mach. Tools	1,500	2,000	3,000	2,000								
Benches	500	500										
Conveyor System	400	300										
Shelving	200											
Assembly Tables	500	200	200									
Miscellaneous	200	200	200	200	200							
Cost of Goods Sold	7,828	11,367	13,073	14,076	14,466	3,450	55,320	110,400	110,400	158,400	158,400	158,400
G. & A. Expenses and Sales	4,422	7,557	6,507	4,930	6,288	6,638	9,650	10,650	12,800	12,900	12,900	
Cost—Spare Parts	-0-	6,300	4,500	4,500	4,500	4,500	4,500	4,500	4,500	4,500	4,500	4,500
Cost—Major Accessories	-0-	-0-	600	-0-	-0-							
Cost—Major Units	-0-	-0-	-0-	-0-	-0-	1,200	1,200	1,200	1,200	1,200	1,200	1,200
Total Outflow	14,250	34,795	28,557	27,580	26,308	26,654	71,108	125,750	126,750	176,900	177,000	177,000

Projected Cash Flow: First Year (*continued*)

	12 MONTH PERIOD											
Cash Income												
Sales												
Spare Parts	-0-	-0-	-0-	10,000	10,000	10,000	10,000	10,000	10,000	10,000	10,000	10,000
Major Accessories	-0-	-0-	-0-	-0-	-0-	1,000	2,000	2,000	2,000	2,000	2,000	2,000
Major Units	-0-	-0-	14,000	-0-	-0-	-0-	-0-	73,600	147,200	147,200	211,200	211,200
Use of Parts Inventory	-0-	6,300	4,500	4,500	4,700	4,700	4,700	15,000	15,000	5,600	-0-	-0-
Depreciation & Amortization												
General & Adminis.	350	350	350	350	350	350	350	350	350	350	350	350
Cost of Goods Sold	1,169	1,169	1,169	1,169	1,169	1,169	1,169	1,169	1,169	1,169	1,169	1,169
Total Income	1,519	7,818	20,019	16,019	16,219	17,219	18,219	102,119	175,719	166,319	224,719	224,719
Cash Income (Outgo) per month	(12,731)	(26,976)	(8,538)	(11,561)	(10,000)	(9,435)	(52,889)	(23,631)	48,969	(10,581)	47,719	47,719
Cash Income (Outgo) for the year	(12,731)	(39,707)	(48,245)	(59,806)	(69,895)	(79,330)	(132,219)	(155,850)	(106,881)	(117,462)	(69,743)	(22,024)

case of office equipment and improvements, the life is 10 years. For the machinery and plant improvements, the life is calculated at 12 years.

ITEM 13. Miscellaneous: This expense item is included to cover items that are difficult to account for but invariably required.

ITEM 14. Cost of Goods Sold

ITEM 15. G. & A. Expenses and Sales
A detailed explanation of both of these expense items is included in section "Cost Projections—First Year."

ITEM 16. Cost—Spare Parts: We are estimating the cost of our spare parts sales at 45% of the sales. This is in line with the recent gross profit margins experienced by Magna American Corporation.

ITEM 17. Cost—Major Accessories: We are planning to price the major accessories to give us a gross profit margin of 40%. Therefore, this cost item is calculated at 60% of the sales volume.

ITEM 18. Cost—Major Units: In the calculation of our costs to determine our cash flow, we are using an average cost of 75% of the sales, even though we will be pricing the unit to give us an approximate gross profit of about 32%. As can be seen in the section "Profit and Loss—First Year," we have calculated our gross profit at 15% of the first month's sales of major units, increasing to 30% by the twelfth month. We have done this in order to reflect the time it will take to attain 100% production efficiency.

ITEMS 19–21. An explanation of how we determined the monthly sales of each of these three product categories is detailed in section "Sales Projection—First Year." In entering these sales into this cash flow projection, we have figured 30 days from the time of the sale until we receive the proceeds from these sales. As we will be offering a discount for payment within 10 days, we are hoping the average age of our receivables will be 30 days or less.

ITEM 22. Use of Parts Inventory: As our purchase from Magna American Corporation includes approximately $160,000 in parts inventory, all our parts sales for the first six months will be filled from this inventory. Altogether, we are estimating that we will be able to use $65,000 of this inventory during the first year. This figure should prove to be very conservative.

ITEM 23. Depreciation and Amortization—G. & A.

ITEM 24. Depreciation and Amortization—Cost of Goods Sold
As these cost items are included in the totals in our cash outflow calculations and are not actually cash expenses, we are offsetting these items by including them in our cash income section.

Five-Year Sales Projections

In this section, we have projected our estimated sales volume, expenses, and profits for each individual year for the next five years. We are also including calculations of how each year's figures were calculated.

The net profit after taxes for these years is listed below. As can be seen, they show an erratic pattern that becomes understandable as we get started.

First Year	$ 72,015			
Second Year	148,017	difference	$ 76,092	105%
		difference	23,937	15.5%
Third Year	171,954	difference	71,900	42.0%
Fourth Year	243,854			
		difference	102,960	42.5%
Fifth Year	346,814			

The above figures show a 51.25% compounded growth rate for the first five years. After the third and fourth years, we will aim for a compounded yearly growth rate of a least 25%.

First Year

How we determined the sales estimates and the projected expenses during our first year are explained in detail in other sections. Comparisons of this year to other years are not possible for several reasons. Our sales and advertising charges during this year are extremely low because we will be working with a limited number of dealers, and we will have very little national advertising. The "Cost of Goods Sold" expenses will normally be included in the calculation of the gross profit. The biggest factor is that during the first six months we have considerable set-up costs and we are actually producing major units during only the last six months of the year.

Sales—First Year (2,504 major units)	$1,130,600	
Gross Profit	307,580	(27.2%)
Cost of Goods Sold (nonrecurring)	76,038	(6.72%)
General and Administrative Costs	63,620	(5.62%)
Sales Expenses	38,390	(3.40%)
Profit before Taxes	127,432	
Federal Income Taxes	55,417	
Net Profit after Taxes	$ 72,015	(6.37%)

Second Year

During our first year we reached a production level of 30 units per day, which works out to 522 units per month or 6,336 per year. We plan to produce at this rate during the second year.

Part of this production will be used to complete replenishing dealer inventories and also to direct consumer sales where there is an existing demand with no dealer coverage.

The balance of the second year's production will need to be sold. Therefore, we will be adding a number of personnel to our sales staff in order to service properly the dealers already established and also to sign up additional large dealers. In addition, we will increase our advertising expenditures considerably. This advertising will be directed to both potential dealers and to the consumer, particularly in *Workbench* and *The Family Handyman*.

During the second year we will also be developing the Shopsmith Craft Centers, as well as the direct mail sales of woodworking supplies and equipment. To begin with, our spending in these areas will be very modest, and we estimate that it will be the fourth or fifth year before they start contributing to our profits.

We have provided detailed estimates of our costs for the first year. The following is a breakdown of those costs that will increase during the second year.

INCREASED GENERAL AND ADMINISTRATIVE COSTS

Additional three secretaries at $5,000 each per year	$ 15,000
Hiring a Vice President, Administrative	15,000
Salary increase—President	8,000
Increased payroll taxes	3,500
Increased telephone expenses	1,000
Total Increase	$ 42,500
First year's G. & A. costs	$ 63,620
Added above	42,500
Total, Second Year	$106,120

INCREASED SALES EXPENSES

Shopsmith Craft Centers	$ 20,000
Catalog sales costs	10,000
Advertising	90,000
Ten salesmen (including demonstrators) at $25,560 per year (including expenses)	255,600
Total Increase	$375,600
First year's sales expenses	$ 38,390
Added above	375,600
Total, second year	$413,990

Sales—Second Year (6,336 major units)	$2,534,400	
Gross Profit (at 32%)	811,008	
General and Administrative Costs	106,120	(4.19%)
Sales Costs	413,990	(16.3%)
Total Costs	520,110	
Profit before Taxes	290,898	
Federal Income Taxes	142,881	
Net Profit after Taxes	$148,017	(5.84%)

Third Year

Because a portion of our second year's sales were to replenish inventories, we are projecting our third year sales at the same volume—or 6,336 major units. We feel that this is justified because of the significantly increased expenditure for our sales organization and for our advertising.

Our General and Administrative expenses should be approximately the same since our sales will be the same.

We plan to increase our advertising in this year from $90,000 to $130,000. We are estimating that the Shopsmith Craft Centers will require a continued expense of approximately $20,000. However, any increased costs for direct mail selling will be offset by profits from these sales.

Because of the increased gross profit from these direct sales and better manufacturing efficiencies, we are projecting our gross profit margins at 35%, rather than the 32% of the second year:

Sales—Third Year (6,336 major units)	$2,534,400	
Gross Profit (at 35%)	887,040	
General and Administrative Costs	106,120	(4.19%)
Sales Expenses	443,990	(17.5%)
Total Costs	550,110	
Profit before Taxes	336,930	
Federal Income Taxes	164,976	
Net Profit after Taxes	$171,954	

Fourth Year

After the first three years, we feel that a 25–35% compounded growth rate for the next several years is not only justified, but possibly very conservative. At that rate, it will still take a number of years to reach the sales volume of 15 years ago.

In projecting the fourth and fifth years, we are utilizing the 25% growth rate, which will include the sales generated through the Shopsmith Craft Centers and the catalog sales.

Our General and Administrative expenses should hold at approximately 5% of sales.

The big difference will be in our sales costs. Our sales expenses in the third year were 17.5%, which is excessive but necessary in establishing the company. While they were still effectively selling, Magna American Corporation kept their sales costs between 8% and 10% of sales, which we feel is somewhat conservative. Therefore, we are projecting our fourth year's sales costs at 15% and our fifth year's costs at 13%, at which point it should remain fairly constant.

Sales—Fourth Year (7,905 major units)	$3,168,000
Gross Profit (at 35%)	1,108,800
General and Administrative costs (at 5%)	158,400
Sales Expenses (at 15%)	475,200
Total Costs	633,600
Profit before Taxes	475,200
Federal Income Taxes	231,346
Net Profit after Taxes	$243,854

Fifth Year

As in the fourth year, we are projecting increased sales of 25%. Our General and Administrative costs should remain at approximately 5% while our sales expenses should drop to about 13%.

Sales—Fifth Year (9,900 major units)	$3,960,000
Gross Profit (at 35%)	1,386,000
General and Administrative costs (at 5%)	198,000
Sales Expenses (at 13%)	514,800
Total Costs	712,800
Profit before Taxes	673,200
Federal Income Taxes	326,386
Net Profit after Taxes	$346,814

Analysis of Dealer Survey, April 16, 1971

On March 29, 1971, I called Mr. Ben Barrett to discuss the option agreement we were negotiating, and I asked him to have Mr. Roy Maddox send me a list of 20 to 30 dealers I could call to get a feel for the former dealer organization. He said he would, and on April 5th I received a list of 52 names and addresses. I do not know how he arrived at this list, but I am inclined to believe they were names he recognized without checking their sales records.

I believe this list included many of their good dealers, but it also included a service center that was never in the business and an individual who became a dealer immediately before Magna terminated production (he was able to have only his first Shopsmith order filled). Of the 52, there were included eight dealers out of approximately fifteen Mr. Maddox called on while he was an area representative. I was unable to contact one of these dealers. When I completed calling, I had talked to the responsible individual at 51 of the 52 dealers listed. The one dealer I was not able to contact must have a phone listing under another name as I was unable to establish that he is still in business at the location listed.

Other than general discussion, I asked the following questions:

1. Were they interested in reestablishing their dealerships?
2. How many Shopsmiths did they feel that they would be able to sell the first year?
3. What would their first order be? (This order would include their first six months' requirements and would be made in three deliveries, three months apart [plus or minus a couple of months].)

To the first question, I had 17 dealers say they would not be interested. Their reasons, except where mentioned below, were primarily because of the way Magna American Corporation left them exposed when they terminated production, their inability to get parts and accessories, and the general deterioration of factory communication and support in later years. However, all but four said that they would be most interested in talking to me once I was operating and they could see how we handle things. The reasons of those four were: a service that actually never sold Shopsmiths; a dealer that has dropped all power tool sales and is selling only unfinished furniture; a dealer that wasn't interested for personal reasons he wouldn't discuss; and another dealer who is selling only overhead cranes at present.

Of the 34 dealers left, all but a few were concerned with price, quality, promotion, factory support, service, and assured fast delivery of units, accessories, and parts. Most of their sales estimates were predicted on the above criteria being taken care of to their satisfaction. However, if these things are done, they are without exception most interested in being dealers. Also, I was very careful to try to get conservative estimates, and most potential dealers feel that, if the company goes at all, the estimates should go much better than they are projecting. These orders can be grouped as follows:

FIRST ORDERS: TOTAL OF 556 MAJOR UNITS

5 or less units	5 dealers
6 to 10 units	19 dealers
11 to 20 units	5 dealers
21 or more units	5 dealers

FIRST YEAR PROJECTIONS: TOTAL OF 1279 UNITS

10 or less units	9 dealers
11 to 20 units	13 dealers
20 to 40 units	7 dealers
40 or more units	5 dealers

By using a factor of $400 for the total sales generated by the sale of a major unit, we arrive at total orders for the first six months of $222,400, and estimated sales for the first year of $911,600. Actually, if these unit estimates are valid, sales should be considerably higher because of pent-up demand for major and minor accessories. The men that want to continue being dealers have all requested that we start getting accessories to them as quickly as possible, and many of the dealers that are presently holding off committing themselves as to whether they will purchase major units want to buy accessories as soon as they can be produced.

The figures I generated from these calls can be stated as follows: 66.7% of the dealers are interested in continuing selling Shopsmiths, their average estimates for the first six months are for 16.3 units, and their first year estimates average 37.4 major units.

In trying to utilize these figures to project sales for the total former dealer organization, I feel the following adjustments would make them more valid, although very conservative:

1. Cut the total dealers from the 866 they were working with in half—to 433.
2. Because three or four of their best dealers were represented on Mr. Maddox's list, cut the order estimates as follows:
   A. From 16.3 to 10 for the first order as an average from each dealer.
   B. Cut the estimated first year's sales from 37.4 to 23 per average dealer.

Using these reduced factors, we can loosely project:

1. 433 × 66.7% equals 288 dealers interested.
2. The first order from these dealers covering their first six-month sales will be 2,880 major units.
3. The estimated sales for the first year will be 6,624 major units.

These figures tend to substantiate those estimates for our first year's sales where we estimate that all the 2,500 units that we can produce in the six months after we actually start production will be required to satisfy the former dealers.

I am attaching the list of dealers I talked to in the order I was able to reach them, with their estimates and appropriate comments.

One additional thing concerning the list is the comments on dealer interest in stock investment. I asked the first 12 dealers I talked to if they were interested and 7 said they were. However, at that point I came to the conclusion that the question complicated the conversation and that the answer actually did not tell me anything. Of the remaining dealers I talked to, 3 of them volunteered an interest in buying stock in the company without my broaching the subject.

Dealer Survey

DEALER NAME	FIRST ORDER	FIRST YEAR	COMMENTS
Omar Greydt 402 Nichols Rd. Madison, Wis. 608-222-4028	18	25	Formally worked for Monky Ward. Rents space to just sell and service Shopsmiths. Interested in investing.
Hobby Models 418 Fulton Peoria, Ill. 309-673-2616	20	45	Wants to work for Shopsmith and thinks he can be of real help. Interested in investing.
Lou Rappaport, Inc. 1149 Front St. Binghamton, N.Y. 607-723-5436	6	12	Not interested in investing.
Gee Lumber Co. 2600 W. 79th St. Chicago, Ill. 312-476-7400	-0-	-0-	Not interested in investing. Wants to see how we do before he becomes a dealer.
Alhart Electric Co. 1110 Culver Rd. Rochester, N.Y. 716-482-8686	6	20	Interested in investing.
Production Equipment Co. 2178 N. Meridian Indianapolis, Inc. 317-925-7508	60	100	Not interested in investing.
Casper Lumber Co. 404 E. Railroad Casper, Wyo. 307-237-2545	10	25	Not interested in investing. Be glad to help in any way possible.
Mendelsohms, Inc. 469 Moddy St. Waltham, Mass. 617-894-3210	25	25	Interested in investing. He said "don't be afraid of the price."
Wiggert Bros. 327 Jay St. La Crosse, Wis. 608-784-4790	6	12	Interested in investing. He would like to be distributor in the area.
Machinery Sales P.O. Box 329 Daleville, Inc. 317-378-3366	-0-	-0-	Thinks we are buying a dead line but would like to talk to us after we get started.
Battel's Hardware 13238 E. Whittier Blvd. Whittier, Calif. 213-696-3218	150	350	Interested in investing. Would like to be the distributor in So. Calif.

Dealer Survey *(continued)*

DEALER NAME	FIRST ORDER	FIRST YEAR	COMMENTS
B. Dulchin, Inc. 170 7th Ave. New York, N.Y. 212-243-6741	9	25	Interested in investing. Would like to be the "N.Y." dealer.
Kaminstein Bros. 29 3rd Ave. New York, N.Y. 212-777-7170	9	15	
Paul Silken, Inc. 21 W. 46th St. New York, N.Y. 212-582-0002	10	20	Wants me to contact him when I'm in area so he can discuss it. Does a big business in radial saws.
Clark Dye Hardware 210 S. Main St. Santa Ana, Calif. 714-547-1633	10	24	Not interested in investing. He was one of the first dealers in the country.
Buena Park Hardware 6586 Beach Blvd. Buena Park, Calif. 714-522-2864	10	20	
Montgomery Hardware 2801 Canton Rd. Jackson, Miss. 601-366-4441	-0-	-0-	Would be interested in talking to us after we get started.
Root's Fix-it Shop 159 Delmar Place Syracuse, N.Y. 315-455-6764	6	6	He was a service dealer. Still doing a pretty good business in parts and service.
Skarie, Inc. 707 N. Howard St. Baltimore, Md. 301-728-6000	12	20	
Capital City Lumber Co. 700 E. Kalamezza Lansing, Mich. 517-482-1115	12	25	They have a "Shopsmith Club" of about 50 members.
Midland Hardware 5228 Chouteau Kansas City, Mo. 816-452-7100	-0-	-0-	Because of personal reasons he wouldn't discuss, he won't be interested.
Von Tobel Lumber Co. 217 S. First St. Las Vegas, Nev. 702-734-8111	-0-	-0-	Would like to talk to us after we get started. Actually feels they have ruined it.

Dealer Survey *(continued)*

DEALER NAME	FIRST ORDER	FIRST YEAR	COMMENTS
Entz-White Lumber Co. 909 Camelback Rd. Phoenix, Ariz. 602-279-2341	-0-	-0-	Would like to see cost sheets, delivery dates, etc. before they go back into it.
Bryant & Trott Hardware 110 E. Main St. Santa Maria, Calif. 805-WA5-2721	3	5	Not interested in Sawsmith.
B & H Hardware 121 S. 4th St. Corvallis, Ore. 503-753-8511	-0-	-0-	Interested after we get started. Very concerned about the price.
Rose's Hardware 4132 Viking Way Long Beach, Calif. 213-HA9-5988	40	250	
Miller Bros. Hardware 395 Pomona Mall E. Pomona, Calif. 714-622-5524	-0-	-0-	Area has deteriorated. However, the son is building a store in Arizona and would be interested in selling it there.
Star Lumber Co. 505 Jackson Amarillo, Texas 806-376-6383	-0-	-0-	Very interested after he sees how we do. They are a "Carter Co." dealer, which helps margins.
Turner Hardware 607 E. Weber St. Stockton, Calif. 209-464-4651	12	20	They have an eleven-store operation.
L. & S. Tool Supply 8625 E. Las Tunas Dr. San Gabriel, Calif. 213-287-0516	-0-	-0-	Probably oldest dealer after Monky Ward. Very interested, but will have to see the way we handle it.
Seiki Hdwe. & Appl. 1620 Post St. San Francisco, Calif. 415-246-5010	-0-	-0-	They are tied in with Ace Hardware. If Ace will buy it, they will handle it.
Fullerton Hardware 106 Harbor Blvd. Fullerton, Calif. 714-526-3351	6	20	
Oceanside Lumber Co. 260 3rd Ave. Oceanside, Calif. 714-722-8281	10	12	

Dealer Survey *(continued)*

DEALER NAME	FIRST ORDER	FIRST YEAR	COMMENTS
Baldwin Park Hardware 4153 N. Main St. Baldwin Park, Calif. 213-338-7371	-0-	-0-	He just bought the business about one year ago and would have to see how it went before he committed himself.
Santa Cruz Hardware 1523 Pacific Ave. Santa Cruz, Calif. 408-423-2926	6	10	
Grandview Hardware 3024 E. Camino Real Santa Clara, Calif. 408-246-1070	6	18	
Commercial Hardware 500 E. 4th St. Reno, Nev. 702-329-0231	-0-	-0-	Would be interested in talking after we get things firmed up.
Ray Sapp Hardware 7210 N. Oak St. Kansas City, Mo. 816-436-4500	6	10	
Woodward Lumber Co. 909 Amador Las Cruces, N.M. 505-526-6622	6	10	
Missoula Mercantile Co. Higgins & Front St. Missoula, Mont. 406-543-7211	6	15	He doesn't think we have to sell it cheap.
Schneider Bros. Hardware 1248 Commerce Ave. Longview, Wash. 206-425-4100	3	5	
Power Tool Center 4808 N. Lombard Street Portland, Ore. 503-289-8762	30	80	They are still a service center.
J. E. Sears Co. Box 576 Appomattox, Va. 703-352-7138	3	6	
Simon Streiffer Co. 2026 Metairie Rd. Metairie, La. 504-833-8288	-0-	-0-	Not interested. All they are selling now is unfinished furniture.

Dealer Survey *(continued)*

DEALER NAME	FIRST ORDER	FIRST YEAR	COMMENTS
Hammond Electric 1510 E. 3rd St. Tulsa, Okla. 918-582-4104	-0-	-0-	Not interested. Not selling any power tools. Now selling Yale Hoist Overhead Cranes.
Bolton's Hardware 123 N. E. 10th St. Oklahoma City, Okla. 405-235-8471	3	6	They took it over when Monky Ward dropped it. Only got one order filled before Magna stopped producing them.
Swenson's Lumber Co. 860 N. 3rd St. Laramie, Wyo. 307-745-4843	-0-	-0-	Would be interested after he sees how we handle dealer service and training.
Farr's 880 1st St. Coos Bay, Ore. 503-267-2137	10	12	Very interested in investing. Thinks I should consider locating in the Seattle, Wash., area.
The Welders' Supply Co. 3301 Polk Houston, Texas 713-223-3356	-0-	-0-	They still do service and plan to continue. They never actually sold the product.
Rhodes Hardware 434 San Mateo Ave. San Bruno, Calif. 415-588-2383	10	20	They would like to be the Northern California distributor.
Pine Tree Hardware 325 N. 72nd St. Omaha, Neb. 402-556-6767	3	5	They think the margin should be at least 33%.

VENTURE: A MAGAZINE FOR ENTREPRENEURS

$35,000 Limited Partnership Interests: These securities are subject to a high degree of risk. Copy number: 47. Date: October 1977.

CONTENTS

Risk Factors

Editorial Concept

The Potential Market for *Venture* readers

Circulation Plan

Advertising Plan

Operational Plan

People Involved
Federal Income Tax Consequences
Exhibits

Summary of Program

This is a plan for a new monthly, general business magazine, called "*Venture* . . . the magazine for entrepreneurs." Included in this plan are a description of the editorial concept, a review of the market for readers and advertisers, and operating plans for the magazine.

Venture will be edited for three principal groups of readers:

1. existing entrepreneurs—the owners and managers of entrepreneurial businesses.
2. potential entrepreneurs—executives and managers of large corporations interested in owning their own businesses.
3. corporate entrepreneurs—executives and managers of large corporations who perceive their job function as one that requires them to think and operate entrepreneurially.

These three groups contain over 10 million potential readers. A quality magazine edited specifically for the entrepreneur does not exist. *Venture's* target audience represents a substantial market for the sale of magazines and advertising for business and consumer products.

Venture's operating plan projects a paid circulation rate basis of 80,000 for the premier issue. The goal of the operating plan is to expand circulation to 320,000 within five years.

The attached exhibits contain projections of management with respect to total investment required and profits. As stated in "Risk Factors," no assurance can be given that these projections will be achieved.

Joseph D. Giarraputo (the "General Partner") offers interests in a limited partnership to be organized under the laws of the State of New York and to be known as The Venture Publishing Company (the "Partnership"). Purchasers of such interests will be referred to herein as Limited Partners.

The Limited Partners will contribute the entire capital of the Partnership, and the General Partner will contribute the concept for the magazine. The Limited Partners in the aggregate will receive a 15.0625% profit-sharing interest in the Partnership, and the General Partner will receive a 84.9375% profit-sharing interest. Without the consent of any of the other Partners, the General Partner may raise additional capital by selling additional Limited Partnership Interests in the Partnership up to a maximum amount, including the amount subscribed for hereunder, of $90,000. The sale of these Partnership Interests shall not dilute the Partnership Interests of the Limited Partners but only that of the General Partner. Thereafter, the General Partner may not raise capital in excess of such amount by selling additional Limited Partnership Interests without the consent of Partners holding in the aggregate a 50% Partnership Interest in the Partnership.

Each Limited Partner will receive a capital account equal to the amount of his subscription.

The Partnership will be formed for the purpose of developing and conducting a mailing to test the feasibility of founding a business magazine called *"Venture . . . the magazine for entrepreneurs."* A positive response to the test mailing in excess of 2% would generally be required before advancing to the next stage of the magazine's development. If the response falls below this, the project will in all probability be abandoned, and no salvage value is anticipated.

If the test is successful, the next step will be to prepare for the start of regular publication of the magazine, which will involve recruiting a staff, selling advertising, establishing relations with suppliers, commencing direct mail promotion, and raising a substantial amount of additional capital (see "Prepublication Phase").

It is projected that the proceeds of the sale of interests in the Partnership will be expended approximately in the following manner.

Direct Mail Test (80,000 pieces)	$24,000
Direct Mail Advertising Agency	4,000
Office and Travel	2,250
Magazine Design	1,750
Legal	3,000
	$35,000

Interests in the Partnership will not be registered with the Securities and Exchange Commission. The Partnership is relying on an exemption from registration for the sale of securities which do not involve a public offering. Accordingly, each purchaser will be required to agree that his purchase was not made with any present intention to resell, distribute, or in any way transfer or dispose of his interest in the Partnership, except in compliance with applicable securities laws, and that he meets the suitability standards described herein.

No person is authorized to give any information or representation not contained in this memorandum. Any information or representation not contained herein must not be relied upon as having been authorized by the Partnership or the General Partner.

Risk Factors

Projections.   This Prospectus contains certain financial projections. Although no representations can be made that the circulation or advertising levels indicated by the projections will be achieved or that projected costs or cash flow will correspond even approximately to actual costs or cash flow, those projections reflect the current estimates of management of the results that are likely if circulation or advertising can be increased and the costs controlled as reflected herein. These projections are subject to the uncertainties inherent in any attempt to predict the results of operations for the next five years, especially where a new business is involved.

Additional Capital.   Assuming the test projections are successful and publication of the magazine is commenced, it is estimated that at least $1 million of new capital will be required before positive cash flow is achieved. There are no commitments for any of these funds, and no assurances can be given that such funds will be available, and if available, no prediction can be made of the terms and conditions of such additional financing. Partners in the Partnership will be given the right to participate in this additional financing. To the extent this right is not exercised, a substantial dilution of the partners' interest will probably result.

Staff.   To commence publication of the new magazine, it will be necessary to recruit a new staff. A full staff has not yet been recruited, and no assurance can be given that a qualified staff can be hired on reasonable terms.

Taxation.   For the tax treatment of gains or losses to Limited Partners of the Partnership, see "Federal Income Tax Consequences."

General Risk.   Starting a new magazine is a highly speculative undertaking and has historically involved a substantial degree of risk. The ultimate profitability of any magazine depends on its appeal to its readers and advertisers in relation to the cost of production, circulation, and distribution. Appeal to readers and advertisers is impossible to predict and depends upon the interaction of many complex factors.

Competition.   The magazine business is highly competitive. In promoting the sale of *Venture*, management will be competing with many established companies having substantially greater financial resources.

Suitability.   Because of the lack of liquidity of an investment in this program and the high degree of risk involved, the purchase of limited partnership interests of the Partnership should be considered only by persons who can afford a total loss of their investment.

Editorial Concept

Venture will be a magazine for entrepreneurs—real ones, would-be ones, corporate ones. It will illuminate the world of new ventures in all its aspects for the 10 million businessmen who are entrepreneurs or have aspirations to be, and the millions more who in the future increasingly will be "running their own businesses" within larger corporations. It is a discrete assemblage with an identity and common interests that are all but ignored by today's major business publications.

Venture will appeal to an influential, upwardly mobile readership. While "business" has its detractors as well as adherents, the entrepreneur retains an admirable image with almost everyone. As a risk-taker, his business venture is one of the closest approximations of true adventure our civilized society offers. Even his success is seldom envied, for it is a reminder to the rest of the world that rags to riches stories are still possible. Dropouts from the corporate world they may be, but entrepreneurs build new worlds in their own image. They are fascinating subjects.

Furthermore, the time for *Venture* is propitious. There is a growing realization that "big won't work." The efficiencies of scale of large organizations, predicated upon planning the actions of everyone from the top, may have peaked. Today, even workers on assembly lines balk at becoming unthinking robots. It is hardly surprising then that managers want to be creators, not mindless functionaries. It is a time when entrepreneurship will flourish— inside the large company as well as in the new venture.

Venture will be the month-by-month chronicle of that world and the personalities who inhabit it. It will be Edwin Land (Polaroid), Ross Perot (Electronic Data Systems), Mary Wells Lawrence (Wells Rich Greene), but *Venture* also will be today's climbers who will be tomorrow's celebrities.

It can be Ken Walker, 35, whose masters degree from Harvard is in architecture, not business, a museum-quality painter turned entrepreneur, whose five-year-old design firm, Walker/Grad, is currently handling $20 million in construction money and who is wondering how fast he should continue to grow.

It can be Jim Sheridan, businessman turned designer. A former vice president of Bankers Trust, Sheridan purchased a design firm (Raymond Loewy) last summer and expects to double its volume by the end of the current fiscal year.

It can be Bruce Westwood, 36, vice-president of a venture capital firm that put $1 million into a Canadian-based soft-drink firm, who then joined the venture as its president and took it to $27 million in sales, with planned expansion just beginning.

It can be Joe Camp, who learned the film business by producing the feature film *Benji* with $550,000 of borrowed money. *Variety* called it 1975's third largest grosser.

Venture will make an impact on the business of its times. It will unashamedly espouse the cause of the entrepreneur as an alternative to corporate giantism. Entrepreneurs will be portrayed realistically, warts and all, but the image of success will never be more than a page or two away.

Venture will be a mosaic of news, gossip, and need-to-know information. Personalities, trends, and "how to" will be interwoven in a fashion that will entertain as well as instruct.

The core of *Venture* will be its feature articles. The format—appropriate for a monthly—will be flexible enough to allow articles, which will be written with style and wit, to run their proper length, whether one page or ten. But each must justify itself as topical and newsy, not merely instructional and significant. Subjects will include management, financing, how-to-get-started, risks, and rewards.

The relationship between government and entrepreneurial business also will be a frequent area of exploration. Much in the system today mitigates against the fledgling entrepreneur and to the advantage of the large corporation, which often in turn seems to subvert the very nature of a free market system. We will expose attempts to erect unwarranted barriers in the way of new ventures and will speak out strongly against them.

While features will comprise most of *Venture's* editorial columns, each issue will include regular departments, front and back, to give the magazine a familiar look and "feel."

One will be a news section, with a small-column format and staccato news items on: PEOPLE (making it, trying to make it, and going bust); LEGISLATION; TAXES; NEW VENTURES; FRANCHISES.

Other regular stand-alone departments will be BOOKS; LETTERS; REWARDS (a feature showing how to spend the big bucks that our upscale readers will aspire to, and presenting the life styles of successful entrepreneurs); YOU AND YOUR_____(Banker, Consultant, Backer, Accountant, Lawyer, Right-hand Man), a feature on building relationship with the entrepreneur's various associates; CAPITALISTS (a regular feature on what the money men are up to and the kinds of ventures they are looking for); FRANCHISES (a rating of opportunities); and HOW TO START A_____(Restaurant, Resort, Tennis Club).

Sample tables of contents of issues show more specifically how *Venture's* concept can be translated into a provocative and entertaining magazine.

CONTENTS: MONTH 1

LETTERS

NEWSPAGE

(Sample lead items):

PEOPLE: Clay Felker, sadder but surely wiser, starts over. . .

LEGISLATION: Going public? the SEC's fuller-disclosure rules could put you at a competitive disadvantage. . .

TAXES: Backers of Broadway musicals find tax shelter benefits as well as glamour. . .

NEW VENTURES: Former banker Jim Sheridan's design company is booming. . .

FRANCHISES: The biggest growth will be in recreation, travel, and entertainment. . .

FEATURES:

Who says technology ventures are passé? Take the case of Frederick Adler, who made $6 million on Data General and is busy incubating a host of companies with names like Lexidata that may make him millions more. Shades of '69?

The second time around. Entrepreneurs don't always make it on their first attempt, but almost 3 out of 4 try again if they fail. Here are 6 who came back from disasters to succeed the second time around.

A Venture Capital Paradise—Santa Clara. In all, some 150 venture capitalists live and work in Santa Clara county, California, a place that offers everything entrepreneurs need to succeed. Already more than 100 company founders have become millionaires there and many are not yet 35 years old.

Seymour Cray: His plans are ambitious. Cray already is famous in his field as the original technical genius behind William Morris Control Data Corporation. Now his own Cray Research Inc. plans nothing less than dominance of the scientific computer market. Cray is contributing his talents—and $1 million of his own money—but he still will be lucky to hold on to 11% of this potential giant.

Half-way House. Corporate executives (at General Mills, GE, and Exxon, among others) sometimes have the chance to act more like entrepreneurs than some of the real ones—and occasionally reap the same kind of rewards.

You don't have to go public to make money. A package of subordinated debentures, convertible preferred, and equity will tide you over in a bad-market pinch.

Franchising's golden dozen. Franchise volume is soaring with sales expected to total $179 billion by 1980. On average, however, sales at individual establishments are abysmally low. Still, the winning industries are well worth your attention.

DEPARTMENTS

BOOKS: *The Entrepreneur's Manual,* Richard M. White, Jr. (Chilton, $15)

REWARDS: *The Sporting Life.* Lamar Hunt's professional sports enterprises—football, soccer, tennis among others—allow him to live very well indeed. (Who else could have afforded to buy Jim Ling's $3 million chateau?) It also helps that daddy was a billionaire.

YOU AND YOUR *LAWYER*

CAPITALISTS: *Personality Test.* Venture firms have their own ideas about what kind of personality profile an entrepreneur should have. It's okay to be a misfit but, yes, these days to get a stake you have to be a super guy.

FRANCHISES: McDonald's vs. Burger King

HOW TO START A *MAGAZINE*

CONTENTS: MONTH 2

LETTERS

NEWSPAGE

(Sample lead items):

PEOPLE: Donald Cook, who made plenty of waves as CEO at American Electric Power, is running Lazard Frères' venture capital fund his own way . . .

LEGISLATION: What you hear is true—the Pension Reform Act is hurting companies without records of success . . .

TAXES: The new laws opened as well as closed some loopholes: Shelters today, . . .

NEW VENTURES: A California book publisher is making money by breaking all the rules . . .

FRANCHISES: Pyramiding, Bait-and-Switch, Sound-Alikes, and other frauds to watch for . . .

FEATURES:

Advice to Corporate Minnows: Being swallowed by a whale isn't all bad. In these times a merger with a larger partner may be the easiest way for backers to turn over their investments. A look at some marriages made in heaven.

Ross Perot: Adjusting to a billion dollar paper loss. But before you pass the hat for him, remember he still has a quarter of a billion left.

The "Entrepreneurial Center." Can these B-School adjuncts—at Wharton, SMU and elsewhere—really show you the ropes in venturing?

The winners are . . . Here's a selling point for your venture: A $1,000 flyer in companies going public can produce some startling dividends if you are lucky. Look at the record—you could have missed Xerox and still be a winner. A 1955 investment of $1,000 in the first public offering of Gearhart Owens, for example, would be worth more than $1 million today.

The small business administration: getting smaller. Its help for entrepreneurs is shrinking along with everybody else's.

And with the left hand . . . Some of the fastest-stepping managers in some of the largest corporations are doing their own thing on the side. Cases in point: Heinz President Tony O'Reilly, who has his ups and downs with his Irish enterprises and City Investing Executive Vice President Peter Huang, who may soon be cashing in some chips.

How to survive in spite of contract law. Lawyers think every sloppily drawn contract results in a legal battle. Don't you believe it. Remember, as an entrepreneur you cannot always afford the legal protection your lawyer says is "Minimal."

DEPARTMENTS

BOOKS: *Running Your Own Business,* Howard H. Stern (Ward Ritchie, $4.95 paper)

REWARDS: *Working couple.* Does Mary Wells Lawrence really need a house in the south of France, a ranch in New Mexico, a hide-away in Acapulco, a mansion in Dallas and an apartment in New York? No. But with her own ad agency she can afford it. Husband Harding Lawrence, Chairman of Braniff, is no slouch in the take-home-pay department either.

YOU AND YOUR *BANKER*

CAPITALISTS: *Sometimes everything is relative.* Face it—first-stage financing isn't apt to come from venture capitalists. But your family and friends are there for the asking.

FRANCHISES: Rating the muffler shops

HOW TO START AN *ART GALLERY*

The Potential Market for Venture Readers

Venture will attract its readership primarily from these groups:

existing entrepreneurs
potential entrepreneurs
corporate entrepreneurs

All of its readers will not be businessmen, however. Subscribers will include doctors, dentists, lawyers, government officials, educators, students, and foreign readers with an interest in entrepreneurship.

But existing, potential, and corporate entrepreneurs represent in themselves a large enough group to support a magazine the size of *Venture.* The section that follows, The Circulation Plan, will show how management presently intends to market to these groups.

Existing Entrepreneurs. The number of entrepreneurs is inferred from the number of entrepreneurial businesses or those in which the managers have an equity interest.

We shall assume a business with less than $50 million in revenue is entrepreneurial. Although some larger businesses also are entrepreneurial and some smaller are not, most businesses of this size are entrepreneurial. There are several sources of data on the number of businesses by their size.

The Internal Revenue Service reports there are approximately 13 million proprietorships, partnerships, and corporations in the United States. Most of these businesses are very small—87% had annual sales of less than $100,000. These very small businesses, while probably entrepreneurial, are not considered a part of the prime market for *Venture* magazine. *Venture* will be too sophisticated for most of this group and it is not the segment of the market *Venture's* advertisers would find most attractive.

Rather than appeal to very small businesses, the existing entrepreneurs *Venture* will seek will be in middle-size businesses. These are businesses with sales of less than $50 million but more than $100,000 for proprietorships and partnerships, and more than $500,000 for corporations.

According to the IRS there are approximately 1.1 million businesses in this size range.

If it is assumed each of these 1.1 million businesses has three potential readers (an owner and two management-level employees) *Venture's* potential market among existing entrepreneurs would total 3.3 million.

U.S. Commerce Department data, which ranks businesses by number of employees, indicates the number of existing entrepreneurs in *Venture's* prime audience range is closer to 4 million.

That the universe of middle-size and smaller businesses is a potential market for *Venture* circulation may be inferred from data provided by other general-interest publications.

Dun's Review indicates that 55%, or 124,000, of its subscribers are from companies with fewer than 1,000 employees.

Forbes indicates that 54%, or 346,000, of its subscribers are from companies with fewer than 1,000 employees.

Executive Newsweek indicates that 48%, or 239,000, of its subscribers are from companies with sales of less than $50 million.

Fortune indicates that 256,000 of its subscribers are with companies employing fewer than 1,000 people—185,000 are with companies employing fewer than 100 people.

Thus, the total market of entrepreneurial owners and managers is large, and subscription to general business magazines is significant.

The Potential Entrepreneur Market.   It is difficult to develop any accurate estimate of the number of potential entrepreneurs. The urge and ambition to become an entrepreneur is wide-spread. Each man's motivation is uniquely his own. One man may be pushed toward entrepreneurship by problems in his present job, while another may be attracted by the chance to make a fortune. Whatever their motivation, potential entrepreneurs undoubtedly outnumber actual entrepreneurs many times over.

However, *Venture* will not attempt to appeal to the entire universe of potential entrepreneurs. Again, the sophistication of the magazine and the reader characteristics advertisers will require preclude this approach. *Venture* will aim at those potential entrepreneurs who are currently executives or managers in large nonentrepreneurial businesses and institutions. These individuals will be equipped to understand the editorial content of *Venture* and, as business decision makers, will be attractive prospects for *Venture* advertisers.

The Corporate Entrepreneur Market.   A corporate entrepreneur works in a large corporation as an executive or senior manager. He perceives that success in his job requires him to be able to function entrepreneurially. Specific jobs these corporate entrepreneurs currently fill are varied. Many of them are merger and acquisition specialists, managers who are leading their companies into new businesses and markets. Most profit center managers also envision themselves as entrepreneurs. They are responsible for bringing together many varied resources and orchestrating them into a successful operation. Profit center managers can be presidents of the largest corporations or managers of sales regions.

Many people in the United States fill managerial and executive positions. U.S. census figures indicate that there are more than 9 million people in such positions. The actual number of these managers who will subscribe to *Venture* can only be determined in the direct mail test. However, for editorial and advertising reasons, *Venture* will probably appeal to upper- and middle-management corporate entrepreneurs.

Reaching the Market for Readers: Circulation Plan

Circulation marketing tests, which will be conducted during the first phase of operations, will determine the exact course of the circulation program, but a general description of a plan can be presented.

Venture will be marketed through both subscription and single copy, or newsstand, sales. Subscriptions, however, are expected to account for the predominant share of *Venture's* circulation. It is expected that 90% of the magazine's circulation will result from subscriptions. The objective of the Circulation Plan is to attempt to sell approximately 220,000 new subscriptions during *Venture's* first two years of operation. The projected sources of these subscriptions are as follows:

	% OF NEW SUBSCRIPTIONS
Direct Mail	73%
Reply Cards	12
Catalogue & School Agents	10
Exchange Advertising	4
White Mail	1
	100%

Direct Mail. During the test phase, a direct mail probe of 80,000 pieces will be made. This probe will determine the most responsive mailing lists, copy, and price offers. The types of lists that will be considered for testing include:

Dun & Bradstreet—particularly those segments of the list selectable by size of business.

Business Week, Nation's Business, and other general interest business publications.

Board Room Reports and other more specific business publications.

Lists of mail order buyers of self-help business books and other business products.

Lists of MBAs, CPAs, and certain attorneys.

Lists of members of organizations such as The Jaycees and National Association of Independent Businessmen.

Lists of owners and managers of specific types of businesses that fall within *Venture's* size requirements, such as auto dealers, business consultants, and building contractors.

Reply Cards.   A significant source of subscribers is expected to be from offers in *Venture* magazine itself. Every issue of *Venture* magazine, newsstand and subscription, will contain a bind-in and blow-in offer for *Venture* magazine. Several successful publishers have made these inserts their most profitable source of new subscriptions.

Catalogue and School Agents.   Subscription agencies are organizations which, for a fee, sell subscriptions to many magazines. They can be useful in building a new magazine's circulation. Past experience indicates that two types of agents produce better revenue and advertising prospects than others. These are catalogue agents, which sell primarily to libraries, and school agents, which sell primarily through students as a fund-raising device. *Venture* is expected to use both of these types of agencies in its initial years to gain exposure and build circulation levels.

Exchange Advertising.   Another significant source of new orders is expected to be through subscription offers in other general business and trade magazines. This can be a relatively inexpensive method of obtaining subscribers. *Venture* need not pay rate card prices for advertisements in other magazines. Instead of paying cash, it may be possible for *Venture* to trade its own advertising space. (This is a common practice among publishers.) Particularly good sources can be other general business publications. Tests will also be conducted of selected trade publications to determine their responsiveness.

White Mail.   Every established magazine receives unsolicited requests for subscriptions. While these will not represent a large portion of the magazine's circulation, they are still very valuable as they require no promotional expenditures.

Several other potential sources of profitable subscriptions for *Venture* have not been included in the projections. All these additional sources have been profitably employed by other publishers. They include the following:

Paid Space.   This entails buying advertising in other publications to promote subscriptions.

Airline Distribution. Selected magazines are able to obtain 10,000 to 20,000 subscriptions annually from distribution through airlines. It would appear that *Venture's* editorial content would make it an attractive prospect for this type of distribution.

Co-ops. There are currently in existence several executive co-op mailings. These are mailings, for a variety of products, to groups of business executives. Obviously a magazine like *Venture* could be included in one of these promotions.

Sponsored Sales. Several magazines have successfully worked with organizations in the sale of subscriptions. *Venture* could enter into arrangements with organizations such as The Junior Chamber of Commerce or The National Association of Independent Businessmen for the sponsorship of subscription sales.

Shows and Exhibits. Several magazines have been successful selling subscriptions at shows and exhibits related to the editorial concept of the magazine, *e.g.,* a boating magazine at a boat show. Most major cities have an annual start-your-own-business show. It is possible that a subscription booth at these shows would be a profitable source of subscriptions for *Venture.*

While subscriptions from these sources are not included in the projections, there will be continuing attempts to create new profitable sources of subscriptions.

Under the Circulation Plan, *Venture* will attempt to attract about 10% of its circulation from newsstand sales. Newsstands can produce profitable sales and newsstand profits can be enhanced by responses to insert offers. *Venture's* operating plan projects total paid circulation of 80,000 for its premier issue—77,000 from subscriptions and 3,000 from newsstand. The goal of the operating plan is to expand circulation to 320,000 within five years—293,000 from subscriptions and 27,000 from newsstand.

Advertising Plan

Efforts to sell advertising will be directed at a wide range of marketers of business and consumer products and services. *Venture's* editorial environment and reader demographics are expected to make it a desirable forum for those companies currently advertising in other general business publications.

The annual advertising revenue in general business publications is substantial and growing. Publishers Information Bureau (PIB) collects information on advertising revenue of most major magazines. According to PIB, advertising revenue for the general business publications it measures increased from $98 million in 1974 to $101 million in 1975. This represented a 3% increase.

General Business Magazines Advertising Pages and Revenue: January–December

	PAGES		REVENUE (000)	
	1975	*1974*	*1975*	*1974*
Black Enterprise	401	373	$ 3,070	$ 2,787
Business Week	3,405	3,698	52,946	51,286
Dun's Review	713	883	3,028	3,321
Forbes	1,464	1,432	14,901	13,775
Fortune	1,432	1,679	21,799	23,113
Harvard Business Review	214	246	706	690
Nation's Business	371	297	4,178	3,097
Total	8,000	8,608	$100,628	$98,069

The general economy and the magazine industry did not experience a particularly good year in 1975. Total advertising in all types of magazines actually declined during the year. General business magazines, however, were able to show an increase in spite of the industry decline. With the recovery of the economy, 1976 developed into an extremely good advertising year for general business publications. PIB data for January through December 1976 issues of the measured magazines follow.

Advertising Pages and Revenue

	PAGES			REVENUE (000)		
	1976	*1975*	*Increase*	*1976*	*1975*	*Increase*
Black Enterprise	443	401	10%	3,398	$ 3,070	11%
Business Week	3,925	3,405	15	67,428	52,946	27
Dun's Review	727	713	2	3,315	3,028	9
Forbes	1,757	1,464	20	19,452	14,901	31
Fortune	1,599	1,432	12	26,687	21,799	22
Harvard Business Review	274	214	28	927	706	31
Nation's Business	404	371	9	5,054	4,178	21
Total	9,129	8,000	14%	$126,261	$100,628	25%

PIB indicates a 25% increase in advertising revenue for this group of publications in 1976. Current projections for 1977 call for continued substantial increases in advertising revenue. Advertising revenue for general business magazines actually increased by 24% during the first seven months of 1977.

The categories of advertisers that will be attracted to *Venture* magazine will be similar to those currently advertising in existing general business publications. During 1975, advertisers in general business publications were in the following product categories.

PIB Measured Business Publications*: 1975 Advertising by Classification

	(000)	%
Consumer Services	$ 29,166	29.0
Industrial Materials	20,072	20.0
Office Equip., Stationery, and Writing Supplies	11,936	11.8
Freight	6,349	6.2
Automotive	6,249	6.2
Insurance	4,408	4.4
Travel, Hotels, Resorts	4,357	4.4
Beer, Wine, Liquor	2,904	2.9
Building Materials	2,838	2.8
Publishing, Other Media	2,423	2.4
Aviation, Accessories	2,245	2.2
Gasoline, Lubricants	1,669	1.7
Optical Goods, Cameras	745	.8
Smoking Materials	641	.6
Household Equipment, Supplies	587	.6
Consumer Electronics, TV, etc.	305	.3
Retail and/or Direct by Mail	256	.3
Sporting Goods, Toys	224	.2
Food, Food Products	191	.2
Entertainment, Amusement	122	.1
Apparel, Footwear, Acces.	109	.1
All Other	2,820	2.8
	$100,616	100.0%

*Black Enterprise, Business Week, Dun's Review, Forbes, Fortune, Harvard Business Review, Nation's Business.

The top five classifications of advertisers account for over 70% of the total revenue in this market. Individual advertisers in these top five categories are expected to be *Venture*'s prime advertising prospects. Included in these five classifications are banks, brokers, credit cards, communications, computers, office machines, metals, papers, chemicals, foreign and domestic cards, and air, sea, and land carriers.

Among the categories of advertisers selling business products and services, *Venture* may prove to be an excellent medium for those with a special interest in reaching decision makers in medium-size and smaller businesses.

Because its editorial content is oriented toward the individual, *Venture* may be able to compete effectively with general business publications for advertisers of personal consumer products. These categories include automotive, travel, hotels, resorts, beer, wine, and liquor.

Venture's advertising plan calls for obtaining a .06% share of the general business magazine advertising market in 1978 and expanding this to a 1.9%

market share in 1982. If one assumes that this market will grow at a 7% annual rate, projected advertising revenues would be as follows:

		VENTURE'S ADVERTISING SHARE ($000)	
	Venture	All General Business Magazines	Venture Share
1978	$ 87.7	$143,112.0	0.06%
1979	487.7	153,130.0	0.3
1980	1,223.0	163,849.0	0.7
1981	2,240.7	175,319.0	1.3
1982	3,607.8	187,591.0	1.9

Operational Plan

The Operational Plan for *Venture* is divided into three phases:

1. Testing and Financing
2. Prepublication
3. Publication

Testing and Financing Phase.   The major objectives of this phase will be (1) a direct mail test of consumer acceptance of the magazine, and (2) obtaining the capital required to launch the publication and carry it through its initial years. This phase is expected to last from approximately October 1977 through May 1978.

A major portion of *Venture's* subscriptions are expected to be obtained from direct mail promotions. Future response to a direct mail promotion can be tested and predicted with a high degree of accuracy. A direct mail test is planned for December 1977. This mailing will be sent to approximately 80,000 names. The test will attempt to determine the following:

the validity of the concept
the most effective copy approaches
the most productive price at which to offer subscriptions

An experienced direct mail circulation advertising agency has been engaged to plan, execute, and evaluate the direct mail test.

Also during this phase, sources of the capital required to launch the magazine will be contacted and exposed to *Venture* as an investment opportunity.

The expected cost of this phase is $35,000.

TEST AND FINANCING PHASE COSTS

Direct Mail Test (80,000 pieces)	$24,000
Direct Mail Advertising Agency	4,000
Office & Travel	2,250
Magazine Design	1,750
Legal	3,000
	$35,000

Prepublication Phase. After the Testing and Financing Phase has been completed, all information gathered will be carefully evaluated. If this evaluation leads to a decision to proceed with *Venture,* the project will enter a seven-month Prepublication Phase.

During the Prepublication Phase, work will begin in earnest on the actual launch of the magazine. The decision to publish will have been made, the financing obtained, and a substantial portion of the required capital will be committed. The major activities occurring during this period will be:

building the staff
dropping a major direct mail subscription promotion
creating a dummy and initial issues of the magazine
selling advertising
establishing relationships with outside suppliers

1. *Building the Staff.* Ideally, the key staff members will be on the job at the start of the Prepublication period, with the remainder of the staff hired during the second, third, and fourth months.

Venture will be located in New York City. There should be no problem in finding qualified professionals in New York to fill required positions.

2. *Direct Mail Promotion.* Current plans call for a direct mail drop in September 1978 of 1.7 million pieces. The preparation of this major promotion will be handled by *Venture's* staff, with the assistance of experienced direct mail advertising agency.

3. *Creating a Dummy and Initial Issues.* A dummy, or prototype, of the actual magazine will be required to sell advertising and assist the editorial staff in planning the eventual publication. The dummy will be created by the *Venture* editorial staff. An experienced design consultant will be used to develop the actual look of the magazine.

Correspondents will be engaged in key areas. Relationships will be developed with qualified free-lance writers and artists. Story and feature ideas will be developed and assigned to staff editors or freelancers. The first issues of *Venture* will be made ready for the printer.

4. *Selling Advertising.* Prime potential advertisers will be identified from the lists of the largest advertisers in other general business publications. Sales approaches will be developed. Pricing strategies will be finalized. Sales calls will be made on advertisers and their agencies by the publisher, sales force, and, where indicated, the editor.

5. *Establishing Relationships with Suppliers.* Arrangements will be negotiated with printers, typesetters, fulfillment houses, newsstand distributors, subscription agents, and other necessary suppliers.

Publication Phase. The Publication Phase will begin when the first issue of *Venture* is mailed to subscribers in January 1979. Previous sections of this proposal have described plans for the editorial, advertising, and circulation of the magazine.

Reference is made to the exhibits herein for certain financial projections.

Competition. *Venture's* direct competition is expected to come from the existing general business magazines. These magazines are established and, for the most part, well financed. Comparisons between these publications and projections for *Venture* follow.

Venture Compared to Other Publications

COMPETITIVE DATA ADVERTISING RATES

Publication	Rate Base (000)	One-Time B/W Page	CPM
Black Enterprise	215*	$ 6,190	$28.79
Business Week	765	12,940	16.92
Dun's Review	225*	4,195	18.64
Forbes	650	9,450	14.54
Fortune	625	12,555	20.09
Harvard Business Review	165	3,170	19.21
Nation's Business	1,030*	9,575	9.30
Venture	80	1,200	15.00

SUBSCRIPTION AND SINGLE COPY RATES

Publication	Issues Per Year	One-Year Subscription Price	Subscription Price Per Issue	Single Copy Price
Black Enterprise	12	$10.00	$ .83	$1.00
Business Week	52	21.50	.41	1.00
Dun's Review	12	12.00	1.00	1.50
Forbes	24	18.00	.75	1.00–1.50
Fortune	12	18.00	1.50	2.00
Harvard Business Review	6	18.00	3.00	3.50
Nation's Business	12	13.50	1.13	1.25
Venture	12	12.00	1.00	1.25

*Includes substantial amount of nonpaid or association subscriptions.

The People Involved

The following people are expected to be involved with *Venture* as the publication develops.

President and Publisher, Joseph D. Giarraputo.   Thirty-five years old, Mr. Giarraputo is a graduate of the Harvard Business School. His publishing experience includes positions with the Ziff-Davis Publishing Co., publishers of *Psychology Today, Popular Photography, Boating, Flying,* and other consumer and business publications. At Ziff-Davis, he was the business manager of the Circulation Division and ran the *Psychology Today* Book Club. Mr. Giarraputo was also Director of Finance at the CBS Education and Publishing Group, and Vice President, Planning and Finance, of CBS Publications. Among the CBS magazines were *Field & Stream, Road and Track, World Tennis,* and others. He is currently Senior Vice President of the Cadence Publishing Division. The company is involved in publishing and publishing services.

Editor-in-Chief.   He is currently employed in a senior editorial position with a major weekly business magazine. He has edited and written numerous cover stories for this publication. He is one of four editors who oversee the editorial closing of the magazine on a rotating basis.

 Prior to this position he served as a bureau manager for this publication. He has also worked as an assistant city editor and reporter for the Dallas *Times Herald.* He graduated with a degree in journalism from the University of Texas, where he was managing editor of the *Daily Texan,* the student newspaper, and president of Sigma Delta Chi, the honorary journalism fraternity.

Direct Mail Consultant.   Bloom & Gelb Inc. will function as the direct mail advertising agency. Carl Bloom, President of the agency, has extensive circulation marketing experience, having been Circulation Manager of both *McCalls'* and *Redbook* magazines. Pete Gelb was formerly Circulation Promotion Manager of *Fortune* magazine. Their present clients include *Book Digest* and *New Times* magazines.

Launch Consultant.   James B. Kobak is acting as overall publishing consultant with specific responsibility for planning and preparation of projections. Formerly the Senior Partner of J. K. Lasser & Co., Mr. Kobak is now an independent publishing consultant whose client list includes such publishers as McGraw Hill Inc., the *New York Times, Playboy, Book Digest,* and *Firehouse* magazine.

Production Services.   Burt Paolucci will be responsible for printing and other production services. Currently an independent consultant, he is a graduate of the Harvard Business School and was formerly Director of Production for Time, Inc. His recent clients include: CBS Publications, ABS Leisure Magazines, *Billboard* Publications, and the *Columbia Journalism Review.*

Finance. Important assistance with respect to finance is being provided by Kenneth Fadner, who was most recently Vice President of Finance of *New York* magazine, the *Village Voice,* and *New West* magazine.

Art Director. David Merrill will function as *Venture*'s Art Director. For four years, until August 1977, Mr. Merrill was the Art Director of *Time* magazine.

Probable auditors. J. K. Lasser & Co.

Federal Income Tax Aspects

THE DISCUSSION OF TAX ASPECTS IN THIS MEMORANDUM RE-LATES PRINCIPALLY TO LIMITED PARTNERS WHO ARE INDIVID-UAL TAXPAYERS. LIMITED PARTNERS WHICH ARE PARTNER-SHIPS, CORPORATIONS, OR OTHER FORMS OF BUSINESS ENTITIES, OR WHICH ARE SUBJECT TO OTHER SPECIAL CATEGO-RIES OF THE INTERNAL REVENUE CODE, SHOULD CONSULT WITH THEIR OWN TAX ADVISERS CONCERNING THE DIFFERENT TAX CONSEQUENCES WHICH THEIR FORM OF ORGANIZATION MAY ENTAIL.

General Principles of Partnership Taxation. Under the Internal Revenue Code (the "Code"), a partnership is not a taxable entity. Instead, each item of part-nership income, gain, loss, deduction, or credit flows through to the partners, such as the Limited Partners of the Partnership, substantially as though the partners had earned or incurred each item directly. Each partner is required to include in his income each year his distributive share of partnership income whether or not any actual distribution is made to such partner during his tax-able year. In addition, each partner may claim as a deduction against income from other sources his distributive share of partnership losses in any taxable year to the extent of his basis for his partnership interest determined as of the close of such taxable year. For this purpose, a limited partner's tax basis does not include any partnership liability for which the partner is not personally liable.

Under present law, the tax basis for the interest of a Limited Partner in the Partnership is generally equal to (1) the amount of money he pays to ac-quire such interest plus (2) the Partner's distributive share of the income of the Partnership, decreased (but not below zero) by (3) his distributive share of losses of the Partnership and (4) the amount of money, and the adjusted basis to the Partnership of any property, distributed to the Partner by the Partnership.

Tax Status of the Partnership. The partnership form has been employed to al-low the Partners to recognize their *distributive* share of the Partnership profits and losses and because a partnership does not pay federal income tax. However, if the Partnership is treated as an association taxable as a corporation, then the Partners would be treated as corporate shareholders and, as such, would not recognize the Partnership's profits and losses on their individual tax returns. In addition, the Partnership would be required to pay taxas on its taxable income, and distributions to the Partners would not be deductible in computing such taxable income. Further, all, or some portion, of distributions to the Partners would be taxed as dividend income.

THE PARTNERSHIP HAS NOT REQUESTED A RULING FROM THE INTERNAL REVENUE SERVICE AS TO ITS STATUS AS A PART- NERSHIP FOR TAX PURPOSES AND THERE IS NO ASSURANCE THAT A FAVORABLE RULING COULD BE OBTAINED IF SOUGHT.

The Internal Revenue Service (the "Service") presently applies four tests to determine whether an entity will be classified as a partnership or as an asso- ciation taxable as a corporation for federal income tax purposes. Generally, an entity will be treated as an association if it has more than two of the follow- ing corporate attributes: (1) continuity of life; (2) centralization of manage- ment; (3) limited liability; (4) free transferability of interests.

It appears that the Partnership will have a limited life and that the Part- nership interests will not be freely transferable. In addition, under applicable regulations, an entity has the corporate attribute of limited liability if, under local law, there is no member who is personally liable for the debts of or claims against the entity. In the case of an entity formed as a limited partnership, the general partner has personal liability for the debts of and claims against the limited partnership unless the general partner has no substantial assets (other than his partnership interest) which could be reached by partnership credit- ors or he is merely a "dummy" acting as an agent for the limited partners. Since it appears that the General Partner of the Partnership is personally lia- ble for the debts and claims against the Partnership and that he is not merely a "dummy" acting as an agent for the Limited Partners, it appears that the Part- nership does not have the corporate attribute of limited liability within the meaning of the applicable regulations.

Notwithstanding the aforementioned rules, in October 1975, the United States Tax Court filed its opinion in *Phillip G. Larson*, 65 T.C. No. 10. There, the Court held that two California limited partnerships were associations taxa- ble as corporations within the meaning of §7701(a) (3) of the Code, despite the fact that the tests generally applied in classifying an entity for tax purposes were apparently satisfied.

In November 1975, the Tax Court withdrew its opinion in the *Larson* case. In April 1976, the Court issued a new opinion (66 T.C. No. 21) holding that the California limited partnerships were partnerships for federal income tax purposes. On September 4, 1976, the Service entered an appeal in the *Larson* case.

In addition, in December, 1976, the Service issued new proposed regu- lations under §7701(a) (3) of the Code which would have prescribed more restrictive tests for determining the status of an entity as a partnership for tax purposes. Shortly thereafter, the Secretary of the Treasury ordered the proposed regulations to be withdrawn.

No prediction can be made as to future developments with respect to the appeal in the *Larson* case, or with respect to potential changes in the income tax regulations. If the Service is successful in the *Larson* appeal, or if the Service amends the regulations under §7701(a) (3) of the Code, such results could be applied retroactively and could adversely affect the classification of the Partnership as a partnership for federal income tax purposes.

Allocation of Profit and Loss.   Under §704(b) of the Code, as amended by the Tax Reform Act of 1976, special allocations of partnership items are disregarded unless the allocations have substantial economic effect. The Service has not yet issued regulations in connection with §704(b). However, explanations of the provision in the applicable Committee Reports indicate than an allocation will be deemed to have substantial economic effect if the allocation may actually affect the dollar amount of each partner's share of the total partnership income or loss, independent of tax consequences.

Since the allocations made by the Limited Partnership Agreement affect each Partner's capital and income accounts, it appears that the profit and loss allocations will be recognized for tax purposes. However, it is not possible to predict the rules that will be adopted by the Service when regulations under §704(b) are promulgated.

Partnership Organizational Expenses.   The Partnership will pay all expenses relating to the organization of the Partnership. Under §709 of the Code, as added by the Tax Reform Act of 1976, no deduction will be allowed to the Partnership, or to any Partner, for any amount paid or incurred to organize the Partnership. Rather, such amounts must be capitalized and, generally, amortized over a period of not less than 60 months, if the Partnership so elects. Expenses incurred by the Partnership to promote the sale of, or to sell, Interests in the Partnership must be capitalized and may not be amortized by the Partnership. Such expenses will be recovered by the Partners as a reduction of gain, or as an additional loss, when the Partnership is liquidated or the Partners sell their interests in the Partnership.

The foregoing discussion is merely a summary of those features that may have a general effect on all investors. It is not intended to serve as a comprehensive explanation of all the technical provisions of the Code and their applications to the particular circumstances of each investor. This summary is based on present laws, regulations, and interpretations and would, of course, be affected by any changes in such laws, regulations, or interpretations.

Each investor in the Partnership should consult his tax adviser as to all matters discussed herein.

Exhibit 1

VENTURE: BASIC ASSUMPTIONS

	Prepublication	Year 1	Year 2	Year 3	Year 4	Year 5
Average circulation	—	80	155	212	267	312
Subscription Price (1 year only)						
Introductory	10.00	10.00	12.00	13.00	14.00	15.00
Regular	14.00	14.00	14.00	14.00	15.00	16.00
Total Mailings/Year (in millions)	1.7	1.7	2.6	2.4	3.4	2.8
Average Bad Debt Mailings	15%	15%	15%	15%	15%	15%
Average Percent Return Mailings (gross)	3%	3%	3%	3%	3%	3%
Renewal Percentage						
1st Renewal (conversion)	—	50%	50%	50%	50%	50%
Renewal	—	60%	60%	60%	60%	60%
Newsstand Draw (in thousands)	—	15	30	35	40	50
Newsstand Percentage of Sale	—	25%	40%	45%	50%	55%
Newsstand Price/Copy	—	$1.25	$1.25	$1.25	$1.25	$1.50
Average Total Pages/Issue	—	88	96	104	112	112
Average Advertising Pages/Issue	—	15	20	33	43	54
Advertising Rate/Black & White Page	—	$1,200	$2,560	$3,850	$5,340	$6,860
Cost/Copy Printing & Paper	—	19.5¢	22.8¢	26.4¢	30.5¢	32.6¢
Number of Full-Time Employees						
Mechanical & Distribution	1	1	1	2	2	2
Editorial	6	6	6	6	6	6
Advertising	4	4	5	6	6	6
Circulation	2	2	2	2	3	3
General & Administrative	6	6	6	6	6	6

This forecast is based on estimates and assumptions contained on this and other pages. No opinion is expressed as to the future accuracy of these projections.

Venture: Cast Projections (In thousands)

	Test	Prepublication	1979 Year 1	1980 Year 2	1981 Year 3	1982 Year 4	1983 Year 5
Subscriptions	$	$ 179.0	$1,516.2	$2,302.2	$2,956.6	$3,838.4	$3,620.0
Newsstand		0.0	29.1	95.2	126.8	166.2	236.2
Advertising		0.0	171.0	637.7	1,454.1	2,563.6	3,814.0
Other		0.0	10.4	25.2	40.1	52.0	65.4
Total Receipts		$ 179.0	1,726.6	3,060.3	4,577.6	6,260.2	7,735.6
Disbursements							
Mechanical & Distribution		4.5	387.8	780.5	1,148.5	1,573.3	1,820.7
Editorial		84.5	345.8	381.8	406.3	429.5	443.1
Advertising		88.4	165.0	190.8	223.9	240.8	256.9
Circulation Promotion		375.6	789.6	857.3	1,070.8	1,209.3	774.5
Circulation Fulfillment		0.0	48.6	96.0	138.5	176.4	211.5
General & Administrative	35.0	124.6	308.6	334.5	364.9	392.1	415.8
Total Distribution	35.0	677.5	2,045.4	2,640.9	3,352.9	4,021.4	3,922.4
Net Cashflow	$–35.0	$–498.5	$–318.7	$ 419.3	$1,224.7	$2,598.8	$3,813.2
Total Cashflow	$–35.0	$–533.5	$–852.2	$–432.9	$ 791.8	$3,390.6	$7,203.8
High Negative Cash Flow		$1,100.0					

This forecast is based on estimates and assumptions contained on this and other pages. No opinion is expressed as to the future accuracy of these projections.

Sources of Help
for Entrepreneurs

Because our office constantly receives a flow of questions from our worldwide membership, we have compiled this directory of original sources of help for presidents of growing businesses. Since our founding in Worcester, Massachusetts in 1978, this list of sources has provided answers to most of the questions asked by our 3,000 members. CEM Inc. has become the world's largest non-profit membership association of small company presidents dedicated to serving the unique information needs of The Entrepreneurial Venture. While the professional manager seeks to protect a resource, an entrepreneurial manager seeks to create it!

This directory was "created" not as a full source of everything that was available because then you'd need a directory to access it. Rather, it was developed to handle all the questions put to use by our members, and, thus far, we are able to handle better than 3 out of 4 questions by referring to the "answer book." We are now offering this guide to our members as another example of our special reports.

APPENDIX H CONTENTS

APPENDIX H CONTENTS

THE TOP SOURCES OF HELP FOR ENTREPRENEURS

A. ADVERTISING AND PUBLIC RELATIONS:

A1. The leading twice-per-weekly newspaper serving the advertising industry is *Advertising Age*. Issues are in excess of 100 pages in a large tabloid format. The newspaper focuses on advertising in the broadest sense: It claims to be the international newspaper of marketing and is widely read and quoted. Write:

> *Advertising Age*
> Crain Communications
> 740 North Rush Street
> Chicago, IL 60611
> (312) 649-5200
> Circulation: about 100,000

A2. *Adweek*, a weekly news magazine, is composed of *Adweek, Adweek/East, Adweek/Midwest, Adweek/Southeast,* and *Adweek/West*. Reports on industry news for each region of the U.S.A. Look in your regional yellow pages. Write:

> *Adweek*
> ASM Communications
> 820 Second Avenue
> New York, NY 10016
> (212) 661-8080

A3. *Directories and Publicity Release Programs*: The procedure for contacting the various trade journals varies from industry to industry. Some journals require black-and-white photographs, while others accept no photographs. To obtain specific information on how to obtain publicity and to obtain a list of relevant trade journals, these six publishers offer you directories and publicity release programs.

A3A. The most comprehensive source of newspaper information is Ayer's Directory of Newspapers and Periodicals. Write:

> IMS Press
> 426 Pennsylvania Avenue
> Fort Washington, PA 19834
> (215) 628-4920

A3B. For the finest overall source of publicity information in the country, (this is a source used by most P.R. firms) contact:

> *Bacon's Publicity Checker*
> 332 South Michigan Avenue
> Chicago, IL 60604
> (800) 621-0561
> or
> (312) 922-2400

A3C. For an excellent overall list of periodicals, use the *Standard Periodical Directory,* published by:

Oxbridge Publishing Company
150 Fifth Avenue
Suite 301
New York, NY 10011
(212) 741-0231

A3D. *Ulrich's Directory of Periodicals* is most often available in libraries. It is published by:

R.R. Bowker Company
205 E. 42 Street
New York, NY 10017
(212) 916-1600

A3E. An extensive source of all data for both print and electronic media:

Standard Rate & Data
3004 Glenview
Wilmette, IL 60091
(312) 256-6067

A3F. We like the Gebbie all-in-one directory of print and electronic media, as well as the very comprehensive *Working Press of the Nation.* The old famous Gebbie listing of company house organs directory is still a good and unusual method of obtaining publicity. It's now called *The Internal Publications Directory.*

Gebbie Press Inc.
Box 1000
New Paltz, NY 12561
(914) 255-7560

Working Press of the Nation
National Research Bureau
310 South Michigan
Suite 1150
Chicago, IL 60601
(312) 663-5580

B. BANKRUPTCY

B1. *How to Get Out of Debt,* by Ted Nicholas (1980), is a large workbook with practical advice on how to get out of debt. They publish some of the best books, especially legally based on small business. Write:

Enterprise Publishing
1725 Market Street
Wilmington, DE 19801
(302) 575-0440

B2. *National Bankruptcy Reporter* is an interesting but expensive newsletter that will inform you of the vital data of business bankruptcy filings all across the country. It's expensive—about $1,000 annually—but it provides useful facts on a subject that can be hard to acquire information about. Write:

Andrews Publications, Inc.
P.O. Box 200
Edgemont, PA 19028
(215) 353-2565

B3. This is a monthly newsletter costing about $60 annually and available from:

Chapter Eleven Reporter
Roth Publishing Company
485 5th Avenue
New York, NY 10017
(212) 692-9388
or
(800) 223-5594

C. BANKS

C1. The most complete source of banks and banking listings.

Polks World Bank Directory
R.L. Polks & Company
2001 Elm Hill Pike
Box 1340
Nashville, TN 37202
(615) 889-3350

C2. The training arm for commercial bankers, excellent sources of financial ratios. Write:

Robert Morris Association
1616 Philadelphia National Bank Building
Philadelphia, PA 19107
(215) 665-2850

C3. The industry trade association. Write:

American Bankers Association
1120 Connecticut Avenue N.W.
Washington, DC 20036
(202) 467-4180

C4. The SBA Hotline number to find the SBA approved bank nearest to you in the preferred lender (PLP) program to obtain a SBA loan—(800) 368-5855.

C5. Want to check up on the financial health of your bank? Write:

Veribank
Box 2963
Woburn, MA 01888
(617) 245-8370

D. BUSINESS ASSOCIATIONS (with political representations)

D1. The largest small business association with over 500,000 dues paying members, strong force in Washington D.C. where they also maintain an office.

John Sloan, President
National Federation of Independent Business (NFIB)
150 West 20 Avenue
San Mateo, CA 94403
(415) 341-7441

or

(NFIB)
600 Maryland Avenue S.W.
Suite 700
Washington, DC 20024
(202) 554-9000

D2. About 50,000 members with strong legislative programs. Work closely with the Small Business Legislative Council (SBLC). Bidders Early Alert System for government contracts, also supplied by NSB.

Herb Liebenson, President
National Small Business Association
1604 "K" Street N.W.
Washington, DC 20006
(202) 296-7400

E. BUSINESS ASSOCIATION (non-political)

E1. Within the American Management Association (AMA), the 2,000 members who are in the President's Association (P/A) are an especially elite group. The P/A runs very effective five-day workshops for chief executive officers (CEOs). Also offers limited Company Membership and has an additional 3,000 small business members in this program.

Limited Company Members
or
President's Association
American Management Association
135 West 50 Street
New York, NY 10020
(212) 586-8100

E2. The Chief Executive Officers Clubs (CEO) consist of 300 CEOs who meet eight times per year in seven cities, including Boston, New York, Chicago, Los Angeles, San Francisco, Houston, Dallas, and Chicago for the purpose of sharing ideas for mutual gain. This is an elite group of CEOs who run businesses of $1M to $50M of annual sales. Contact:

Joseph Mancuso, President
Chief Executives Officers Clubs (CEO Clubs)
83 Spring Street
New York, NY 10012
(212) 925-7306

E3. Several hundred R&D-based small businesses belong to:

> American Association of Small Research Companies
> 1200 Lincoln Avenue
> Prospect Park, PA 19076
> (215) 522-1500

E4. A nationwide group of 5,000 young presidents with strong local chapters.

> Y.P.O.
> Young Presidents Organization
> 52 Vanderbilt Avenue
> New York, NY 10017
> (212) 867-1900

E5. A group of several hundred founders of businesses, headed by Mr. Arthur Lipper III, the owner of *Venture* magazine.

> Venture Founders
> 521 Fifth Avenue
> New York, NY 10175
> (212) 682-7373

E6. There are 22 TEC groups in California, and 30 others in New Mexico, Texas, Wisconsin, Michigan, Florida, Illinois, and in Japan. Groups of a dozen CEO meetings monthly for about $6,000 annual fees.

> Pat Hyndman, Director
> The Executive Committee (TEC)
> 3737 Camino Del Rio South
> Suite 206
> San Diego, CA 92108
> (619) 563-5875

F. BUSINESS OPPORTUNITY SOURCES

F1. A monthly magazine of business opportunities, specializing in retail and franchising. A good listing of pamphlets for hundreds of small businesses you can operate out of your home.

> *Business Opportunity Sources*
> Chase Revel
> *Entrepreneur Magazine*
> 2311 Pontius Avenue
> Los Angeles, CA 90064
> (213) 477-1011

F2. An excellent original source of financial and lending information, especially mortgages, business plans, and bank loans. Also publishes monthly newsletters called *Dollar & Sense*.

> Jay Cameron
> Diversified Financial Corporation
> 1145 Reservoir Avenue
> Cranston, RI 02910
> (401) 943-7551

G. BUSINESS PLANS

G1. *The Business Planning Guide* by David Bangs and William Osgood (1976) is one of the better documents available on this subject. It was originally offered free by the Federal Reserve Bank of Boston and received wide distribution. Write:

> David Bangs
> Upstart Publishing Company
> 50 Mill Street
> Dover, NH 03820
> (603) 749-5071

G2. *How to Prepare and Present a Business Plan* (1983), Prentice-Hall, 400 pages, by Dr. Joseph Mancuso, is a complete guide to preparing the business plan that will attract venture or debt capital. The most widely used book on this subject according to *Venture* magazine. They also offer audio tapes on this subject, plus an archive of old original business plans which launched major U.S. based businesses. Write to:

> Center for Entrepreneurial Management, Inc.
> 83 Spring Street
> New York, NY 10012
> (212) 925-7304

> or

> General Publishing Division
> Prentice-Hall
> Englewood Cliffs, NJ 07632
> (201) 592-2000

G3. Many accounting firms give out free booklets on Business Plans. One we especially like is given out free at any of the regional offices of Arthur Young & Company, or you can write to:

> G. Steven Burrill, Partner
> Arthur Young & Company
> 1 Post Street
> Suite 3100
> San Francisco, CA 94104
> (415) 393-2731

H. COLLEGIATE ENTREPRENEURS

H1. An association of MBAs has membership available for $55 annually ($25 for students) and it has 20,000 members:

> Association of MBA Executives (AMBA)
> 305 Madison Avenue
> New York, NY 10165
> (212) 682-4490

H2. A national group of collegiate entrepreneurs is a collection of student entrepreneur chapters at leading business schools. Write:

> Fran Jabara, Director
> Association of Collegiate Entrepreneurs (ACE)
> Wichita State Univeristy
> Box 40A
> Wichita, KS 67208
> (316) 689-3000

H3. The School of Entrepreneurs is not really for college students but for persons seeking to explore entrepreneurship as a way of life. It's a two-weekend program at the estate of Bob Schwartz, the person who makes the weekends happen. Write:

> Robert Schwartz
> School of Entrepreneurs
> Tarrytown Conference Center
> East Sunnyside Lane
> Tarrytown, NY 10591
> (914) 591-8200

H4A. The International Council for Small Business (ICSB) is an academically oriented organization open to anyone with an interest in small business management, including educators, government officials, trade association executives, professionals, and small business owners. ICSB also publishes an academic journal, Journal of Small Business Management, four times annually.

> International Council for Small Business Management Development (ICSBMD)
> University of Wisconsin Extension
> 929 N. Sixth Street
> Milwaukee, WI 53203
> (414) 224-1816

H4B.

> Dr. Robert Brockhaus, President
> International Council for Small Businesses (ICSB)
> St. Louis University
> 3550 Lindell Boulevard
> St. Louis, MO 63103
> (314) 658-3800

H4C.

> *Journal of Small Business Management*
> Bureau of Business Research
> West Virginia University
> Morgantown, WV 26506
> (304) 293-0111

H4D.

Jack E. Brothers
Small Business Institute
Directors Association
6601 West College Drive
Palace Heights, IL 60463
(312) 861-0831

H5. M.I.T. ENTERPRISE FORUM

The Enterprise Forum at Massachusetts Institute of Technology (M.I.T.) offers companies seeking advice and assistance an opportunity to present their case before a panel of experts and entrepreneurial peers. Each month, the panel reviews a company's history, its ongoing business situation, and its future plans; the panel offers constructive advice on resolving the problems. A participating audience of about 200 is also present, along with business executives and entrepreneurs who donate their time and services. There are M.I.T. Forums in a dozen locations throughout the country. They also offer a monthly newsletter. Contact:

Paul E. Johnson, Executive Director
MIT Enterprise Forum
MIT Alumni Center
77 Massachusetts Avenue
Cambridge, MA 02139
(617) 253-8240

I. COMPUTERS IN SMALL BUSINESS

I1. Control Data Business Centers are a unique and growing resource for small businesses. Apart from the U.S. Small Business Administration, they provide the most complete one-stop source of help to young and growing firms. The centers, which number 115 nationwide, offer financial services, business training, and data processing. Contact:

Dave Leahy
Control Data Business Centers, Inc.
22 West Padonia Road
Suite 152C
Timonium, MD 21093
(301) 561-1800

I2. The largest circulation magazine for small business computers, about 300,000 readers.

Byte Magazine
70 Main Street
Peterborough, NH 03458
(603) 924-9281

I3. A comprehensive guide to developing and selling software.

> *The Complete Software Marketplace* (1984–1985), by Roger Hoffman
> Warner Books
> 666 Fifth Avenue
> Box 690
> New York, NY 10019
> (212) 484-2963

I4. American Electronics Association (AEA)—Forty years old, 2,000 electronics industry member companies.

> American Electronics Association (AEA)
> 2670 Hanover Street
> Palo Alto, CA 94304
> (415) 857-9300

I5. Association of Data Processing Service Organization (ADAPSO)—a good association of software developers, of any size. Membership fees are on a sliding scale based on your sales revenues. ($400 annual minimum for companies $250,000 and under.)

> ADAPSO
> 1300 North 17 Street
> Suite 300
> Arlington, VA 22209
> (703) 522-5055

J. CONSULTING SERVICES

J1. If you need specialized professional help, lists of consultants are available from an organization founded in 1929 which screens the companies which apply for membership. They pledge a code of ethics and professional conduct.

> ACME, Inc.
> 230 Park Avenue
> New York, NY 10169
> (212) 697-9693
> (800) 221-2557

J2. Directory of Members and a list of individual management consultants certified by the institute of Management Consultants, along with a capsule description of their areas of competence/fields of practice. There are no firm memberships in the Institute—every member must qualify on his or her individual merits.

> Institute of Management Consultants, Inc.
> 19 West 44 Street
> New York, NY 10036
> (212) 921-2885

J3. Free catalog available from the Consultant Bookstore, also a monthly newsletter on inside information about consultants for $66 annually. Lives and works in big wonderful New Hampshire farmhouse.

> James Kennedy
> "Consultants News"
> Pempleton Road
> Fitzwilliam, NH 03447
> (603) 585-2200

J4. Catalog free on request, large selection of books. Consultants Library.

> Mr. H. Bermont
> Post Box 309
> Glenelg, MD 21737
> (202) 737-6437

J5. Send for a free "Resource Guide." "The Professional Consultant," monthly, $60/yr.

> Howard L. Shenson, Inc.
> 20121 Ventura Blvd., Suite 245
> Woodland Hills, CA 91364
> (818) 703-1415

J6. The Control Data Business Resource Centers are a walk-in clinic for small businesses. Check with the Minneapolis office for locations nationwide. Contact:

> Control Data Business Center
> 5241 Viking Drive
> Bloomington, MN 55435
> (612) 893-4200

J7. Small Business Administration—Consult your local telephone directory for over 100 regional offices. Write:

> SBA
> 1141 "L" Street N.W.
> Room 317
> Washington, DC 20416
> (202) 653-6881
>
> or
>
> HOTLINE:
> (800) 368-5855

J8. A resource of books and seminars on consulting:

> Jeffrey Lant
> Jeffrey Lant Associates
> 50 Fallen Street
> Suite 507
> Cambridge, MA 02138
> (617) 547-6372

K. CORPORATE AND GOVERNMENT ENTREPRENEURSHIP

K1. A source of seminars for government on job creation, a non-profit corporation founded in 1975.

> Jan Zupnik
> Entrepreneurship Institute
> 3592 Corporate Drive
> Suite 100
> Columbus, OH 43229
> (614) 895-1153

K2. A source of seminars for government, including Third World countries for job creation.

> William McRae
> I.C.E.
> International Congress for Entrepreneurs
> 1 North Capital Avenue
> Suite 460
> Indianapolis, IN 46204
> (317) 639-3325

K3. A good source of community economic developments programs.

> Stewart Perry
> Institute for New Enterprise Development
> 1430 Massachusetts Avenue, Suite 310
> Cambridge, MA 02138
> (617) 491-0203

K4. The only school for Intrapreneurs (corporate entrepreneurs) is headquartered in Stockholm, Sweden. Headed by:

> Gustav Delin
> Sefram-Gruppen
> The Foresight Group
> Uppsalavagen Z5
> S–19300 Sigtuna, Sweden 0760 575–14

L. DIRECTORIES

L1. Standard & Poor's *Register of Corporations, Directors & Executives* is an excellent two-volume directory of information. Many other directories also available, ranking credit of corporations. Write:

> Standard & Poor's Corporation
> 25 Broadway
> New York, NY 10004
> (212) 208-8736
> (800) 221-5277

L2. One of the leading publishers of Who's Who on a variety of subjects:

Marquis Who's Who Inc.
4300 West 62nd Street
Indianapolis, IN 46268
(317) 298-5484

or

Marquis Who's Who
200 East Ohio Street
Chicago, IL 60611
(800) 621-9669

L3. A directory of association on a wide range of subjects. Also an excellent reference book of small business information sources. Write:

Encyclopedia of Associations
Gale Research Company
Book Tower
Detroit, MI 48226
(313) 961-2242

M. DIRECTORS

M1. A national membership association of corporate directors, mostly for middle-sized companies. Conducts seminars and offers books on the subject. Formerly owned by the American Management Association (AMA).

John Nash
National Association of Corporate Directors (NACD)
450 Fifth Street N.W.
Suite 1110
Washington, DC 20001
(202) 347-3123

M2. This non-profit membership association offers books and seminars on this subject and maintains a registry of companies seeking directors and of individuals seeking directorship. This service is available only to CEM members.

Joseph Mancuso, President
The Center for Entrepreneurial Management, Inc.
83 Spring Street
New York, NY 10012
(212) 925-7304

M3. Myles L. Mace, a former professor at the Harvard Business School, has authored a number of papers in *The Harvard Business Review* on this subject including July/Aug 1978, Nov/Dec 1976, March/April 1972. Incidentally, this publication has a feature in each issue on small business, called growing concerns—write to David Gumpfret. For a more current list, write:

Harvard Business Review
Soldiers Field
Boston, MA 02163
(617) 495-6182

N. FAMILY BUSINESSES

N1. A good source of books and seminars on the subject. Personal consulting also available.

> Leon Danco
> Family Business Institute
> P.O. Box 24268
> Cleveland, OH 44124
> (216) 442-0800

N2. An industry association of family-run businesses.

> John Messervey
> Executive Director
> National Family Business Council
> 8600 West Bryn Mawr
> Suite 720 South
> Chicago, IL 60631
> (312) 693-0990

O. FOUNDATIONS & GRANTS

O1. The single most comprehensive source of information with regional offices and libraries. A wide range of directories, computer searches, and seminars. Write:

A) The Foundation Center
79 Fifth Avenue (16th Street)
New York, NY 10106
(212) 975-1120
(headquarters)

C) The Foundation Center
1001 Conecticut Avenue N.W.
Washington, DC 20036
(202) 331-1400

B) The Foundation Center
Hanna Building
Cleveland, OH 44113
(216) 861-1933

D) The Foundation Center
312 Sutter Street
Suite 312
San Francisco, CA 94109
(415) 397-0902

O2. Arranges seminars on how to get grants, also offers magazines.

> The Grantsmanship Center
> 1031 South Grand Avenue
> Los Angeles, CA 90015
> (213) 749-4721

O3. There are four good government sources for contracts and grants. 1. The Federal Register. 2. The Commerce Business Daily. 3. The Congressional Record. 4. The Catalog of Federal Domestic Assistance. All of the above documents are available in public libraries, through local legislators, or from the Superintendent of Documents, U.S. Printing Office, Washington, DC 20402. You can contact the Printing Office for the respective costs, or many of the larger cities have their own branch office.

P. FRANCHISES

P1. A monthly magazine with a franchising directory issue.

> *Entrepreneur Magazine*
> 2311 Pontius Avenue
> Los Angeles, CA 90014
> (213) 477-1011

P2. A good source of information.

> *Dow Jones-Irwin Guide to Franchises*
> Richard D. Irwin, Inc.
> 1818 Ridge Road
> Homewood, IL 60430
> (312) 798-6000
> $17.50

P3. Another good book.

> *Handbook of Successful Franchising*
> Van Nostrand Reinhold
> 135 West 50 Street
> New York, NY 10020
> (212) 265-8700

P4. One of the better sources for a complete list of the titles on the subject of franchising, call or write:

> Pilot Books
> 103 Cooper Street
> Babylon, NY 11702
> (516) 422-2225

P5. Their quarterly publication is *Franchising World,* which is quite good. The Trade Organization for franchising is:

> The International Franchise Association
> 1025 Connecticut Avenue N.W., Suite 707
> Washington, DC 20036
> (202) 659-0790

P6. *Venture* magazine is offering a list of seminars on franchising. Write:

> Chris Lehman, President
> *Venture*
> 521 Fifth Avenue
> New York, NY 10175
> (212) 682-7373

P7. A group of experts on this subject is headed by:

> Edward Kushell
> The Franchise Consulting Group
> 2049 Century Park East
> Suite 2290
> Los Angeles, CA 90067
> (213) 552-2901

Q. GOVERNMENT INFORMATION

Q1. An excellent source of government data with a very extensive ability to get answers.

> Washington Reseachers
> 2612 "P" Street N.W.
> Washington, DC 20007
> (202) 333-3499

Q2. For a list of publications, send to the government printing office. A detailed source of many sources of government data.

> Superintendent of Documents
> Government Printing Office
> Washington, DC 20402
> (202) 783-3238

Q3. An excellent source of data on both small and large businesses in the U.S.A.

> Chamber of Commerce USA
> 1615 "H" Street N.W.
> Washington, DC 20062
> (202) 659-6000

Q4. In addition, SBA's Office of Procurement and Technical Assistance has a Procurement Automated Source System (PASS) that maintains capability profiles of small businesses interested in Federal Government procurement opportunities. This system is used by Federal agencies and major prime contractors to identify small concerns with capabilities needed by the agencies or prime contractors. Contact:

> U.S. Small Business Administration
> Office of Procurement and Technical Assistance
> 1441 "L" Street N.W.
> Washington, DC 20416
> (202) 655-4000

Q5. The Small Business Administration (SBA). There is no *one* mailing list for all SBIR Program Solicitations. You must request solicitations from each individual Federal agency. If you wish to be added to the master SBA–SBIR mailing list, contact:

> U.S. Small Business Administration
> Office of Innovation, Research and Technology
> 1441 "L" Street, N.W.
> Washington, DC 20416
> (202) 655-4000

PARTICIPATING AGENCY SBIR REPRESENTATIVES

Q5A. *Department of Agriculture*

Dr. W. K. Murphey
Office of Grants and Program Systems
Department of Agriculture
West Auditors Building, Rm. 112
15th & Independence Avenue, S.W.
Washington, DC 20251
(202) 475-5022

Q5B. *Department of Commerce*

Mr. James P. Maruca
Director, Office of Small and Disadvantaged Business Utilization
Department of Commerce
Room 6411
14th & Constitution Avenue., N.W.
Washington, DC 20230
(202) 377-1472

Q5C. *Department of Defense*

Mr. Horace Crouch
Director, Small Business and Economic Utilization
OSABU Office of Secretary of Defense
Room 2A340-The Pentagon
Washington, DC 20301
(202) 697-9383

Q5D. *Department of Education*

Dr. Edward Esty
SBIR Program Coordinator
Office of Educational Research and Improvement
Department of Education
OERI Brown Building
Mail Stop 40
Room 717
Washington, DC 20208
(202) 254-6413

Q5E *Department of Energy*

Ms. Gerry Washington
c/o SBIR Program Manager
U.S. Department of Energy
Washington, DC 20545
(301) 353-5867

Q5F. *Department of Health and Human Services*

Mr. Richard Clinkscales
Director, Office of Small and Disadvantaged Business Utilization
Department of Health and Human Services
200 Independence Avenue, S.W.
Room 513D

Washington, DC 20201
(202) 245-7300

Q5G. *Department of the Interior*

Dr. Thomas Henrie
Chief Scientist
Bureau of Mines
U.S. Department of the Interior
2401 "E" Street, N.W.
Washington, DC 20241
(202) 634-1305

Q5H. *Department of Transportation*

Mr. George Kovatch
SBIR Program Manager
Transportation Systems Center
Department of Transportation
Kendall Square
Cambridge, MA 02142
(617) 494-2051

Q5I. *Environmental Protection Agency (EPA)*

Mr. Walter H. Preston
Office of Research and Development
Environmental Protection Agency
401 "M" Street, S.W.
Washington, DC 20460
(202) 382-5744

Q5J. *National Aeronautics and Space Administration (NASA)*

Dr. Carl Schwenk
National Aeronautics and Space Administration
SBIR Office Code RB
600 Independence Avenue, S.W.
Washington, DC 20546
(202) 655-4000

Q5K. *National Science Foundation (NSF)*

Mr. Roland Tibbetts
Mr. Ritchie Coryell
SBIR Program Managers
National Science Foundation
1800 G Street, N.W.
Washington, DC 20550
(202) 357-7527

Q5L. *Nuclear Regulatory Commission (NRC)*

Mr. Wayne Batson
Office of Nuclear Regulatory Research
Nuclear Regulatory Commission
Washington, DC 20555
(301) 427-4250

R. IMPORT & EXPORT

R1. A monthly magazine for entrepreneurs outside the USA patterned after *INC* and *Venture* in the USA, $48 annually, including airmail delivery to U.S.A.:

> *Your Business*
> 60 Kingsly Street
> London IR 5LH England
> Telephone: 01 437-5678

R2. ICC Publishing Corporation is an affiliate of the International Chamber of Commerce. They have excellent resources available:

> Ms. Rachelle Bijou
> ICC Publishing Company
> 156 5th Avenue
> Suite 820
> New York, NY 10010
> (212) 206-1150

R3. Small Business Administration Hotline on import and export:

> (800) 424-5201
> (202) 653-7561 (in Washington DC)

R4. The export-import bank is:

> Export-Import Bank
> Office of Small Business
> 811 Vermont Avenue N.W.
> Washington, DC 20571
> (800) 424-5201
> (202) 566-8860 (in Washington DC)

R5. A national non-profit consulting group for anyone interested in using one of the 600 free trade zones in the world.

> Mark Frazier, President
> Free Zone Authority Services Inc.
> 317 "C" Street, N.E.
> Washington, DC 20002
> (202) 546-1344

S. INCORPORATING

S1. The benefits of incorporating in Delaware are worth investigating—a booklet for $4.00 is available from:

> Gauge Corp.
> 113 W. 8th Street
> Wilmington, DE 19801
> (302) 658-8045

S2. Ted Nicholas' book, *How to Incorporate for under $75.00 Without a Lawyer*, is well worth reading. They also provide forms for state-by-state incorporations for all states.

> Enterprise Publishing Company
> 725 Market Street
> Wilmington, DE 19801
> (302) 654-0110

S3. *Form Your Own Corporation*, by John Howell, is a low-cost paperback guide:

> General Publishing Division
> Prentice-Hall
> Englewood Cliffs, NJ 07632
> (201) 592-2000

S4. If you should want a corporate outfit (including a seal and by-laws) and don't need a lawyer, write or call:

> Corpex Bank Note Company, Inc.
> 480 Canal Street
> New York, NY 10013
> (212) 925-2400 (in New York City)
> (800) 522-7299 (in New York State)
> (800) 221-8181 (outside New York State)

T. INDUSTRY-BY-INDUSTRY STUDIES

T1. Technical reports.

> Theta Technology Inc.
> 462 Ridge Road
> Wethersfield, CT 06109
> (203) 563-9400

T2. A major source of technical information and studies.

> Stanford Research Institute (SRI)
> 333 Ravenswood Avenue
> Menlo Park, CA 94025
> (415) 326-6200

T3. Many industry studies.

> Frost & Sullivan
> 106 Fulton Street
> New York, NY 10038
> (212) 233-1080

T4. A good source of electronic industry data.

> Venture Development Corp.
> Electronic Industry Specialists
> 1 Washington Street
> Wellesley, MA 02181
> (617) 237-5080

T5. A good source of lists, names, and directories.

> Dun & Bradstreet
> 99 Church Street
> New York, NY 10007
> (212) 285-7000

T6. Industry-by-industry data.

> Morton Research Corp.
> 1745 Merrick Avenue
> Merrick, NY 11566
> (516) 378-1066

T7. Offers a directory of market research reports, studies and surveys.

> FIND/SVP
> 500 5th Avenue
> New York, NY 10110
> (212) 354-2424

T8. A good group of state-by-state directories of manufacturers is available from:

> Commerce Register
> 190 Godwin Avenue
> Midland Park, NJ 07432
> (201) 445-3000

> or

> Manufacturers News Inc.
> 4 East Huron Street
> Chicago, IL 60611
> (312) 337-1084

U. LEGAL SELF-HELP & FORMS

Conducts seminars and has excellent audio and video tapes on a range of subjects. Non-profit organization founded in 1933.

> Practicing Law Institute (PLI)
> 810 7th Avenue
> New York, NY 10019
> (212) 765-5700

U2. Good source of forms and supplies, used widely by lawyers.

> Bowne & Company
> 345 Hudson Street, 10th Floor
> New York, NY 10014
> (212) 924-5500

U3. A good source of books and help, including incorporation kits and minutes books. We especially like the looseleaf book called "The Complete Set of Corporate Forms."

Enterprise Publishing
725 Market Street
Wilmington, DE 19801
(302) 645-0110

V. LOBBYING

The five best political *lobbying* groups for small business:

V1.

Thomas Cator, Counsel
Small Business United
c/o Neece, Cator, Assoc.
1050 17th Street., N.W.
Suite 810
Washington, DC 20036
(202) 887-5599

V2.

Herbert Liebenson
National Small Business Association (NSB)
NSB Building
1604 "K" Street., N.W.
Washington, DC 20006
(202) 293-8830

V3.

John J. Motley III
Director of Legislation
National Federation of Independent Business (NFIB)
Capital Gallery East
Suite 695
600 Maryland Avenue., S.W
Washington, DC 20024
(202) 554-9000

V4.

Ivan C. Elmer, Manager
Small Business Center
Chamber of Commerce of U.S.
1615 "H" Street., N.W.
Washington, DC 20062
(202) 659-6000

V5.

Lewis A. Shattuck
Smaller Business Association of New England (SBANE)
69 Hickory Drive
Waltham, MA 02154
(617) 890-9070

W. MAGAZINES

W1. The magazine for growing businesses, with a circulation close to 500,000. Publishes the *INC.* 100.

Bernard Goldhirsh, Publisher
INC Magazine
38 Commercial Wharf
Boston, MA 02110
(617) 227-4700

W2. A great source of initial public offerings and venture capital sources. Also publishes the *Venture* 100. The magazine for entrepreneurs. Circulation about 300,000.

Arthur Lipper III, Publisher
Venture Magazine
521 Fifth Avenue
New York, NY 10175
(212) 682-7373

W3. Monthly magazine for independent innovative individuals, with a stress on smaller home-based businesses. Circulation less than 100,000.

Jerome Goldstein, Publisher
In Business Magazine
Box 351
Emmaus, PA 18049
(215) 967-4135

X. MAIL-ORDER MARKETING

X1. An industry association with newsletters, banks, and seminars.

National Mail Order Association
5818 Venice Boulevard
Los Angeles, CA 90019
(213) 934-7986

X2. Seminars, books, and a weekly newspaper, which is free, well read, and informative.

Direct Mail Marketing Association
6 E. 43rd Street
New York, NY 10017
(212) 689-4977

X3. Good source of small business mailing lists.

Liza Price
American List Counsel
88 Orchard Road, CN-5219
Princeton, NJ 08540
(800) 526-3973
(201) 874-4300

Y. MANUFACTURERS AGENTS OR REPRESENTATIVES

Y1. The Direct Selling Association is composed of about 100 firms engaged in selling products and services to consumers primarily in their homes. Several directories of members are available. Write:

Direct Selling Association
1730 "M" Street., N.W.
Suite 610
Washington, DC 20036
(202) 293-5760

Y2. Your low-cost ad in the *Manufacturers Agents Newsletter* reaches agents and manufacturers throughout the United States and Canada and in some foreign countries. Your ad in the newsletter can let them know who you are, where you are, which territory you cover, or wish to cover. Write:

Manufacturers Agents Newsletter
23573 Prospect Avenue
Farmington, MI 48024
(313) 474-7383

Y3. A comprehensive directory of manufacturers agents and the products they represent. *Marketing Through Manufacturers Agents and Representatives*, a directory. Write:

MacRae's
87 Terminal Drive
Plainview, NY 11803
(516) 349-1010
$100

Y4. About 10,000 members, founded in 1947.

James J. Gibbon, President
Manufacturers Agents National Association (MANA)
Box 3467
Laguna Hills, CA 92654
(714) 859-4040

Y5. A good source of information on representatives, with newsletters and a regular flow of solid information.

Albee-Campbell
Rep World
Sinking Springs, PA 19608
(215) 678-3361

Y6. An organization of manufacturers agents.

United Association of Manufacturers Representatives
P.O. Draw 6266
Kansas City, KS 66106
(913) 258-9466

Z. BEST SOURCE OF MAPS (geographical)

Z1. The best source of maps of all kinds.

> Rand McNally
> 8255 North Central Park Avenue
> Skokie, IL 60076
> (312) 267-6868

Z2. A good source of buying power and maps of consumer and industrial usage of products by state and metropolitan statistical areas. Best source of marketing maps.

> *Sales & Marketing Management*
> 633 3rd Avenue
> New York, NY 10017
> (212) 986-4800

AA. MARKETING

AA1. Dun & Bradstreet's *Million Dollar Directory* (1984) contains marketing information on approximately 45,000 businesses, each with a net worth of $1,000,000 or more.
Write:

> Dun & Bradstreet
> 99 Church Street
> New York, NY 10007
> (212) 285-7000

AA2. *The Klein Guide to American Directories,* 12th, edition, is a directory of directories. Indexing is by specific name, and broken down by general industry and associated categories. They also offer an excellent mail order directory. For information, write:

> B. Klein Publishing Inc.
> P.O. Box 8503
> Coral Springs, FL 33065
> (305) 752-1708

AA3. Standard Rate and Data Service, Inc. (SRDS). Some sections include "market data summary" estimates and Standard Metropolitan Statistical Area (SMSA) rankings. They also offer a guide to magazines and periodicals for publicity and promotion. SRDS is one of the fundamental services for the advertising industry because it provides numerous publications that contain all the information necessary to place an advertisement. For information on these, write:

> Standard Rate and Data Service, Inc.
> 3004 Glenview Road
> Wilmette, IL 60091
> (312) 256-6067

BB. MINORITY BUSINESS

A minority business, or a business owned by a disadvantaged minority person, is offered special assistance from government programs. The Minority Enterprise Small Business Investment Corporation (MESBIC) is an example of the government's help in businesses owned, or controlled by, minority groups. The following are the best sources of help for minority entrepreneurs.

BB1. A listing of all Minority Enterprise Small Business Investment Companies (MESBIC) is available via a monthly newsletter called *AAMESBIC News*. Write:

> *AAMESBIC NEWS*
> 915 15th Street., N.W.
> Suite 700
> Washington, DC 20005
> (202) 347-8600

BB2. The Minority Business Information Institute, Inc. is a research and reference center in New York City, partially funded by the U.S. Department of Commerce, Office of Minority Business Enterprise. MBII was formed in June 1971 to answer the need for a specialized reference center focusing on minority economic development. There is no charge for the services of the library. Write:

> The Minority Business Information Institute, Inc.
> 130 Fifth Avenue
> New York, NY 10011
> (212) 242-8000

BB3. Monthly magazine listing issues for minority businesses.

> *Black Enterprise* Magazine
> 130 Fifth Avenue, 10th Floor
> New York, NY 10011
> (212) 242-8000

CC. NEWSLETTERS & NEWSPAPERS

CC1. A good directory.

> *Oxbridge Directory of Newsletters*
> Oxbridge Communications
> 150 Fifth Avenue
> Suite 301
> New York, NY 10011
> (212) 741-0231

CC2. Has a directory and a monthly newsletter on newsletters, offers seminars.

Newsletter Clearing House
Box 311
Rhinebeck, NY 12572
(914) 876-2081

CC3. Newsletter Association of America
1341 "G" Street., N.W.
Suite 603
Washington, DC 20005
(202) 347-5220

CC4. NEWSPAPERS—The best newspaper for entrepreneurs is the *Wall Street Journal*. Write:

Wall Street Journal
22 Cortlandt Street
New York, NY 10017
(212) 285-5000

Every Monday, Sandy Jacobs' small business column is widely read. It's on the left hand corner of the second front page.

DD. PATENTS AND INVENTIONS

DD1. For entrepreneurs seeking assistance on their inventions or patents, there are several sources of help.

Arthur D. Little, Inc.
Invention Management Corporation
25 Acorn Park
Cambridge, MA 02140
(617) 864-5770

DD2. National Technical Information Service sells technical reports and other information products of specialized interest. Customers may quickly locate summaries of interest from among some 500,000 federally sponsored research reports completed and published from 1964 to date, using the agency's on-line computer search service (NTISearch) or the more than 1,000 published searches in stock. About 70,000 new technical summaries and reports are added annually. Write:

National Technical Information Service
U.S. DEPARTMENT OF COMMERCE
5285 Port Royal Road
Springfield, VA 22161
(703) 487-4600

DD3. A small inventor membership organization in America, write:

Inventors Club of America	Alexander Marinaccio, Pres.
Box 3799	Inventors Club of America
172 Chestnut Street	4005 Brown Road
Room 222	Tucker, GA 30084
Springfield, MA 01101	(404) 938-5089
(413) 737-0670	About 6,000 members

DD4. "How to Get a Patent" is about America's patent law. For a free copy of the booklet, write:

Consumer Information Center
Department 126E
Pueblo, CO 81009
(303) 948-3334

DD5. The United States Trademark Association is a non-profit organization dedicated to the protection, development, and promotion of the trademark concept. Write:

The United States Trademark Association
6 East 45th Street
New York, NY 10017
(212) 986-5880

EE. REFERENCE BOOKS on all subjects

EE1. A wide range of information.

Gale Research Company
Book Tower
Detroit, MI 48226
(313) 961-2242

EE2. A wide range of information.

B. Klein Publishing, Inc.
Box 8503
Coral Springs, FL 33065
(305) 752-1708

EE3. Offers more than one million sources of supply for 55,000 plus products and services. 17 volumes for about $160—a real storehouse of who makes what.

The Thomas Register of American Manufacturers
Thomas Publishing Company
1 Pennsylvania Plaza
New York, NY 10019
(212) 695-0500
Telex–12-6266

FF. REGIONAL SMALL BUSINESS ASSOCIATIONS

FF1. Oldest small business group in the USA, headed by Lewis A. Shattuck for dozens of years, several thousand members, very good politically.

Lewis A. Shattuck
Small Business Association of New England
69 Hickory Drive
Waltham, MA 02154
(617) 890-9070

FF2. Started in 1945, it has about 1,800 member companies.

Smaller Manufacturers Council
339 Boulevard of the Allies
Pittsburgh, PA 15222
(412) 391-1622

FF3. Division of Chamber of Commerce with about 4,000 members.

Council of Smaller Enterprises (COSE)
690 Huntington Building
Cleveland, OH 44115
(216) 621-3300

FF4. Founded in 1970, has under 1,000 members, but is well supported.

Independent Business Association of Wisconsin (I.B.A.W.)
415 East Washington Avenue
Madison, WI 53703
(608) 251-5546

FF5. A group of several hundred high technology companies in Los Angeles. Conducts monthly meetings and holds seminars.

Dr. Steven Panzer, Executive Director
Southern California Technology Executives
12011 San Vicente Boulevard
Suite 401
Los Angeles, CA 90049
(213) 476-0618

FF6. A group of several hundred San Francisco businesses which hold meetings. Originally founded by Nolan Bushnell.

Nancy Kelly, Director
Entrepreneur Alliance
3396 Steven Creek
Santa Clara, CA 95117
(408)554-0855

FF7. A group of Massachusetts high technology businesses which attempt to influence legislation favorably for Massachusetts businesses. Originally founded by Mr. Ray Stata, President and founder of Analog Devices, Norwood, Massachusetts.

Massachusetts High Technology Council
60 State Street
Boston, MA 02109
(617) 227-4855

GG. RESEARCH SERVICES

GG1. Supplies bibliographies.

Bibliographic Retrieval Services
200 Route 7
Mason, NY 12110
(518) 783-1161

GG2. An information source, especially a Dow Jones and Wall Street Journal publication.

> Dow Jones News Retrieval Service
> 22 Cortlandt Street
> New York, NY 10007
> (212) 286-5214

GG3. A good source of all sorts of data.

> Information on Demand
> P.O. Box 9550
> Berkeley, CA 94709
> (415) 841-1145 or (800) 227-0750

HH. SMALL BUSINESS DEVELOPMENT CENTERS

The Small Business Development Center (SBDC) Program is sponsored by the Small Business Administration, and is a cooperative effort by the Federal, state, and local governments, with universities and the private sector, to provide management techniques and technical assistance to the small business community. SBDC assistance is available to anyone interested in entrepreneurship. Listed below are the directors and addresses of the 23 SBDC centers. We've alphabetized the states to make it easier to find yours.

1. Dr. Fred Myrick, SBDC Director
   School of Business
   University of Alabama
   717 Eleventh Avenue
   Suite 419
   Birmingham, AL 35294
   (205) 934-7260

2. Dr. Ray Robbins, SBDC Director
   New Business Building
   University of Arkansas
   33rd & University Avenue
   Little Rock, AR 72204
   (501) 569-3353

3. Mr. John O'Connor, SBDC Director
   School of Business Administration
   University of Connecticut
   Box U–41D
   Storrs, CT 06268
   (203) 486-4135

4. Mr. Charles G. Maass, SBDC Director
   Coll. of Business and Economics
   University of Delaware
   005 Purnell Hall
   Newark, DE 19716
   (302) 451-8401

5. Mr. Eugene Sawney, Acting Director
   Howard University
   2361 Sherman Avenue, N.W.
   Washington, DC 20059
   (202) 636-7187

6. Mr. Gregory Higgins, SBDC Director
   University of West Florida
   Pensacola, FL 32514
   (904) 474-2000

7. Mr. Frank Hoy, Acting SBDC Director
   University of Georgia
   Brooks Hall, Room 348
   Athens, GA 30602
   (404) 542-5760

8. Ms. Louise Brinkman, SBDC Director
   Center for Ind. Research & Services
   Room 205, Engineering Annex
   Iowa State University
   Ames, IA 50011
   (515) 294-3420

9. Mr. Jerry Owens, SBDC Director
   Coll. of Business and Economics
   University of Kentucky
   18 Porter Building
   Room 18
   Lexington, KY 40506
   (606) 257-1751

10. Mr. Warren Purdy, SBDC Director
    Small Business Development Center
    University of Southern Maine
    246 Deering Avenue
    Portland, ME 04102
    (207) 780-4423

11. Mr. John Ciccarelli, SBDC Director
    School of Management
    University of Massachusetts
    Room 203
    Amherst, MA 01003
    (413) 549-4930, Ext 304

12. Mr. Terry Cartwright, SBDC Director
    St. Thomas College
    2115 Summit Avenue
    P.O. Box 5009
    St. Paul, MN 55105
    (612) 647-5840

13. Mr. Robert Wilkinson, Acting SBDC Director
    School of Business
    University of Mississippi
    3825 Ridgewood Road
    Jackson, MS 39211
    (601) 982-3825

14. Mr. Felipe Garcia-Otero, Acting SBDC Director
St. Louis University
Tegeler Hall–3rd Floor
3550 Lindell Boulevard
St. Louis, MO 63103
(314) 658-2222

15. Mr. Robert Bernier, SBDC Director
Peter Kiewit Center
University of Nebraska
1313 Farman
Omaha, NE 68182
(402) 554-2391

16. Ms. Adele Kaplan, SBDC Director
Rutgers University
Ackerson Hall–3rd Floor
180 University Avenue
Room 202
Newark, NJ 07102
(201) 648-5627

17. Ms. Susan Garber, SBDC Director
The Wharton School
University of Pennsylvania
343 Vance Hall/CS
Philadelphia, PA 19104
(215) 898-1219

18. Mr. Thomas Sullivan, SBDC Director
Bryant College
Smithfield, RI 02917
(401) 231-1200

19. Mr. Casey R. Blonaisz, SBDC Director
College of Business Administration
University of South Carolina
Columbia, SC 29208
(803) 777-5118

20. Mr. Richard Haglund, SBDC Director
University of Utah
BUC 410
Graduate School of Business
Salt Lake City, UT 84112
(801) 581-7905

21. Mr. Ed V. Owens, SBDC Director
Coll. of Business and Economics
Washington State University
Todd Hall–441, 4740 Campus
Pullman, WA 99164
(509) 335-1576

22. Mr. Cecil Underwood
University of Charleston
2300 MacCorkle Avenue, S.E
Charleston, WV 25304
(304) 357-4800

23. Dr. Robert Pricer, SBDC Director
University of Wisconsin
602 State Street
Madison, WI 53703
(608) 263-7794

II. SOURCES OF SMALL BUSINESS INFORMATION

III. An excellent book ($20), subtitled Sources of Help For Entrepreneurs.

Small Business Survival Guide
Joseph R. Mancuso
Prentice-Hall
Englewood Cliffs, NJ 07632
(201) 592-2000

112. *The Insiders Guide to Small Business Resources* by David Gumpert and Jeffrey Timmons.

Doubleday Inc.
501 Franklin Avenue
Garden City, NY 11530
(516) 294-4561

113. A good directory of information.

Small Business Information Book
Gale Research Company
Book Tower
Detroit, MI 48226
(313) 961-2242

114. The Walter E. Heller International Corporation Institute for the Advancement of Small Business Enterprises was formed in late 1979 with three general objectives, according to the Heller Corporation's 1979 annual report: "to help small businesses survive"; "to give the small business person a greater sense of self-esteem"; and "to make sure that small businesses and entrepreneurs do not disappear."

Walter E. Heller
105 West Adams Street
Chicago, IL 60603
(312) 621-7000

115. There are more than 50 titles in the Small Business Reporters series. There is a postage and handling charge for these reports, but a Publication Index is available without charge. Approximate circulation is 300,000. Write:

Small Business Administration
Bank of America
211 Main Street
4th Floor
San Francisco, CA 94105
(415) 974-0649

116. A worldwide non-profit association of several thousand entrepreneurs— and the source of the guide.

> The Center for Entrepreneurial Management, Inc.
> 83 Spring Street
> New York, NY 10012
> (212) 925-7304

JJ. SPEAKERS

JJ1. A national association of speakers with annual conventions.

> National Speakers Association
> 4323 North 12th Street
> Suite 103
> Phoenix, AZ 85014
> (602) 265-1001

JJ2. A monthly newsletter for speakers.

> *Sharing Ideas*
> Dottie Walters
> Royal CBS Publishing
> 18825 Hicrest Road
> Glendora, CA 91740
> (213) 335-8069

KK. TAX INFORMATION

KK1. Excellent source of newsletters and tax bulletins.

> Research Institute of America (RIA)
> RIA Building
> 589 5th Avenue
> New York, NY 10017
> (212) 755-8900

KK2. A good source of reference books and tax interpretations.

> Commerce Clearing House (CCH)
> 4025 W. Peterson
> Chicago, IL 60646
> (312) 583-8500

KK3. A tax service used by lawyers and accountants.

> Matthew Bender & Co.
> 1275 Broadway
> Albany, NY 11201
> (518) 462-3331

KK4. Offers tax advice in many forms.

Prentice-Hall Tax Guide
Prentice-Hall
Englewood Cliffs, NJ 07632
(201) 592-2000

KK5. The Internal Revenue Service (IRS) offers free assistance on Federal tax questions.

(800) 424-5454
(202) 633-6487 (Washington D.C.)

LL. TELEPHONE NUMBERS, ADDRESSES, AND ZIP CODES

LL1. Given that long distance directory assistance now costs 50¢ per inquiry, we recommend:

National Directory of Addresses and Telephone Numbers
Concord Reference Books, Inc.
111 West 50th Street
Suite 4694
New York, NY 10020
(212) 307-1491

LL2. Telephone books do not give zip codes—so you'll need a second directory of zip codes. We list this item in this section in hopes that someone will combine the two. It has most popular numbers, and it is only $22.50.

Zip Code Directory
National Information Data Center
P.O. Box 2977
Washington, DC 20013
(301) 565-2539

Hint: Mailers seeking the nine-digit ZIP code for any address in the country can call the Postal Service's new toll-free number, (800) 228-8777. Operators will provide ZIP codes for as many as 25 addresses per call and also verify the accuracy of street spellings.

MM. VENTURE CAPITAL

MM1. Howard and Company publishes an excellent guide for borrowing capital. It also publishes a monthly newsletter, *The Initial Public Offering*, which is a complete guide to capital sources and techniques. This information on Initial Public Offerings is excellent. In addition, *Private Placements* and *Growth Capital* are monthly newsletters which provide excellent information on venture capital underneath, and debt capital. Write:

Graham Howard
Howard and Company
1528 Walnut Street, 20th Floor
Suite 220
Philadelphia, PA 19102
(215) 735-2815

MM2. A source of most original venture capital information includes a directory and a newsletter and a large data book of venture capital statistics.

> Stan Pratt
> Venture Economics Inc.
> 16 Laurel Avenue, Box 348
> Wellesley Hills, MA 02181
> (617) 431-8100

MM3. The *Directory of State and Federal Funds* is a single source for basic data on the financial assistance programs of the 50 states and 12 federal agencies. The book helps management to shop, compare, select, and discard a wide range of aid programs without having to go through mountains of promotional literature. Write:

> Pilot Books
> 103 Cooper Street
> Babylon, NY 11702
> (516) 422-2225

MM4. Membership directory is available for a $1.00 handling fee. Requests in writing only. An association of 700 SBIC's monthly newsletter and excellent annual conference on venture capital.

> The National Association of Small Business Investment Companies (NASBIC)
> 1156 15th Street, NW
> Washington, DC 20005
> (202) 833-8230

MM5. Membership directory is free with a telephone request. A rather loose federation of venture capital sources. Does not provide much information.

> National Venture Capital Association
> 1655 North Fort Myer Drive
> Suite 700
> Arlington, VA 22209
> (703) 528-4370

MM6. An association of venture capital sources.

> Western Association of Venture Capital
> 3000 Sand Hill Road
> Suite 260
> Menlo Park, CA 94025
> (415) 854-1322

NN. WOMEN ENTREPRENEURS

NN1. A non-profit group of women in small business.

> Beatrice Fitzpatrick
> American Women's Economic Development Corporation (AWED)
> 60 East 42 Street
> New York, NY 10165
> (212) 692-9100

NN2. Established in Washington D.C. in 1974. Dues-based membership group of women business owners.

National Association of Women Business Owners
2025 California Street, NW, Suite 304
Washington, DC 20008
(202) 223-3835

NN3. Holds annual conference and has a membership of women business owners.

National Association of Female Executives
120 E. 56 Street
New York, NY 10022
(212) 371-0740

NN4. Women's business magazine which annually lists the top sixty U.S. businesses run by women.

Savvy Magazine
111 Eighth Avenue
New York, NY 10011
(212) 225-0990

APPENDIX H CROSS INDEX

Glossary

Acid Test Ratio. Cash plus those other assets that can be used *immediately* converted to cash should equal or exceed current liabilities. The formula used to determine the ratio is as follows:

$$\frac{\text{Cash plus Receivables (net) plus Marketable Securities}}{\text{Current Liabilities}}$$

The acid test ratio is one of the most important credit barometers used by lending institutions, as it indicates the abilities of a business enterprise to meet its current obligations.

Aging Receivables. A scheduling of accounts receivable according to the length of time they have been outstanding. This shows which accounts are not being paid in a timely manner and may reveal any difficulty in collecting long overdue receivables. This may also be an important indicator of developing cash flow problems.

Amortization. To liquidate on an installment basis; the process of gradually paying off a liability over a period of time, *i.e.,* a mortgage is is amortized by periodically paying off part of the face amount of the mortgage.

Assets. The valuable resources, or properties and property rights owned by an individual or business enterprise.

Balance Sheet. An itemized statement which lists the total assets and the total liabilities of a given business to portray its net worth at a given moment in time.

Breakeven Analysis. A method used to determine the point at which the business will neither make a profit nor incur a loss. That point is expressed in either the total dollars of revenue exactly offset by total expenses (fixed and variable); or in total units of production, the cost of which exactly equals the income derived by their sale.

Capital Equipment. Equipment that you use to manufacture a product, provide a service, or use to sell, store, and deliver merchandise. Such equipment will not be sold in the normal course of business, but will be used and worn out or be consumed over time as you do business.

Cash Flow. The actual movement of cash within a business: cash inflow minus cash outflow. A term used to designate the reported net income of a corporation plus amounts charged off for depreciation, depletion, amortization, and extraordinary charges to reserves, which are bookkeeping deductions and not actually paid out in cash. Used to offer a better indication of the ability of a firm to meet its own obligations and to pay dividends rather than with the conventional net income figure.

Cash Position. See *Liquidity*.

Corporation. An artificial legal entity created by government grant and endowed with certain powers, a voluntary organization of persons, either actual individuals or legal entities, legally bound to form a business enterprise.

Current Assets. Cash or other items that will normally be turned into cash within one year, and assets that will be used up in the operations of a firm within one year.

Current Liabilities. Amounts owed that will ordinarily be paid by a firm within one year. Such items include accounts payable, wages payable, taxes payable, the current portion of a long-term debt, and interest and dividends payable.

Current Ratio. A ratio of a firm's current assets to its current liabilities. The current ratio includes the value of inventories which have not yet been sold, so it is not the best evaluation of the current status of the firm. The acid test ratio, covering the most liquid of current assets, provides a better evaluation.

Deal. A proposal for financing business creation or expansion; a series of transactions and preparation of documents in order to obtain funds for business expansion or creation.

Depreciation. A reduction in the value of fixed assets. The most important causes of depreciation are wear and tear, the effect of the elements, and gradual obsolescence that makes it unprofitable to continue using some assets until they have been exhausted. The purpose of the *bookkeeping charge for depreciation* is to write off the original cost of an asset (less expected salvage value) by equitably distributing charges against operations over its entire useful life.

Entrepreneur. An innovator of a business enterprise who recognizes opportunities to introduce a new product, a new production process, or an improved organization, and who raises the necessary money, assembles the factors of production, and organizes an operation to exploit the opportunity.

Equity. The monetary value of a property or business that exceeds the claims and/or liens against it by others.

Illiquid. See *Liquidity*.

Liquidity. A term used to describe the solvency of a business and which has special reference to the degree of readiness in which assets can be converted into cash without a loss. Also called *cash position*. If a firm's current assets cannot be converted into cash to meet current liabilities, the firm is said to be *illiquid*.

Long-Term Liabilities. These are liabilities (expenses) that will not mature within the next year.

Market. The number of people and their total spending (actual or potential) for your product line within the geographic limits of your distribution ability. The *market share* is the percentage of your sales compared to the sales of your competitors in total for a particular product line.

Net Worth. The owner's equity in a given business represented by the excess of the total assets over the total amounts owing to outside creditors (total liabilities) at a given moment in time. Also, the net worth of an individual as determined by deducting the amount of all his personal liabilities from the total value of his personal assets.

Partnership. A legal relationship created by the voluntary association of two or more persons to carry on as co-owners of a business for profit; a type of business organization in which two or more persons agree on the amount of their contributions (capital and effort) and on the distribution of profits, if any.

Pro Forma. A projection or estimate of what may result in the future from actions in the present. A pro forma financial statement is one that shows how the actual operations of the business will turn out if certain assumptions are realized.

Profit. The excess of the selling price over all costs and expenses incurred in making the sale. Also, the reward to the entrepreneur for the risks assumed by him in the establishment, operation, and management of a given enterprise or undertaking.

Sole Proprietorship or Proprietorship. A type of business organization in which one individual owns the business. Legally, the owner *is* the business and personal assets are typically exposed to liabilities of the business.

Sub-Chapter S Corporation or Tax Option Corporation. A corporation that elected under Sub-Chapter S of the IRS Tax Code (by unanimous consent of its shareholders) not to pay any corporate tax on its income and, instead, to have the shareholders pay taxes on it, even though it is not distributed. Shareholders of a tax option corporation are also entitled to deduct, on the individual returns, their shares of any net operating loss sustained by the corporation, subject to limitation in the tax code. In many respects, Sub-Chapter S permits a corporation to behave for tax purposes as a proprietorship or partnership.

Take-Over. The acquisition of one company by another company.

Target Market. The *specific* individuals, distinguished by socioeconomic, demographic, and/or interest characteristics, who are the most likely potential customers for the goods and/or services of a business.

Working Capital, Net. The excess of current assets over current liabilities. These excess current assets are available for carrying on business operations.

Afterword

Most books on business plans are simply boring and restatements of the obvious. This book undoubtedly suffers from the same restrictions about the issues and meanings of terms like goal setting, mission statement, purposes, reason-to-be and what-business-am-I-in. So to combat this inherent difficulty I've added this last chapter as an afterword. Now that the business plan is fully done, I call it The Secret to Raising Capital. Please do not read it until you are done with the entire book. Thank you.

THE SECRET TO RAISING CAPITAL!

Here's the situation. You've been in a financial negotiation for three months, but the deal just won't close. You've got a terrific business plan—even your venture capitalist admits that—but no matter what you do, you just can't come to terms. So now you're meeting for the umpteenth time, and half of you is thinking, "maybe I should just get up from the table and leave the room, I'm just wasting my time." But the other half of you is thinking "I've got three months invested in this deal; they've got the money; they like my plan; I'd be a fool not to stick it out." What do you do? Well, there's a six-word phrase that will help you close the deal. But before I tell you what that six-word phrase is, I need to show you how and why it works.

The biggest mistake an entrepreneur can make in dealing with a venture capitalist is to lose sight of what the venture capitalist is really after. It may sound like he wants too much equity or too much control, but what it really comes down to is money—his job and his goal is to make profit on his investments. So when the venture capitalist makes what you consider an unreasonable offer ("Just give me my terms and we're ready to go"), you don't have to panic. You don't automatically have to give up control of your business in order to get financed (which is what it may sound like when he says "my terms").

But what *do* you try next? Do you shop the deal around, hoping to arouse enough interest to play one source off against the other? That might be a good ploy, in theory. But in reality, you have to remember that you're playing on his turf. And shopping a deal around tends to alienate venture capitalists rather than entice them, more often than not.

Then what's the secret to closing the deal? Good old-fashioned persistence? I've always subscribed to the theory that if a batter stands in the batter's box long enough, the pitcher will eventually hit the bat with the ball. But all by itself, persistence won't raise a nickel. So maybe you should try to get the financier to go over everything he thinks looks good about the deal and everything that attracted him to it in the first place. That will bring you back to square one, but unfortunately it won't get you any closer to closing the deal than you were when you first got started. That's because as special as you may think your company is, chances are the venture capitalist has seen, and maybe even turned down, deals similar to yours in the past. Getting your business off the ground might be your dream, but the art of raising capital isn't the art of selling dreams. The art of raising capital is the art of reducing risk!

And the dream sellers will always get into trouble during negotiations, because when their backs are up against the wall, they come out and say something like "You ought to see how beautiful she looks. She's tall and thin and she's got this and that. . . " But that's not the way raising capital works, in fact, it's just the opposite. When you're back is to the wall, what you want to be able to say is "the risk on this deal is zero—the down side is *zero*! Now let's talk about the up side." The following are some examples of what I mean by the up side.

Let's say I have a piece of land up at Cheboque Point, in Yarmouth, Nova Scotia—a piece of ocean-front property. This is a good example because it's true. I bought the land 18 months ago, and it's really a gorgeous piece of property. If you take the ferry up from Portland (Maine) you can walk to it from the dock. Eighteen months ago, I paid $100,000 for this property (100 acres), but then a few months later, I needed some cash, so I decided to sell off a piece of it. The first thing I did was to divide it into two parcels of equal value. Next, I put one of the parcels on the market. So how much do you think the asking price for it was? Before I tell you, I want you to guess. Remember, 18 months ago I bought the full 100 acres of land for $100,000.

If you guessed $100,000, you guessed right. And what this illustrates is perhaps the single most important thing to remember about investors. An investor's first and foremost concern in making an investment lies in getting his money back. Investors aren't just in the business of making investments, they're also in the business of recouping their investments.

Here's a second example. Did you ever watch the gamblers in the casinos in Las Vegas or Atlantic City? Most of them are sensible enough people—

when they're at home. But put them at a slot machine or a crap table and they go crazy. But if you watch long enough, you'll notice that a funny thing begins to happen with some of them. At about two or three in the morning, they pull all the money out of their pockets and put it down on a table and count it. Then they divide it into two piles and they put one of the piles back into their pocket. Then they continue to play with the other pile of money. So what did they put back into their pocket? Cab fare? the money for a phone call home? No. What a smart gambler puts back into his pocket is his initial stake—the money he came in with.

In my third example I'll show you how the best money-raisers in the world raise money. And who do you think are the best money-raisers in the world? No, not politicians, and not the banker's brother. The best money-raisers in the world are the venture capitalists. A successful venture capitalist can pick up the phone, and in under an hour, raise 100 million dollars. Most entrepreneurs have trouble getting someone to co-sign a 10-thousand-dollar note, but a venture capitalist can raise 100 million in under an hour. But why is a venture capitalist so successful when it comes to raising money? The answer lies in that same six-word phrase I mentioned before. And after one more example, I'm going to tell you what those six words are.

I speak at a number of conferences where venture capitalists are assembled, and it's always interesting for me to watch two of the giants come into a room and meet. And when they do meet, what do you think they say? Let's say that Bill from Widget Venture runs into Frank from Mega Venture. What do you think they talk about? Does Bill say I made 600 million in the last quarter? Or does Frank say that my average annual rate of return for the past 17 years has been 41.26 percent? Or do they just say hello, and leave it at that? No. What they talk about is the success of their *last* fund.

Widget Venture may run four or five different funds of 100-200 million dollars each, but Frank from Mega Venture is only really interested in Widget's last fund. The rest is already history. So Frank may say, "I understand you put together $120 million for Fund #6. Is that true?" And Bill will say, "Yes, that's true." So Frank will ask him, "Well how long did it take you to get your principal back to your partners in Fund #6?" And Bill might answer, "Eleven months." So then Bill will ask Frank how long it took Mega's last fund to get it's principal back to his partners. And so on and so on. The only thing that venture capitalists ever compare is how fast they returned the original investment back to their partners.

When the gambler puts his original capital back into his pocket he's doing the same thing that the venture capitalist does. He returns the original investment and continues playing on his winnings. Of course the venture capitalists are a little more sophisticated. They raise their money in ten-year limited partnerships. But their strategy is the same. They try to rush the original investment back to their partners as soon as possible, and then they "play with the winnings" for the balance of the ten-year period. The partnership has to wait the full ten years to get their winnings, but they get their principal back right away.

The main point here is, that no matter who the investor is, his first concern is getting his initial investment back. So when a negotiation seems like it's come to an impasse, the six key words you have to say to get the signatures on the agreement are *"*You get your money back first.*" Nothing else that you could possibly say will strike closer to the heart of a venture capitalist than these six words: *"*You get your money back first.*"

Now let me offer you one last example. Let's say a young company goes public at ten dollars a share, but a few months after the Initial Public Offering (IPO), the company runs into some problems, and the stock drops down to five dollars a share. All of a sudden the entrepreneur is breaking his back to get the earnings and the stock price back up. And after a superhuman effort, it seems like he's succeeded, because the earnings have reached, and even begin to exceed, the original projections. But after a slow climb back up, the stock price hits ten and then just sits there. Why? Because despite the strong performance, the stockholders (investors) remember the initial setback, and when the stock gets back to its original price, they begin to bail out. It's what's known as the "jump-off" point. Independent of performance, the initial investors bail out, and the stock price gets hung up at ten. And this further illustrates the same principle I've described in the other three examples: the investor is adamant, almost fanatical, about recovering his initial investment. In this case, he isn't left with any winnings to play with, but he's recovered his initial investment and he's ready to start all over again.

Despite the very different approaches of these three categories of investors (the land owner, the gambler, and the venture capitalist) their thinking is the same—protect the original capital. That's why selling dreams will never work with a venture capitalist. He wants to make sure the risk on his investment is held to a minimum. He wants to be assured that his original capital will be protected. So, after you've tried everything you know to close a deal and it still seems to hang up on a few points, try my little six-word phrase and see what happens. And always remember that, as great as your dream for your company may be, you're on the venture capitalist's turf. You have to talk his language, not your own. So talk about *his dream*. Tell him "You get your money back first."

Index